SHORTER, FASTER, FUNNIER

SHORTER, FASTER, FUNNIER

COMIC PLAYS AND MONOLOGUES

EDITED BY *Eric Lane*
AND *Nina Shengold*

VINTAGE BOOKS

A DIVISION OF RANDOM HOUSE, INC. NEW YORK

A VINTAGE ORIGINAL, MAY 2011

Copyright © 2011 by Eric Lane and Nina Shengold

Library of Congress Cataloging-in-Publication Data
Shorter, faster, funnier : comic plays and monologues / edited by Eric Lane and Nina Shengold. —1st ed.
    p. cm.
  ISBN 978-0-307-47664-7
  1. American drama (Comedy).   2. Monologues, American.
I. Lane, Eric.   II. Shengold, Nina.
  PS627.C65 S56 2011
  812'.052308—dc22
  2011001949

www.vintagebooks.com

Printed in the United States of America
10 9 8 7 6 5 4 3 2 1

CONTENTS

vi CONTENTS

INTRODUCTION

Asian chefs cite five flavor notes—sweet, sour, salty, bitter, and spicy—without which no meal is complete. While assembling the plays in this anthology, the editors enjoyed a dazzling range of comedic hors d'oeuvres. From laugh-out-loud funny to subtly amusing, caustic, witty, or outrageous, there are as many flavors of comedy as there are senses of humor.

We read over 400 short plays and monologues to create this all-you-can-eat comic buffet. We found delectable morsels by celebrated humorists Christopher Durang (*Funeral Parlor*), David Ives (*The Blizzard*), Warren Leight (*Norm-Anon*), Mark O'Donnell (*You Know Who Else I Hate?*), and Theresa Rebeck (*The Contract*); inspired monologues by actor/playwrights Halley Feiffer (*Thank You So Much for Stopping*), Dan Berkowitz (*Sourpuss*), and Tony Award winner Mary Louise Wilson (*Tirade*); plus enough superb audition pieces, two-handers, and ensemble plays to satisfy laugh-hungry actors, readers, and audience members.

We chose monologues of all lengths, from Liz Ellison's swift *Gabrielle* and Elizabeth Wong's spiky *Ripper Girl* to Jeffrey Hatcher's epic *Match Wits with Minka Lupino,* from his monologue trio *Murderers.* Pete Barry's irascible businessman extends his free fall from a plane to hilarious lengths in *Nine Point Eight Meters per Second per Second.* Jane Shepard's *Long Distance* reveals a man's thorny encounter with a former classmate, while Edwin Sánchez's *Ernesto the Magnificent* fiercely paints a performance by an embittered sword swallower.

There's also a wealth of plays for two actors. Amy Herzog's *Christmas Present,* Mark Harvey Levine's *The Rental,* and Garth

Wingfield's *Mary Just Broke Up with This Guy* put unique spins on that staple of comedy, boy meets girl. In Anton Dudley's romantic *Getting Home*, boy meets hunky Indian cabdriver. The couple in Eric Lane's *Curtain Raiser* tackles an abandoned Woolworth building; in Wayne Rawley's *The Scary Question,* another couple bonds over zombies.

There are graceful duets for young actors, including Samara Siskind's *Bar Mitzvah Boy*, Megan Mostyn-Brown's *The Woods Are for Suckers and Chumps*, Michael Mitnick's *Life without Subtext,* and Ean Miles Kessler's bullet-paced *Brotherly Love.* Senior actors will cherish Peter Handy's bittersweet *Friendship* and Drew Larimore's *The Anniversary,* quite possibly the first play about retirees in postapocalyptic Siberia.

Three plays for two actresses—Nicole Quinn's lyrical *Sandchair Cantata,* Laura Shaine's poignant *The Whole Truth & Nothing but the Bluetooth,* and Barbara Wiechmann's salty duet for obsessed Realtors, *36 Rumson Road*—treat women's darkest anxieties with a refreshingly light touch.

On the testosterone side, Dan Kois's *The Rumor* outs a surprising scandal in men's sports, Gary Winter's *I Love Neil LaBute* deftly skewers the playwright dubbed "America's reigning misanthrope," and Dana Yeaton's *Men in Heat* bares the mysteries of the male biological clock.

Genders bend freely in Adam Bock's *Three Guys and a Brenda,* in which all four title characters are played by actresses. Nina Shengold's *Double Date* upends political correctness by taking "joined at the hip" at face value, while Jacquelyn Reingold's *A Very Very Short Play* sparks an airplane romance between a one-foot-tall woman and a twelve-foot-tall man, both played by actors of average height.

Rob Ackerman's *You Have Arrived* also encourages *very* nontraditional casting, as one of its actresses plays a GPS monitor. Other three-character plays include John Augustine's uproariously acerbic cell-phone-age comedy *PeopleSpeak* and Caleen Sinnette Jennings's *Uncovered,* which finds gallows humor in the post-Katrina cleanup. Eric Coble's physical comedy *H.R.* is equally topical, observing a quartet of cubicle workers whipping themselves into a froth at the prospect of being downsized.

Three plays with larger casts go back to school for laughs. Billy Aronson's *Reunions* offers a wonderfully demented spin on catching-up small talk among high school alumni, Philip Dawkins's whimsical *Nothing* riffs on an alien invasion at school, and the gruff coach in Daryl Watson's hilarious *Snap* tries to whip his dozens insult team (including a stuttering girl with unforeseen gifts) into shape.

For divinely inspired slapstick humor, try Mikhail Horowitz's *Mere Vessels*, a fearless inquiry into the spiritual lives of ventriloquists' dummies, or Elizabeth Meriwether's *Particle Board,* which gives the pompous Great Man documentary a well-deserved plank in the face.

As editors of more than a dozen play anthologies, we've been gratified to hear of many multiplay productions culled from our previous books. We urge readers of *Shorter, Faster, Funnier* to enjoy these plays in any way you can: read them aloud with friends; mount a staged reading, full production, or evening of short plays. As always, be sure to acquire the proper rights *first*—playwrights don't take kindly to finding unauthorized performances in online listings or YouTube postings. Contacts for performance rights are listed in the back of this book, along with playwrights' biographies and an index by cast size.

Whatever your comic taste, you're sure to find something within these pages to make you laugh. You'll also find heartache and suspense, poetic language and raunchy jokes. Comedy is a many-flavored banquet, and we invite you to pull up a chair. Enjoy!

ERIC LANE AND NINA SHENGOLD,
June 2010

ACKNOWLEDGMENTS

Many people contributed greatly to the creation of this anthology. We'd like to thank the many literary managers, theaters, agents, publishers, playwrights, and friends who led us to such terrific plays and helped us secure the rights.

In particular, we'd like to thank John McCormack at Summer Shorts and INTAR, Meghan Beals McCarthy at Northlight Theatre, Lorca Peress at MultiStages, Sarah Chodoff, Roxanne Heinze-Bradshaw at Samuel French, Craig Pospisil at Dramatists Play Service, Brendan Conheady, Jason Pizzarello, and the entire staff at Playscripts.

Deep gratitude to Actors & Writers, Orange Thoughts Productions, the Drama Book Shop, and the Corporation of Yaddo. As always, we are indebted to our wonderful agent, Susan Cohen, and our superb editor at Vintage, Diana Secker Tesdell. And Bob Barnett and Maya Shengold for bringing laughter to our lives on a daily basis. Many thanks to the playwrights for their amazing plays.

SHORTER, FASTER, FUNNIER

THE ANNIVERSARY

Drew Larimore

The Anniversary made its U.S. debut with Artistic New Directions' "Boxers & Briefs" New Play Festival March 15–28, 2010, in New York City at Theatre 54. It was directed by Nick Stimler and featured Anita Keal and Jane Marx.

The Anniversary premiered at the Short & Sweet New Play Festival in Melbourne, Australia, on December 15, 2007. It was directed by Claire Wearne and featured Debra Zuckerman and Tiffany Loft.

CHARACTERS
DORIS; MARGE: Two New York women, late sixties/early seventies.

TIME
2008.

PLACE
Tunguska, Russia (Siberia).

SETTING
A park bench between two homes.

The play begins. Except nothing at first—only darkness. A surge of some sort, like the rising of a firework but more intense—then nothing again, until a few seconds later . . .

A GIGANTIC EXPLOSION.

Lights slowly rise to DORIS *and* MARGE *entering from opposite ends of the stage, covered in black soot from said explosion, their hair sticking straight up. They look at one another in acknowledgment, then begin walking to center stage.*

DORIS: I'm not even gonna say it.

MARGE: Oh, Doris—

DORIS: A rumble here—a spark there—

MARGE: You'll get yourself all worked up—

DORIS: Never did I think it'd come to this—so quick, so terrible—

MARGE: It could've been worse, it could *always* be worse—

DORIS: One minute you're minding your business, the next you're fifty feet from where you thought you were—

MARGE: You know how you get upset—

DORIS: *Marge!* This is the *worst one yet!*

(*They sit on the bench. Pause.*)

Where were you this time?

MARGE: The kitchen.

(DORIS *scoffs.*)

Making the pirozhkis Harry likes so well.

DORIS: Oh, God...Did it—?

MARGE: Of course. They're everywhere.

DORIS: Are you...?

MARGE: Eh, just a little—a mark on my elbow. It's the *pirozhkis* I'm worried about.

DORIS: Then, at least—

MARGE: The windows blew in—the oven exploded. The cabbage went to the ceiling. The meat, too. The insides—they get *stuck.*

DORIS: Stuck?

MARGE: Like spitballs. Used to be I'd call Vladimir and have him bring over a ladder. That was before we lost him.

DORIS: Sheesh.

MARGE: I can't climb up there. My legs, they get—

DORIS: Weary.

MARGE: *And* tired. Standing so long.

DORIS: And it takes a while, you know, to—

MARGE: Scrape them off the ceiling. And such delicate pirozhkis. (*Turning to* DORIS.) You?

DORIS: Oh, the garden.

MARGE: At least *outside.*

DORIS: This time, anyway.

MARGE: You find cover?

DORIS: Eh... I used my hands... You know...

(*She places her hands over her head, covering the back of her neck.*)

MARGE: Like you're in an earthquake!

DORIS: Exactly—an earthquake.

MARGE: But no—no trees falling or...?

DORIS: No, none-a-that this time.

MARGE: Thank God. When it gets like that, you never know—

DORIS: Except my lilies. They were bright yellow and I couldn't wait to take them inside. I was gonna give it another day. Just when you think they can't get any more yellow they do. That pigment. Hard to believe it's natural. Lloyd loves the lilies.

MARGE: Aww.

DORIS: Says they keep longer than other kinds.

MARGE: Longer than *other* lilies?

DORIS: Mm-hmm. And it's havin' 'em around the house that makes him...well...It *gets* him.

MARGE: *Gets* him?

DORIS: Makes him, you know...

(DORIS *makes an ambiguous gesture with her hands, attempting to symbolize "emotion."*)

MARGE: Right.

DORIS: But when it *happened*, of course—when it *happened*—they turned black. I tried to touch one and it fell apart in my hands. Dust.

MARGE: (*Sympathetic.*) Oh, *Doris.*

DORIS: Have to wait a whole 'nother year to get them that yellow again.

MARGE: And with winter comin' so soon...

DORIS: If I've said it before, I've said it a thousand times...Of *all* the places to spend the golden years—

BOTH: *Siberia.*

(*They sigh. Beat.*)

DORIS: (*Growing perturbed.*) I mean, you'd think they could give us a warning. A sign.

MARGE: (*Pointing in the distance.*) There we go—another one! Off in the distance! Didn't Edith used to live out that way?

DORIS: A loudspeaker—or through the radio.

MARGE: Edith was such a lovely host when we'd play bridge on Sundays. Don't you remember what a lovely host Edith was?

DORIS: 'Cause if it was Moscow—St. Petersburg—it'd be different. But it's not *happening* in Moscow or St. Petersburg. You have to look at where it's *happening,* Marge.

MARGE: Now I bet all that's left of her house is a pile of ash. I bet you couldn't find a deck of cards if you tried!

DORIS: It's the end of the world. It gathers momentum. Don't you know it when you see it?

MARGE: *See* what? I can barely see anything the way the air is.

(*A flash of light.*)

(*Pointing.*) Look—over there! Another!

DORIS: When I'd go to buy yams, Denny at the store would always remind me the first one hit in 1908. I always asked him why the hundred-year wait—and he'd say it was a domino effect. Once one hits, the others can't help themselves. Course, that was before the store blew to smithereens.

MARGE: (*Still looking off in the distance.*) I wonder if that one was near Shirley Feldman—you know, Judy's sister, who lost a foot when her living room caved in on her?

DORIS: At first it was fun to look at. All the colors. Purple—pink—blue.

MARGE: It was better than television—a *Streisand concert*.

DORIS: Until they started blowin' folks into trees.

MARGE: Oh, I'll never forget *my* first time being blown into a tree.

DORIS: Innocent folks—minding their own business.

MARGE: I was finding twigs in body parts I didn't know I had!

DORIS: But nearly a hundred years later—*all this time*—can't anyone sit down and explain to me why asteroids keep hitting Siberia?

MARGE: If they could explain it, then we'd *know*.

(*Moment.*)

DORIS: I'll tell you one thing. I'd love to blow *Lloyd* into a tree.

MARGE: What's that?

DORIS: When I start to think about it, makes me so damn angry.

MARGE: What does?

DORIS: Havin' to move out here like he wanted to—away from civilization. "It's the Palm Springs of the twenty-first century"—he'd tell me.

MARGE: Florida without the traffic.

DORIS: Oh, I hate it—how it builds up inside.

MARGE: Doris, you can't let things build up inside.

DORIS: Asteroid after asteroid. God, I cringe when I hear the *word*.

MARGE: Now, Doris—

DORIS: All the times I've wanted to *tell* him...I should just tell him right now. While the anger's fresh.

MARGE: Tell who?

DORIS: *Lloyd*. I should walk right up there—

MARGE: You wanna tell him *now*? What—with the *explosion*—

DORIS: Marge, it's the last straw. I'm gonna *march* right up there and tell him—tell him straight to his face: "I'm leavin'."

MARGE: You wouldn't.

DORIS: *Try* me. I'd say to him—"Enough is enough, Lloyd, I'm outta here." To his face—right between his eyes, that's where I'd look. "I'm leavin', Lloyd, and you can stay or you can leave with me."

MARGE: To his face, you'd say that?

DORIS: I would. And then I'd pack a bag.

MARGE: A bag!.... And—and *leave*? Just like that?

DORIS: I'd say—"Lloyd, you have the night to think about it." And whether he comes with me or not, the next morning

I'd take a train somewhere. Anywhere. *Sayonara*, Russia. Kiss my ass.

MARGE: But where would you go? Where's there to go if it's just you with Lloyd behind? Surely you wouldn't—

DORIS: Paris. Milan. Iowa City. Anyplace where there's people to look at. People to talk to. Where there's life. *This isn't life*, Marge. *We are not living life.*

MARGE: Maybe you should think about it, Doris. Let yourself cool off.

DORIS: It doesn't have to be this way. You don't have to hide to be safe anymore. What is safety, anyway? Who's ever really safe?

MARGE: (*Growing panicked.*) To just leave like that—I mean, Doris, *to just pack up and leave*—

DORIS: I mean, they convince us to move out here with their crazy ideas that places like Park Avenue or Columbus Circle—where we've lived our whole lives—are gonna suddenly cave in on us—fall to pieces in the blink of an eye. So we pack up and come to *Siberia*, because it's supposed to be *safer*. Because it's a new time—a new age where you hafta seek out your safety, where you guard it like a watchdog. But ya know what? Ya know what I'm gonna tell Lloyd when he's doing his crossword puzzle and sittin' back in his La-Z-Boy? I'm gonna march right in there and tell him: "The biggest bitch of all is that no one's safe." It's a riot—a God damn *riot*, 'cause even in the farthest most remote corner of the world where there may not be a big building to blow up or a plane to crash, you have to worry about asteroids—asteroids—*asteroids* coming down from outer space. It's a joke, Marge. It's all coming to one big joke.

MARGE: But *leaving*, Doris—leaving with no rhyme, no reason—

DORIS: And when I think back—when I think back to all the times when he sweet-talked me into moving here, sweet-talked me into the one part of the world where we could live to be a hundred—where they got new golf courses and all-you-can-eat buffets—

MARGE: Who would I talk to? Where would I get my lilies in the spring?

DORIS: Oh, you wait and see, Marge. 'Cause I'm gonna tell him. I'm gonna tell him and they're gonna be able to hear me all the way in Severomorsk! 'Cause from now on, Marge, *I'm* makin' the decisions. *I'm* tellin' us where we go and what we do. *I'm* the one who is packin' up and movin' to where *I* think is safe—where *I* think is good. And this time *he's* the one who's gonna come with me. Or maybe he doesn't. 'Cause this far along, it doesn't even matter. It's the principle of it, Marge. The *principle*.

(DORIS *has grown intensely empowered.* MARGE *stands, shaking with terror.* MARGE *grabs her chest, a deep sigh, closing her eyes a moment, then opening them, as if back in reality, relieved.*)

MARGE: You know . . . I believed it this time.

DORIS: Did you?

MARGE: It was different from all the others.

DORIS: Yeah?

MARGE: This time I felt it in my stomach. When you raised your voice like that, that's right where it went. Right to my stomach.

DORIS: That's what I'm going for. Precision.

MARGE: You think it'll work?

DORIS: How do we know? Do I look like an expert?

MARGE: Then you should. While it's fresh—before it gets dark.

DORIS: Yes.

(*The two walk over to stage right, which now becomes lit, revealing two gravestones several feet apart.* MARGE *stands near one and* DORIS *the other.* DORIS *takes out wilting black flowers from her coat and sets them down by the grave.*)

MARGE: Hard to believe it's been this long.

DORIS: Three years. Who knew.

MARGE: I think about him most in the morning. When it's quiet.

DORIS: Mornings are long.

MARGE: Time—is long.

(*Moment.*)

　…You gonna do it?

DORIS: (*Beat.*) Do what? (*Moment; sighs.*) I don't think so. Not— right now.

(MARGE *takes* DORIS's *arm.*)

MARGE: You wouldn't really leave like that, would you, Doris?

DORIS: Nah.

MARGE: 'Cause I can't grow lilies like you can. I never could. (*Beat.*) If I scrape off some cabbage from the ceiling, will you eat some?

DORIS: Maybe a little.

MARGE: The heat from the explosion'll keep 'em warm.

DORIS: Tender.

(*They begin walking offstage.*)

MARGE: You know what got me this time, though? Is when you raised your voice like you did.

DORIS: When?

MARGE: When you started repeatin' yourself like that.

DORIS: Uh-huh...

MARGE: I felt it, ya know? I felt it right here.

DORIS: Where?

MARGE: In my gut, you know? Where it all matters. Right in the middle...

(*A slow fade as they walk offstage.*)

END OF PLAY

BAR MITZVAH BOY

Samara Siskind

CAST OF CHARACTERS
SAMUEL: Thirteen, has just become a man.
STACIE: Twelve, just starting to like boys.

SETTING
A Bar Mitzvah reception.
Evening.

ACKNOWLEDGMENTS
Bar Mitzvah Boy was first produced by City Theatre, Coral Gables, Florida, March 2007.

For Ian

Darkness. A sappy slow-dance song plays faintly in the background. We hear an angry voice in the darkness, followed by a slap.

STACIE: Hey!

(*Lights rise on* SAMUEL *and* STACIE *facing each other on a dance floor. They are both dressed in fancy evening attire.* SAMUEL *clutches his sore face.*)

SAMUEL: Oww! You hit me!

STACIE: Your hand was on my butt.

SAMUEL: My hand was nowhere near your butt!

STACIE: C'mon, Samuel, your hand was totally touching my butt!

SAMUEL: One—I wouldn't touch your butt with a ten-foot pole. Two—Even if I did touch your butt, it's no reason to resort to physical violence.

STACIE: Well, if your hand goes anywhere near my butt again, I'm cutting it off.

SAMUEL: Oh that's nice. I'm sure they'll let you off on the popular "he touched my butt" defense. Now can we just finish this dance already, please? Everyone's watching.

(*Beat.* STACIE *puts* SAMUEL'S *right arm high up on her waist, and takes his left hand in hers. They dance, rather awkwardly.*)

My face is stinging. I can't believe you hit me. It better not leave a mark.

STACIE: I didn't hit you that hard. Don't be a wuss.

SAMUEL: Don't be a ruffian.

STACIE: Uh, ruffian?

SAMUEL: Savage, bully . . . barbarian.

STACIE: Oh you're so smart. This is a party, not honors English. (*Beat.*) God, how long is this song?

SAMUEL: It just started.

STACIE: I'm only dancing with you because my mom made me.

SAMUEL: I'm only dancing with you for the photo op.

(SAMUEL *smiles, posing for a photographer. Sound of a flash going off.*)

STACIE: Just because it's your birthday, doesn't mean you're better than everyone else.

SAMUEL: It's not just my birthday, it's my *Bar Mitzvah.*

STACIE: So?

SAMUEL: So?! (*Proud.*) I am a man today.

STACIE: Yeah, right.

SAMUEL: I am!

STACIE: I see no man before me. I see a dork in a beanie.

SAMUEL: It's not a beanie. It's a yarmulke. A religious head covering.

STACIE: Yeah, that makes it cooler.

SAMUEL: I'll have you know, Bar Mitzvah literally translates to "son of commandment" and implies "responsible male."

STACIE: Big whoop.

SAMUEL: Did you hear me read from the Torah?

STACIE: Yeah, and I've got news for you…the Torah is a snore-ah.

SAMUEL: You weren't impressed?

STACIE: I was ready to hit the door-ah.

SAMUEL: Gee, thanks.

STACIE: On a scale of one to ten, I give it a four-ah.

SAMUEL: Okay, you didn't like it. I get it.

(*Beat. They continue dancing.* STACIE *scopes out the dance floor.* SAMUEL *is annoyed.*)

Why did you even come? If you hate me so much.

STACIE: Hello? We've lived next door to each other since we were four, Samuel. My whole family's here. We've had it marked on our calendar since August.

SAMUEL: You could've gotten out of it. You get out of everything else your parents want you to do.

STACIE: Well, maybe I didn't want to get out of it.

SAMUEL: (*Perking up.*) Really? Why?

STACIE: No reason.

SAMUEL: There's gotta be a reason. Tell me.

STACIE: Ow!! That's my foot!

SAMUEL: Why'd you want to come, huh? Say it.

STACIE: God, Samuel, what's the big deal?

SAMUEL: C'mon, Stacie, just give it up. Tell me.

STACIE: Okay, fine! You invited Kyle Fischer and Justin Flint.

(*Beat.* SAMUEL's *spirits plummet once again.*)

SAMUEL: I didn't invite them. Mom did. She's in the PTA with Mrs. Fischer and did Habitat for Humanity or something with Justin's mom.

STACIE: Do I look like I care? The point is they're here.

SAMUEL: So, what? You're dating them both?

STACIE: Samuel! Hello, I'm twelve.

SAMUEL: But you like them both.

STACIE: One of them likes me.

SAMUEL: Which one?

STACIE: I don't know.

SAMUEL: (*Confused.*) If you don't know which one likes you, how do you know if either of them like you?

STACIE: Jeez, Samuel, you're like, clueless. (*Beat.*) One of them is my secret admirer.

SAMUEL: Your secret admirer.

STACIE: Valentine's Day was last week, and I got a dozen pink carnations in my locker.

SAMUEL: And you think one of those dorkwads did it?!

STACIE: When I found the flowers in my locker they were at the lockers across the hall... looking at me, smiling.

SAMUEL: Oh, and that's like, proof.

STACIE: Shut up.

SAMUEL: You shut up.

STACIE: At least I got something. What did you get for Valentine's Day? Let me guess, a big heart-shaped cookie your mom made you.

SAMUEL: You're so dumb. (*Beat.*) It was a Cupid.

STACIE: They're looking over here. Oh my God, I'm gonna die. I am so gonna die.

SAMUEL: One—You're not gonna die. And two—They're not

looking at you, they're looking at my cousin Sharon. She's seventeen, and a thirty-four double D.

STACIE: Go ask them which one did it.

SAMUEL: Which one did what?

STACIE: Put the flowers in my locker.

SAMUEL: What?! No! No way!

STACIE: C'mon, Samuel, please?!

SAMUEL: I'm not talking to those Neanderthals. Uh-uh.

STACIE: Why not?

SAMUEL: Because one—I'm not your messenger boy, and two—I am enjoying my dance.

STACIE: One—What is with the one and two everything? God. And two—You're just jealous.

SAMUEL: Of who? Those guys? Please.

STACIE: YOUR HAND'S ON MY BUTT!!

SAMUEL: Sorry, it slipped!

STACIE: (*Breaking free.*) That's it, Bar Mitzvah boy. Son of commandment or not, my dad is gonna kick your ass!

SAMUEL: (*Holding on to her.*) Wait! Wait. Stacie, I'm sorry. Look, if you leave me up here by myself Mom is gonna make me dance with my little sister. It'll be more embarrassing than that life-size photo of me in the lobby. Please.

(*A popular, upbeat song begins to play.*)

STACIE: Fine, but only 'cause I like this song. (*Beat.*) Don't touch me.

(*They dance without touching, more awkwardly than the slow dance.*)

You're a really bad dancer.

SAMUEL: I've taken dance lessons at Arthur Murray since October.

STACIE: You should get your money back.

SAMUEL: They never got to fast tempo.

STACIE: Seriously, you look like Milton Smidel when he had that epileptic seizure during bio.

SAMUEL: Yeah, well, you're no Fergie either.

STACIE: I'm sure Kyle and Justin would disagree.

SAMUEL: Kyle and Justin are a few brain cells shy of being mentally retarded.

STACIE: Samuel!

SAMUEL: Haven't you heard the rumors? They like, still eat their boogers.

STACIE: Take it back!

SAMUEL: And they're in love with each other.

STACIE: They are not!

SAMUEL: Look, they're dancing together! See? (*Waving.*) Hi, guys! You look super!

STACIE: (*Trying to cover his mouth.*) Samuel, ssshhh!

SAMUEL: Like they could even figure out your locker combination, yeah, as if. How would they even know pink carnations are your favorite flower?!

(*Beat.* STACIE *stops dancing.*)

STACIE: How did *you* know pink carnations were my favorite flower?

(*A few beats. The song changes to another slow one.* STACIE *puts* SAMUEL's *hand on her waist. They start to slow dance again.*)

It was you, wasn't it? My secret admirer.

SAMUEL: No.

STACIE: Samuel.

SAMUEL: I mean, well...yeah. Kind of. (*Beat.*) Kyle and Justin saw me put them in there, hence the staring.

STACIE: Why?

SAMUEL: They thought they were trick flowers that were gonna squirt you in the face.

STACIE: No, I mean...why'd you do it?

SAMUEL: I dunno. It's kind of obvious, don't you think?

STACIE: But we haven't...I've been so...(*Beat.*) I haven't been very nice to you.

SAMUEL: Yeah, true dat.

STACIE: Well then, why?

(*Beat.*)

SAMUEL: When we were in third grade, Bobby Proctor wanted to fight me after school because I wouldn't let him cheat off me. After he threw the first punch you stepped in and kicked him in the balls. He never touched me again after that.

STACIE: I don't remember that.

SAMUEL: I never forgot it.

(*A few beats.*)

STACIE: Well, thank you. I mean, for the flowers.

SAMUEL: You're welcome. (*Beat.*) Y'know . . . I know I'm not cool, or popular enough for you or anything. But I just wanted to do something nice to pay you back for that day and . . . well, 'cause you deserve it.

STACIE: (*Smiling.*) Who knew Samuel Rosenbaum could be so sweet?

SAMUEL: (*Shrugging.*) I am a man today. I've matured.

(STACIE *wraps her arms around* SAMUEL'*s neck. They continue to dance even closer together, but both still a bit shy. They sway back and forth to the music. After a few beats:*)

STACIE: (*Soft.*) Samuel.

SAMUEL: (*Dreamlike.*) Yeah?

STACIE: Your hand's on my butt again.

SAMUEL: Sorry.

(*Blackout.*)

END OF PLAY

THE BLIZZARD

David Ives

The Blizzard was created as part of the 24 Hour Plays series (Tina Fallon, artistic director). It was first presented at the American Airlines Theatre in New York City on October 23, 2006. It was directed by Bennett Miller. The cast was as follows:

JENNY	Anna Paquin
NEIL	Fisher Stevens
SALIM	Aasif Mandvi
NATASHA	Gaby Hoffmann

A country house, toward evening. Cold winter light in the windows. In the course of the play, the lights gradually dim around center stage to nighttime. At curtain, JENNY *is onstage alone.*

JENNY: (*Calls.*) Neil?—Neil! (NEIL *enters from outside, stage right.*)

NEIL: It's still coming down. Some of those drifts are three feet deep already. What's the matter?

JENNY: Nothing. I just wondered what happened to you.

NEIL: Got scared, huh?

JENNY: No, I wasn't *scared.* The food's all ready. Do you really think they'll make it up here in this?

NEIL: Joe's got those new chains on the car. The ones that Sandy made him fork out for? Just what you'd expect from Miss Rationality.

JENNY: Right. Mr. *List Maker.* Mr. My-Pencils-Have-to-Be-Laid-Out-in-the-Right-Order-on-My-Desk. No, you're not rational. Sandy is rational.

NEIL: What about the TV?

JENNY: Nothing. Not a thing.

NEIL: The electricity's on. You'd think with a satellite dish we'd pick up *some*thing.

JENNY: The telephone's still out.

NEIL: They've probably been trying us since they left the city.

JENNY: There's no radio either.

NEIL: No *radio*?

JENNY: Isn't it *great*? It's just like an Agatha Christie.

NEIL: Thanks for that. I'm still not used to it. Being so remote. Nature's always scared the living crap out of me. Now I'm living in it. Or visiting it on weekends, anyway. You know I saw a bat flapping around out there? I didn't know there were bats in blizzards. No *radio*? The world could be ending out there, for Christ's sake. And we'd be the last ones to hear about it. No *radio*…

JENNY: Yes, we have no radio and a beautiful blizzard and a house and woods and a mountain that are all ours.

NEIL: All ours in twenty-nine years and three months.

JENNY: I kind of wish they weren't coming up tonight. It's so cozy. I wouldn't mind curling up with a book.

NEIL: I wish you hadn't said "Agatha Christie."

JENNY: You inflict *Torturama* One, Two and Three on people and I can't say "Agatha Christie"?

NEIL: Those are movies, not a real house in the middle of the real country with the lines down. And *Torturama* paid for our little mansion on a hill, babe.

JENNY: You know what it is about murder mysteries? No, listen. I think the reason people like murder mysteries is that, in a murder mystery, everything is *significant*. The people in murder mysteries are living in a *significant world*. A world where everything is there for a reason. Even before the murder's happened, you know that one is going to happen and you know that everything is a *clue*. Or rather, you know that some things are clues and some things are just obfuscation, they're snow. And you know that everybody has a secret of some kind. A secret that's like a soul. Murder mysteries are religious, in a way. Don't laugh. They're life the way you feel it when you're in love. When everything's in a special light. Incandescent. They're a couple of hours of everything *meaning* something, for God's sake. And then they're over and you're back to your old life, to real life. To mortgages and pork loin and potatoes and making a cherry pie.

NEIL: So real life doesn't feel like it means something to you these days?

JENNY: Sure it does. I'm just saying . . . Well, don't we all wish for that in real life? One of those moments when everything feels charged with meaning? When the air is electric?

NEIL: Well here's your opportunity. Listen, we're probably going to be totally snowed in. Why don't we all do something different this weekend.

JENNY: Different, what does different mean?

NEIL: I don't know. Something unusual. Something unexpected. Not you and Sandy holing yourself up in the kitchen and talking about whatever you talk about, not me and Joe sitting around talking about Mom and Dad and what happened in the third grade. Not the usual pour-a-glass-of-Jack-Daniel's, bullshit bullshit bullshit, what've you guys been doing, go in to dinner and break out the Margaux '01, have you seen any movies, did you catch that episode of blah blah blah. I don't know, something we've never done before, or let's talk about something we've never talked about before. Anything, instead of all the things we usually talk about.

JENNY: Okay. Something unusual. I love it.

SALIM: (*Offstage.*) Hello——? Neil?

NEIL: There they are. (SALIM *and* NATASHA *enter from the front door at stage left.* SALIM *carries a black plastic valise.*)

SALIM: Hello! Neil and Jenny, right? Sorry for the cold hand, I'm freezing. God, you're just like Joe and Sandy described you. I can't believe I'm finally meeting you, Neil. I am such a fan of *Torturama*. All of them. Natasha can't watch them herself. Natasha is squeamish.

NEIL: I'm sorry, I don't understand…

SALIM: Salim. And Natasha.

NATASHA: Hello. I'm so happy to encounter you at last. And you, Jenny, you are just as beautiful as Sandy told me. You are exquisite.

SALIM: And God, what a place up here! But so remote! Wow! We brought this for you. (*Holds up the black valise.*) A little house-warming gift.

NEIL: Whoa, whoa, whoa. I'm sorry, maybe there's been a mistake…

SALIM: I mean, this is the place, isn't it? You're Neil and Jenny? Oh, right, right. *Where are Joe and Sandy.* Middle of a snowstorm. Two strange people walk in. You're spooked. Totally natural. Natasha?

NATASHA: Joe and Sandy couldn't make it, so they sent us instead.

NEIL: They sent you instead. Wait a minute. They sent *you* instead ...

SALIM: They caught some kind of bug. God, Joe and Sandy have been telling us all about you two for I don't know how long.

NATASHA: A long time.

SALIM: A very long time.

NEIL: I don't think Joe and Sandy ever mentioned knowing a ... I'm sorry ...

SALIM: Salim.

NEIL: A Salim and a Natasha.

SALIM: You've been out of touch with your brother for too long, brother. They were really broken up they couldn't make it tonight. I'd say call them up and ask them but hey, are your cell phones as down as ours up here?

JENNY: How do you know Joe and Sandy?

SALIM: (*The black valise.*) You know what's in here? Just for showing us your hospitality? It's this new tequila, a hundred bucks a bottle. Olé, right? Let's support those oppressed brothers churning this stuff out for ten pesos a day. Neil, you want to pour?

JENNY: You didn't answer me.

NATASHA: How do we know Joe and Sandy.

SALIM: How do we know Joe and Sandy. How do we know them, Natasha?

NATASHA: Intimately.

SALIM: Intimately. Good word. We know them intimately.

JENNY: Neil... *Neil*...

NEIL: Look, I'm very sorry, but I'm going to have to ask you to leave.

SALIM: To leave? But... okay, I get it, I get it, you want some kind of proof that we're not just what...

NATASHA: Imposters.

SALIM: Imposters. Ten points, Natasha. We're not imposters! We're the real thing! I'm sorry if I'm coming on kind of strong, it's my personality, you know what I mean? God, how do you prove that you know somebody? Let's see. Where do I start? Do I start with Joe or Sandy? You know she made him get these hotshot snow chains for the car. That is so Sandy. No imagination, but always thinking ahead. So *rational*. (*Pause.*) Listen. Listen, I'm sorry we barged in on you like this. Maybe we should leave, but... hey, are you really going to turn two freezing strangers back out into the storm? Neil, you're the guy who inflicted *Torturama* on the world, more killings per square frame than any movie in history. You're pouring blood in the aisles, man. Don't tell me you're scared. What are you scared of? What am I, the wrong color? And what am I going to do to you, huh? If I was going to do something to you I'd've done it already, wouldn't I? (*Pause.*) So do we leave? Or do we stay? Aw, have a heart, Neil.

NEIL: Well, we can't turn you out in this weather...

JENNY: Turn them out, Neil.

NEIL: Honey, I...

JENNY: Turn them out.

NEIL: It's a blizzard out there, honey.

SALIM: Your wife is so sweet. Really. She is a doll.

NATASHA: You know, with so much snow, it's like we're in a murder mystery here.

SALIM: Natasha adores Agatha Christie. You know what I hate about murder mysteries? It's that everybody in them's got a secret. People don't have secrets. People are open books. I don't know you personally, Neil, but just looking at you I'd say you're probably the kind of guy who makes lists, for example. Lines his pencils up on the desk. Likes things neat and tidy. Am I right? A Jack-Daniel's-before-dinner kinda guy. You're not the kind of guy who, what, secretly worked for the CIA once upon a time, you're not a guy with a secret history of killing people, I mean *really* killing people, offscreen, you don't have any real blood on your hands. You're in the entertainment industry. You have nothing to hide.

JENNY: Send them away, Neil.

SALIM: And Jenny, she probably made her usual dinner for tonight, let's see what would it be, pork loin and some kind of special potato recipe and a cherry-rhubarb pie for dessert. The perfect American housewife. Nothing to conceal. I'm sorry, I'm sorry, there's that personality of mine again. I'm brash. I'm insensitive. I'm loud. Call me American.

NEIL: You know I have a gun in the house.

SALIM: Oh, that's rich. What a liar! "I have a gun in the house." Right. That's so cute. This isn't a movie, this is *real life*, Neil. And I'm your brother for the night. I'm a stand-in for Joe. Remember me? Your brother?

JENNY: Where are Joe and Sandy?

SALIM: They're very sick in bed is where they are.

JENNY: What have you done with them?

SALIM: They can't move is what they are. Aren't I your brother? Neil? Come on. (*He puts his arm around* NEIL's *waist.*) Am I your brother?

NEIL: Sure . . .

SALIM: Am I your brother? Am I your brother? Am I your brother?

NEIL: You're my brother.

SALIM: There you see? How hard was that? Now we can talk about all those kids we used to beat up in third grade. Just like old times. Well, brother, what do you say? We're here for the duration. You gonna play the good host here or what? You want to show me around the grounds?

NEIL: Sure.

SALIM: Sure what?

NEIL: Sure, brother.

SALIM: Attaboy! (SALIM *follows* NEIL *off through the back door. A pause.*)

NATASHA: You know what I love about murder mysteries? Is that everything in them seems to mean something. The people in murder mysteries are living in a significant world. Everything holding its breath. Waiting. The air is electric. And then, bang, it happens. The irrevocable. Whatever that is. Changing everything. It's a kind of poetry. To me, it's almost a religious feeling.

JENNY: I don't want any more fucking significance. I don't want it. I don't want it.

NATASHA: Poor Jenny. Afraid over nothing. Why? Why?

JENNY: You have the wrong people.

NATASHA: You're the right people. Neil and Jenny. We're just here for dinner with you. And you have nothing to be afraid of. Really. Absolutely nothing.

JENNY: (*Calls out.*) Neil...? *Neil...?*

NATASHA: Absolutely nothing... (*The lights fade.*)

END OF PLAY

BROTHERLY LOVE

Ean Miles Kessler

Brotherly Love was first performed as part of the Rutgers Playwriting Festival, 2007. The production was directed by Ean Miles Kessler, with special help from Louis Wells. The cast was as follows:

GORDON	David Delaney
WALLY	Andrew Isaac Rosenberg

The same cast performed the play at Manhattan Repertory Theatre's Summerfest, opening June 16, 2010. Produced by Byron Bronson, lights and sound by Devon Malik Beckford.

For Dave Delaney and Andrew Rosenberg:
For all their hard work and friendship.

At Rise: A small den/living room in a house in Lynchburg, Virginia. A pull-out bed/couch with doily on the back, a dresser; other furniture as seen fit. The house belongs to GORDON *and* WALLY'S *parents, and has a very homey feel.*

Throughout the piece, GORDON *unpacks from his overnight bag, pulls out the bed and makes it, and generally makes the room more comfortable for himself and the arrival of his guest.*

Production Note: The entire piece should fly.

Lights up quick; WALLY, *with beer in hand, and* GORDON, *with suitcase, unpacking.*

WALLY: This is ridiculous—how did you—?

GORDON: I don't know what you want me to say.

WALLY: I want you to say that you're full a' shit, that you're lying to me.

GORDON: I'm full a' shit, and I'm lying to you. (*Moment.*) It was a joke, Wally.

WALLY: That's not funny.

GORDON: I'm just—

WALLY: No, that's not funny, Gordon. Seriously. Come on.

GORDON: I don't know what you wanna hear.

WALLY: Have you seen someone about this?

GORDON: There's no one to see—

WALLY: I mean a doctor or something.

GORDON: There's nothing *wrong*—

WALLY: According to you.

GORDON: Yes. According to me.

(*Beat.*)

WALLY: I didn't—it wasn't me, right? I mean—

GORDON: Oh Jesus . . .

WALLY: At the pool—

GORDON: No, Wally—

WALLY: We were kids, I was stupid; I would flash anyone—

GORDON: That's—

WALLY: I thought it was funny—!

GORDON: Wally, it's not—

WALLY: I was just eleven—! Naked was funny back then—!

GORDON: Wally, you can't turn someone *gay*.

(*Beat.*)

WALLY: No, I know, but yanno, I mean I didn't, I mean, I didn't make you a homo, right?

GORDON: Wally. You can't turn someone gay.

WALLY: No, I know, but—

GORDON: Wally!

WALLY: I'm just sayin'—

GORDON: Fine. Fine, you made me gay.

WALLY: What?

GORDON: No seriously. Your eleven-year-old dick made me a fag.

WALLY: That's not funny—

GORDON: Runnin' around the pool, butt-naked, two inches of flop—you goddamn homo-maker, you.

WALLY: That's—

GORDON: The fuckin' fag-wizard over here—

WALLY: Wait, two inches—?

GORDON: Wally: Lord of the Queers!

WALLY: I am not—I do not—I do not make people gay! (*Slight moment.*) *I have a girlfriend!*

GORDON: Fine.

WALLY: I know you don't make someone gay, I just—I mean if I had done something by accident—I just—I would never try to make you—yanno—like that.

GORDON: Thanks, Wally.

WALLY: What?

GORDON: Nothing.

(*Slight beat.*)

WALLY: You gonna tell Dad?

GORDON: Reason I'm here.

WALLY: You can't do that—

GORDON: Why not?

WALLY: Walk right in there all-of-a-sudden-gay?

GORDON: I repeat: Why not?

WALLY: They're gonna be back from T.G.I. Friday's in twenty— (*checks watch*)—six minutes—! You can't be gay—!

GORDON: They're gonna have to—

WALLY: You've been at NYU for three semesters—!

GORDON: They're gonna have to hear it, Wally—

WALLY: Three semesters, Gordon! Mom and Dad go out for

cheeseburgers and baby back ribs, their firstborn comes back a homo—!

GORDON: I'm not—

WALLY: Have you met Dad?

GORDON: Wally—

WALLY: He was in *Vietnam*—

GORDON: I don't give a fuck what war—

WALLY: He voted for Reagan—

GORDON: Or century—

WALLY: Twice! He voted for Reagan twice!

GORDON: Or—

WALLY: He's got Billy Graham, Live in Concert T-shirts—!

GORDON: Or lifestyle he comes from—

WALLY: Eight of them—!

GORDON: I'm bringing my boyfriend home.

WALLY: Boyfriend, what is boyfriend? The hell can you call him boyfriend?

GORDON: You're very smart, Wally, I'm sure if you think about it, you can figure it out.

WALLY: Cut the smart shit, all right? *Boy*friend! I mean my God, what about you and, and—yanno what's-her-tits—?

GORDON: What's-her-tits doesn't really narrow anything down, Wally—

WALLY: Stacey Feeskin—!

GORDON: Oh my God—that was *high school*—

WALLY: So?

GORDON: So, it didn't mean anything—

WALLY: Didn't mean anything—?

GORDON: We watched *Pretty in Pink* together; that was all.

WALLY: Vicky Bassman?

GORDON: Class lesbian.

WALLY: Sarah Shellder—?

GORDON: (*Pointing to self.*) Gay, not blind—

WALLY: Debbie Fawson—?

GORDON: Not even with your dick, Wally—

WALLY: Oh come on!

GORDON: Oh come on, what—?

WALLY: What about Maureen Dellnick—?

GORDON: Yeah, but who didn't—?

WALLY: *Ha!*—you're straight—!

GORDON: Wally, it's a bit more complicated than that—

WALLY: Complicated my balls: you had sex with a *girl*—

GORDON: *Yeah*—but I was thinking about the *football team* while I was doing it—

WALLY: Don't—

GORDON: Soon as I jumped in I wanted to jump out—

WALLY: No, don't say that—

GORDON: What?

WALLY: About the—the—football team—

GORDON: Wally—

WALLY: Just—it makes me uncomfortable.

GORDON: I wasn't—

WALLY: It makes me *uncomfortable*—

GORDON: Fine.

WALLY: Just—

GORDON: I said fine.

WALLY: Thank you.

(*Slight beat.*)

GORDON: Yanno, if I had a dollar every time I had to listen to you, "she's so hot," "her tits this," "her ass that," I'd be a fucking millionaire.

WALLY: Yeah, well it's different.

(*Beat.*)

You don't—I mean, this guy, you, you don't...yanno ...you...

GORDON: What? Sex?—Do we have sex?

WALLY: No, God—!

GORDON: What? Ask.

WALLY: No, I don't—I—

GORDON: It's fine, ask.

WALLY: I don't want to ask!

GORDON: Fine.

WALLY: I don't care what you do.

GORDON: Whatever.

WALLY: Fucking disgusting...

(*Long beat. Finally:*)

Gordon, that is where poop is made.

GORDON: Well, I'm very glad you figured that out.

WALLY: You really want to put your (*makes a motion*) in somebody's—(*makes another motion*)?

GORDON: Yeah, that's *much* worse than a vagina. Much worse.

(*Slight beat.*)

WALLY: Yes. Yes it is.

GORDON: You are absurd.

WALLY: No. No, no, no. No you are absurd. You want to fuck butts. That is absurd.

GORDON: You telling me you never tried to do that with Rachael?

WALLY: Don't you fuckin'—

GORDON: You *never tried?*

WALLY: Don't you fuckin' talk about my girlfriend like that.

GORDON: Have you, Wally?

(*Beat.*)

WALLY: That's different.

GORDON: For whom?

WALLY: For—for everyone involved!

GORDON: How's it different?

WALLY: (*Counting off the reasons on his fingers.*) It's not a man!

GORDON: It's still a butt.

WALLY: But it's not a man's butt. It's a girl butt—a lady butt! There's a difference.

GORDON: Yanno what, Wally?—you're right. What I do? That's disgusting; what you do—that just takes a bottle of Jäger and a cheerleader—

WALLY: No! No, mine is—mine is about love! And commitment. And yours—yours is—

GORDON: Is what, Wally?

WALLY: Queerin' don't make the world work, Gordon!

(_Slight beat._)

GORDON: I'm sorry, I couldn't hear you over the incessant pounding of your bigotry—what did you just say?

WALLY: It's the birds and the bees, Gordon; not the birds and the birds—

GORDON: _What_—?

WALLY: With the—the stingers, and—the—the wings—

GORDON: What are you—?

WALLY: Feathers...

GORDON: That doesn't even make sense, Wally—

WALLY: _Cross-pollination_—

GORDON: What are you talking about?

(_Slight beat._)

WALLY: Vagina is better than penis! Vagina is better than penis!

GORDON: Oh my God—

WALLY: Vagina is, yanno, good, and yes, and everything good—
And penis is just, yanno, you just look at it and you wonder
how things ever got that bad—yanno? I mean what happened, Gordon?—*what happened?*

(*Beat.*)

GORDON: Sometimes you talk and I just, I don't understand—

WALLY: No, you—

GORDON: Anything, anything at all; you just—

WALLY: This isn't about understanding or not understanding! This
is about birds and bees and you and—your—your ugh! Ugh!

GORDON: . . . My boyfriend?

WALLY: No, God, no—! Stop saying that!

(*Beat.*)

You uh (*Makes a masculine gesture.*)—or—? (*Makes a feminine
gesture.*)

GORDON: What?

WALLY: Your—you and the guy, you—? (*Another masculine gesture.*) Or—? (*Another feminine gesture.*)

GORDON: What are you *doing*—?

WALLY: Do you, yanno— (*Makes a masculine gesture of "thrusting"
or "pumping."*) Or—? Yanno?

GORDON: What—?

(WALLY *makes a feminine gesture of being "taken by surprise."*)

I don't know what that means, Wallace—

WALLY: Are you—I mean, do you—?

(WALLY *makes a "baseball pitcher" motion.*)

Or—

(WALLY *makes a "baseball catcher" motion.*)

GORDON: I—what—?

(WALLY *continues to make motions, thrusting and pumping, getting more and more into it as the guessing goes along, trying to act out what he can't bring himself to ask.*)

Are you skiing? Did you hurt your ass—? The fuck are you doing—? I don't—

WALLY: Oh come on, you know what I'm saying—!

GORDON: No, Wally, I don't—

WALLY: Oh *come on*—!

You're gonna argue with me about what I understand? Really, Wally—?

WALLY: Don't be a fucking asshole about this—

GORDON: "Fucking asshole"; interesting choice of words—

WALLY: Don't start—!

GORDON: I'm not *being* an asshole, I just don't speak retard—

WALLY: *For the love of God, are you the fucker or the fuckee—?*

GORDON: Depends on the day, Wally—

WALLY: Oh my God!

GORDON: For fuck's sake, he's my *boyfriend*—!

WALLY: Oh my *God*! Don't touch me ever again!—Don't touch me—!

GORDON: You fucking *hillbilly*—

WALLY: Yeah, well, you're a fucking faggot, faggot!

GORDON: Good one, Wally; really. Like I've never heard *that* before.

WALLY: No! No, this is just your gayness—

GORDON: My "gayness"—?

WALLY: Your icky, fucking gayness!—your gayness!—How did you—how are you even like this? I mean, Jesus Christ—there aren't any gay people in our family!

GORDON: Well, first time for everything...

WALLY: No—! No not "first time for everything"! Fuck "first time for everything." Go back to being straight!

GORDON: Wally, I was never straight.

WALLY: Yes, you were.

GORDON: No. I wasn't.

WALLY: Yes—you—were!

GORDON: No, Wally, I wasn't. Believe me. I was there.

WALLY: No—*no*!

(WALLY *goes to the couch and gets several porn magazines and DVDs from underneath it.*)

You see those titties—?

GORDON: Why do you have porn in the living room—?

WALLY: We don't have time for questions, Gordon, we only have time for titties! You see the shirt puppies—?

GORDON: *Shirt puppies*—?

WALLY: Nice big—

GORDON: Who says *shirt puppies*—?

WALLY: Mahatmas—

GORDON: Don't—don't do that; don't say that—don't call them—

WALLY: Mahat—

GORDON: For God's sake, the man was a legend—!

WALLY: Moo-moos—

GORDON: Moo-moos? What are you five—?

WALLY: Meat balloons—

GORDON: *Meat balloons? Meat balloons*, Wally?

WALLY: Whatever; look at that pussy! Look!

GORDON: I—

WALLY: Look at that!

GORDON: I—

WALLY: You see that—?

GORDON: I—yes—

WALLY: You see the little—honey pot—

GORDON: Honey pot—? What are you, Winnie the Pooh—?

WALLY: Ham wallet—furburger—

GORDON: That doesn't even sound appealing—!

WALLY: Beef curtains; love canal—little panty hamster—

GORDON: Jesus, *Wally*—

WALLY: Seafood pit—the child-slide—

GORDON: Oh my God—

WALLY: The cock-vacuum—skin chimney—bearded love clam—!

GORDON: Oh my God—!

WALLY: Mud flaps—

GORDON: *Oh my God*—!

WALLY: Slammin' salmon canyon—vajingle-jangle—

GORDON: Wally, I don't even know what that *means*—"vajingle-jangle"; what is it, a Christmas carol—?

WALLY: Look at it, it just makes you wanna— (*Makes a growling sound; bares his teeth; sticks out tongue; licks the air vigorously.*)

GORDON: Were you raised by retarded wolves—?

WALLY: What? No—

GORDON: When did feminism cease completely in Virginia—?

WALLY: These are all well-known terms—

GORDON: Well-known terms? Well-known by whom? Lucifer—?

WALLY: They're in the dictionary, okay—?

GORDON: What kind of dictionary do you read—?

WALLY: The American kind—!

GORDON: Wait—Wally; hold on—

WALLY: You don't wanna (*repeats the motion he did several lines back*)—?

GORDON: Let me see that?

WALLY: Yes—Good; yes—!

GORDON: Wally—

WALLY: Yes! This is good; this is *awesome!*

GORDON: Wally—

WALLY: Awesome, I'm *winning*—!

GORDON: Wally, all this porn is anal.

WALLY: Yeah, naw—yeah—

GORDON: Wally, "Butt Pilots 36"—?

WALLY: Naw, that—wait—

GORDON: There were thirty-five other "Butt Pilots"—?

WALLY: Gimme those—

GORDON: "Ass-Clowns: The Saga Begins"—?

WALLY: Those are mine—!

GORDON: It's a *saga*—?

WALLY: Stoppit—!

GORDON: "Dookie Pirates: Plunder Down Under"—

WALLY: Gimme that—!

GORDON: Starring—Dame Judi *Drench*—Does Mom know you
   watch this stuff—?

WALLY: No, this—gimme that—!

(GORDON *throws the porn back to* WALLY.)

GORDON: I don't like women, Wally! Nothing you're gonna do is gonna make me want to sleep with these women. This pornography is abhorrent.

(WALLY *points to the picture.*)

WALLY: Vagina.

GORDON: Wally. That wasn't even a full sentence—

WALLY: But—(*Points.*)

GORDON: I know; it's a vagina—I've heard really good things; I'm just not interested—

WALLY: Panty hamster—

GORDON: I—stop calling it that—

WALLY: I—

GORDON: I know—it's all right; it's gonna be all right, man—

(GORDON *gives* WALLY *a pat on the back, or some other such show of reassurance; then resumes his activity of cleaning up or unpacking. Beat.*)

WALLY: You don't—I mean—

GORDON: What?

WALLY: You don't touch kids, right? (*Beat.*) I'm asking— that's all, I just—

GORDON: No, Wally. I don't. How the fuck you gonna ask me that?

WALLY: I just, I mean most a' those guys—

GORDON: What?

WALLY: You know exactly what. Those fuckin' people are—

GORDON: "Those fucking people"? Excuse me; "those fucking people," Wally?

WALLY: Yes, *those* people—!

GORDON: Just shut the fuck up, Wally—just shut the fuck up.

(*Beat. Then very small:*)

WALLY: . . . You taught me how to pee standing up.

GORDON: What, I'm gonna touch you twelve years ago? I'm your brother for Christ's sake—!

WALLY: We took baths together—

GORDON: Like I'm gonna get in my big gay *time machine*—?

WALLY: *Baths*, Gordon—

GORDON: I *know*, Wally; I remember—

WALLY: My penis saw your penis!

GORDON: We're not talking anymore; you're a fucking idiot—

WALLY: If our penises were people, they'd be on a first-name basis—!

GORDON: I'm not having this conversation right now—

WALLY: My penis cannot take a bath with a faggot penis—!

GORDON: *I'm not having this conversation right now, Wallace—!*

(GORDON *goes back to unpacking.*)

Oh, and uh, by the way—Uncle Simon? (*He lets his wrist go limp in an "effeminate" hand gesture.*)

WALLY: Are you serious?

GORDON: Wally. Aunt Betsy and Uncle Simon haven't had sex since 1973.

WALLY: He's not gay: he's subtle—doesn't mean he's gay, means he has morals. Maybe he just doesn't—

GORDON: What? Like vaginas?

WALLY: *Want to be condemned to hell,* you sick bastard. And don't talk about Aunt Betsy's vagina. She's a beautiful woman.

GORDON: Yeah. For a dyke.

WALLY: Are you serious?

GORDON: Wally, she's built like a Mack truck and she has the face of Brian Dennehy—

WALLY: She's a lesbian—?

GORDON: Is Tom Cruise gay?

WALLY: Don't say that.

GORDON: Oh God...

WALLY: He made *Risky Business*.

GORDON: Wally—

WALLY: He fucked a girl in that.

GORDON: That doesn't mean—

WALLY: And *Top Gun*?

GORDON: Are you kidding me?

WALLY: What?—I love that movie.

GORDON: Wally.

WALLY: I can't love a gay movie.

GORDON: Well you might want to rearrange your top ten, then.

(*Beat.*)

WALLY: I have a girlfriend—

GORDON: I know—

WALLY: We have lots of sex—

GORDON: I don't—

WALLY: And I played football in high school—

GORDON: I don't care what your favorite movie is, Wally.

(*Beat.*)

WALLY: Am I gay?

GORDON: Oh my God—

WALLY: Am I *gay?*

GORDON: *No, Wally*—

WALLY: Oh my God: "volleyball scene"—oh my God…!

GORDON: You're not gay, Wally; but if you'd like, I know some people, maybe we can work something out—

(WALLY *sticks his fingers in his ears. Production Note: He keeps his fingers in his ears until it is noted that he takes them out.*)

WALLY: I can't hear you, I can't hear you—I'm not listening—I can't hear you—!

GORDON: Get you a nice little man-friend—

WALLY: I have sex with my girlfriend; I have so much sex with my girlfriend—!

GORDON: Some Latin lover—

WALLY: So much heterosexual sex! So much heterosexual sex! Pussy! Vagina! No cock! No cock!

GORDON: Pablo *y* Wally—*los amores*—!

WALLY: *No cock!*

GORDON: You're a fucking idiot—

WALLY: Yeah, well I'm not a faggot!

GORDON: *Stop using that word——! Jesus!*

(*Slight beat;* WALLY *mutters "fucking homo" under his breath.*)

What?

WALLY: Nothing——

GORDON: What did you just say——?

WALLY: *Nothing——*

(*Slight beat.* WALLY *mutters it again;* GORDON *smacks him upside the head.* WALLY *takes one finger out of his ear and whacks* GORDON *on the arm.* GORDON *whacks* WALLY *on the arm;* WALLY *whacks* GORDON; GORDON *whacks* WALLY; WALLY *slaps* GORDON *on the shoulder.* GORDON *slaps* WALLY *on the shoulder. They slap each other, back and forth, over and over, getting faster and faster and more livid, until:*)

I'll fucking kill you——!

(*An all-out slap-fight ensues.* WALLY *takes his fingers out of his ears and hits with both hands for this portion. They get wilder and wilder until they both stop simultaneously, exhausted.* WALLY *puts his fingers back in his ears. Beat.*)

Ow.

(*They both sit, recovering from their fight;* WALLY *stares at* GORDON *without blinking;* GORDON *stares off at nothing in a completely different direction. Long awkward beat. Finally:*)

GORDON: *Oh my God, what do you want from me——?!*

WALLY: If I didn't make you a fag——

GORDON: Jesus *Christ!*

WALLY: And Mom and Dad didn't make you a fag—

GORDON: *What did I just say about using that word*—?

WALLY: What the fuck am I gonna tell people—?

GORDON: I don't care; tell them I'm gay—

(WALLY *takes his fingers out of his ears.*)

WALLY: No!—no, not *gay*—I don't have a gay brother. I have a—a sexually unpredictable brother.

GORDON: Sexually unpredictable? The fuck does that mean, Wally? What? I unpredictably fuck men?

WALLY: No, *Gordon,* what it *means* is that we don't have gay where we come from. We have Confederate flags and shot-guns on walls. So hide your fuckin' rainbows and shut the fuck up! Jesus Christ, you wanna get fuckin' killed!

(*Beat.*)

GORDON: I'm bringing him home with me.

WALLY: No, you're not.

GORDON: Yes. I am.

WALLY: We're from Lynchburg, Virginia, Gordon! *Lynch-Burg!* That's a burg of lynches! Think about it—!

GORDON: I—

WALLY: Have you met my friends?—

GORDON: I don't see your point.

WALLY: You're not gay in Virginia: you're a beating waiting to happen—

GORDON: Yeah, Wally; I *know*—

WALLY: Gordon—

GORDON: I'm not going to be fucking *cowed*, Wally! You, Dad, Mom—the fuck you think I am?

WALLY: It's just; you're my brother, okay?—you're—and I just—you're gonna—

GORDON: *What*—?

WALLY: You're gonna get hurt, all right? What if you get hurt? I mean, I just; you're my brother and I love you and what if you get hurt?

(*Beat.*)

GORDON: I will not be cowed, Wally.

WALLY: I'm not asking you to—

GORDON: Then what are you asking? Huh? Play ball? I've been playing ball since the fourth fucking grade.

(*Tense beat.*)

WALLY: You bring him home?—you don't call him that—your boyfriend. You don't; you don't say that word. All right?

GORDON: Hey, Wally, go fuck yourself—

WALLY: Yeah, you too!

(WALLY *storms out; storms right back in.*)

GORDON: What do you want?

WALLY: I just—when, when I said I loved you, that was, yanno, in a non-un-not-homo-sex kinda way.

GORDON: No, I know—

WALLY: I'm just makin' sure—

GORDON: You are an idiot—

WALLY: Yeah fuck you too—

(*Beat.*)

GORDON: You remember Randall Merkins?

(*No answer.*)

Come to school, he'd wear his ma's perfume— (*Slight beat.*) Said he wanted to be a nurse— We were in gym class once; he said—in front of the whole class, he said when he grew up he wanted to be a nurse— Me, Danny Reeder, Mark Vannson— we got him back behind a Dumpster—

WALLY: Gordon—

GORDON: Did you see him afterwards—?

WALLY: No—

GORDON: You see what we did to him—?

(*Long beat.*)

I didn't know what I was supposed to do—

WALLY: Gordon—

GORDON: It was sixth grade; bunch a' little *boys*—I didn't know what the fuck was I supposed to *do*—I don't—

WALLY: *Gordon*—

GORDON: I don't *know* what I'm supposed to *do*—

WALLY: Kid shouldn't a' acted that way—

GORDON: We put him in the hospital, Wally—

WALLY: He shouldn't a'—

GORDON: *We put him in the hospital, Wally.* You understand that?

WALLY: He just pretended to be straight, nothin' woulda happened. Flaunt that shit around—?

(*Slight beat.*)

GORDON: You wanna see straight—

WALLY: I'm just sayin'—

GORDON: No, you wanna see straight? Huh? (*He pushes* WALLY.) You wanna—?

WALLY: Don't fuckin'—

GORDON: You wanna see a macho man, motherfucker—*here*—

(*He shoves* WALLY.)

WALLY: Don't fuckin' push me—

GORDON: You wanna see straight—

(*He shoves* WALLY *again.*)

WALLY: Don't fuckin'—

GORDON: You wanna—

(*Another shove.*)

WALLY: Get the fuck off me—!

GORDON: Huh!

(*Another shove.*)

WALLY: Fuckin' faggot—

(GORDON *grabs* WALLY *by the collar.*)

GORDON: What did you say?

WALLY: Get the fuck off me—

GORDON: What'd you fuckin' say?

(*Tense moment.*)

WALLY: Y' fuckin' faggot.

(*Tense moment;* GORDON *slams* WALLY *up against the wall. Tense moment. He lets go of* WALLY. *Long tense moment.*)

They have guns. No, I'm serious—Gordon, it's Virginia. We went to "George Wallace High." The—"segregation today, segregation tomorrow, segregation *forever*"—George Wallace, high school. And you! Dad wanted to name you Strom. *Strom*, Gordon! This is not the place to air out that kinda bullshit.

GORDON: Bullshit—?

WALLY: You know what I mean—

GORDON: You're not my fuckin' father, Wallace—

WALLY: Gordon—

GORDON: I'm a *grown man*. No one's gonna fuckin' shoot me—

WALLY: Naw, but they might drag you behind a Dumpster.

(*Long beat. Eventually* GORDON *goes back to unpacking.*)

Stoppit— Gordon; would you just—? Gordon—Jesus Christ!— (*He tries to take the suitcase away from* GORDON.) Gordon, would you just—stop! Just stop! *Stop!*

(WALLY *grabs the suitcase from his brother and throws it against the wall. Long beat of silence;* WALLY *looks at the suitcase.*)

Is that mine?

GORDON: What?

WALLY: Is that—?

GORDON: No—

WALLY: That's my suitcase— (*He picks up the suitcase.* GORDON *goes over and gets the other end—tug-of-war.*)

GORDON: That doesn't belong to you, Wally—

WALLY: Give it back—

GORDON: Grandpa gave that to me two years ago—!

WALLY: Give it back, you ass-face—!

GORDON: Fuck you—

WALLY: You fuckin'—dick-titty!

GORDON: Get the fuck outta here—

WALLY: Fuckin—

GORDON: Cock-wad—!

WALLY: Fuck-ass—!

GORDON: Cock—!

WALLY: Fuck—!

GORDON: Shit—!

WALLY: Goddamn—ass-cock—*fuck-shit*—!

(GORDON *yanks the suitcase from his brother. Slight beat as they both catch their breath.*)

Y'fuckin'—kumquat.

(*Beat.*)

Ma's gonna cry.

GORDON: I know.

(*Beat.*)

WALLY: You wanna be gay in New York, fine, okay, but—but here—

GORDON: Wally—

WALLY: Just not here—

GORDON: Do you love Rachael?

WALLY: Don't be stupid.

GORDON: Do you love Rachael?

WALLY: Don't fucking—

GORDON: Answer the question.

WALLY: Yes! Okay? Yes, I do; she's my girlfriend.

GORDON: Same thing.

WALLY: No—it's not.

GORDON: I—

WALLY: It's a man.

GORDON: I'm not—

WALLY: It's a *man*. That goes against everything we were ever brought up with. Everything.

GORDON: He's a good person.

WALLY: We can do that for you—your family can do that—

GORDON: It's not the same—

WALLY: We'll get you help—

GORDON: No.

WALLY: We'll find someone—

GORDON: No; I am—I am paralyzed—

WALLY: Gordon—

GORDON: I am fucking *paralyzed*, Wally, and sometimes I sit in my apartment and it gets hard to breathe, okay—?

WALLY: Gordon—

GORDON: It gets hard to breathe, because if the rest of my life—*if the rest of my life* is like this—like—like—like—like, Randall Merkins and Danny Reeder and Mark Vannson then I don't know what the fuck to do—I've never had a boyfriend in my life, Wally. In my *life*. What you have with Rachael—I don't even—I don't even have a concept of what that feels like— Now I'm bringin' my boyfriend home; you can either be my brother on this, or you can be an asshole. Which is it?

(*Long moment.*)

WALLY: This guy from New York?

GORDON: Yeah.

WALLY: He's not Jewish, right?

GORDON: No—what—?

WALLY: Just, we can only take it in little increments, all right? I got nothing against Jews, it's just, yanno, you come home with the Fiddler on the Roof, Dad'll probably kill himself.

GORDON: No, he's not Jewish.

WALLY: Thank God. (*Small beat.*) He's not Muslim, is he?

GORDON: *What—?*

WALLY: I just don't want some Mohammad Al-Jawid blowing himself, or anything else up, okay—?

GORDON: How are you my fucking brother—?

WALLY: Beheading the fucking sofa—

GORDON: Just be quiet. Just shut up.

WALLY: What time's his plane come in?

GORDON: Huh—?

WALLY: I'll drive you to the airport—he's not riding up front, though; neither are you, fuck-head—

GORDON: Oh, no; no, my boyfriend—

WALLY: Don't do that, don't—

GORDON: My *boyfriend* didn't fly; he drove.

WALLY: From New York?

GORDON: Only way he could afford it.

WALLY: Christ, that's—

GORDON: Yeah—

WALLY: Really nice. Of him. Really.

GORDON: I know.

WALLY: Jesus; where in New York?

GORDON: Yeah, uh actually it's kinda funny—

WALLY: Yeah—?

GORDON: Yeah, you're gonna laugh, you're gonna—yeah—

WALLY: Yeah—?

GORDON: He's got an apartment over in—um—Harlem—

WALLY: . . . *Harlem?*

(*Lights cut to blackout.*)

END OF PLAY

CHRISTMAS PRESENT

Amy Herzog

Christmas Present was first produced at Ensemble Studio Theatre as part of the 2008 Marathon of One-Act Plays. RJ Tolan directed the following cast:

BENJI	Jake Hoffman
JESS	Julie Fitzpatrick

BENJI *enters a hallway or living room area from the bedroom. He wears pants and an undershirt and socks. His belt is unbuckled. He carries a sweater and his shoes. He pulls on his shoes and his sweater. He buckles his belt. He is heading for his coat when* JESS *enters, unseen, in a bathrobe.*

JESS: Hi. Sorry, hi.

BENJI: Good morning. I didn't want to wake you, I just couldn't sleep—

JESS: Don't worry, I don't want to talk or anything, I just—

BENJI: (*Overlapping.*) No, no I—

JESS: What?

BENJI: Sorry, I interrupted you.

JESS: I don't mean to hold you up, I just wanted to exchange...contact info, or whatever. Not for—I mean, I get it, I'm not delusional. Just, you know. In case.

BENJI: In case...?

JESS: I'm not trying to date you. I know this isn't how dating begins. I'm not actually a total lunatic whatever you may—

BENJI: No, whoa—

JESS: I don't even need your number, just... an e-mail, maybe? I almost definitely won't use it. Just...

BENJI: What?

JESS: In case something goes wrong.

BENJI: We were careful.

JESS: Yeah, I'm always careful, and I'm usually pretty unlucky. So. I'm not trying to freak you out, I'm sure it will be fine.

BENJI: You said you're on the pill.

JESS: Totally.

BENJI: And we used a—

JESS: I happen to be a very fertile person, which I've had opportunity in the past to discover, unfortunately, so... obviously the huge likelihood is that I'll never use your e-mail, which, if it's that much of a problem, I'm not gonna force you to—

BENJI: Actually I—

JESS: But there's also, you know. STD.

BENJI: I just had a physical so I took like a whole battery of tests—

JESS: Okay, that's great. I mean— (*She does air quotes.*) "me too," but things don't show up, or—

BENJI: (*Overlapping.*) You think I'm lying?

JESS: I don't know you.

BENJI: We used a condom.

JESS: Which doesn't protect against several diseases.

BENJI: Which ones?

JESS: Herpes. You don't know this? HPV, which everyone has anyway—

BENJI: Everyone?

JESS: Well like seventy percent of the sexually active population.

BENJI: I don't have it.

JESS: How do you know?

BENJI: I didn't test positive for it.

(*She laughs.*)

    What?

JESS: Men never test positive for it. The test for men sucks. So all these men go around claiming to be HPV free but meanwhile like every sexually active woman has it so it's coming from *somewhere*.

BENJI: I honestly don't think I have it.

JESS: Well, ya do now.

BENJI: *Great.*

JESS: Oh relax, there are no symptoms for men.

BENJI: Which is the one that gives you genital warts?

JESS: Well, HPV. But that's a different HPV. The one I have gives you cervical cancer. If you get cervical cancer, I'll owe you a big apology.

BENJI: You didn't think about telling me this last night?

JESS: Everyone has it! You already had it!

BENJI: I've only slept with one other woman in my life.

(*Brief pause.*)

JESS: You might not have had it.

BENJI: Yeah.

JESS: One other woman?

BENJI: I was in a long relationship.

JESS: Oh. Oops. Sorry.

(*Brief pause.*)

Well, it's a virus, so technically it never completely goes away. But usually your immune system kicks it in two to three years.

BENJI: That's good news, I guess.

JESS: But in the meantime you'll probably just get infected with a different strain. There are more than thirty kinds of HPV.

BENJI: And how many did you just give me?

JESS: I honestly don't know. Wait. Was that a joke?

BENJI: Yes.

JESS: (*Stony-faced.*) It was funny.

BENJI: Thanks.

JESS: Look, I legitimately feel shitty about this. I didn't know you had only slept with one... I mean, I couldn't tell from...

BENJI: Thank you?

(*She looks away, shy for the first time.*)

　　Cervical cancer, huh?

JESS: Yeah.

BENJI: But you don't...?

JESS: Have cervical cancer? No. My last Pap smear was a little weird so I had to get a colposcopy but that came back totally normal.

BENJI: Good.

JESS: Yeah.

BENJI: Are you Jewish?

JESS: What?

BENJI: Are you—

JESS: I heard you, I just—no, I'm not, but anyway I'm pretty sure that's not contagious.

BENJI: No! I mean, if it were, I already have it, so. Got *that* one from my mom.

JESS: Huh. Why . . . ?

BENJI: Because it's the twenty-fifth. And you don't have a tree and we're talking about Pap shmears.

JESS: Smears.

BENJI: What?

JESS: Pap *smears*. Not shmears.

BENJI: Right. Shmears would be like bagels. Like, I'd like a scallion Pap shmear. I'd like mine with lox.

(*He cringes at his bad joke.*)

JESS: Uh-huh. Anyway I wasn't really raised religious, but we do celebrate Christmas, so I'll head to Connecticut in a few hours.

BENJI: I thought Christmas morning was like a *thing*.

JESS: Yeah, it is. Can we not talk about it?

BENJI: Sure. I don't really know what I'm talking about. We always did movies and Chinese food on Christmas, which is sort of a Jewish cliché, but my parents recently moved to Florida, which is also a cliché, incidentally, so . . . guess there's no reason I can't see a movie by myself. It's only because our culture is so fucking Christian-centric that I feel bad about myself if I spend Christmas alone. I mean, what is Christmas to me? It's not Christ. It's not Mass. So if on any other day I'd feel perfectly fine about going to a movie by myself, I shouldn't let Christmas stop me. Right?

JESS: A movie sounds great. I wish I could go to a movie.

BENJI: Not looking forward to the fam?

JESS: I didn't mean to do this, you know.

BENJI: What?

JESS: Lure you into conversation, I was seriously just—

BENJI: (*Overlapping.*) You don't have to—

JESS: (*Overlapping.*)—gonna get your e-mail and not use it. I get what a one-night stand is. I get it.

BENJI: You do that a lot.

JESS: What?

BENJI: "I get it." "I'm not delusional." "I'm not a lunatic."

JESS: Oh.

BENJI: I'm the amateur here, you don't have to justify yourself to me.

JESS: I know.

BENJI: I'd like to hear about Christmas in Connecticut. Really.

JESS: Well. For the past three years I've spent Christmas morning in New Jersey with my boyfriend's family. Ex-boyfriend. 'Cause they were the really religious ones. Catholic. And then

we'd drive together to Connecticut for an early dinner. So...
I haven't exactly told my family yet that he's not coming.

BENJI: When did you break up?

JESS: Just last Christmas.

BENJI: Oh.

JESS: So I'm relatively new to HPV, too. To bring it, you know,
full circle.

BENJI: You haven't told your family you broke up?

JESS: Not with words. They liked him.

(*Brief pause.*)

BENJI: He was really Catholic.

JESS: Not him exactly, his family. But him actually too, in a weird
way, yeah.

BENJI: And you're really fertile.

(*He looks at her. She looks back. Something snaps.*)

JESS: What are you, Nancy Drew?

BENJI: I'm sorry, I—

JESS: Look, if you have some huge aversion to giving me your
e-mail address... it's just something I do, to make myself
feel more responsible, but forget it. It was nice meeting you.
Merry Christmas.

BENJI: (*Gently.*) Hey, listen—

JESS: No no, you don't have to do that. You're very nice. You're not an asshole. Go see your Jewish movie.

BENJI: You want me to go?

JESS: I have to get moving. Pick up the Zipcar. Brave the holiday traffic.

BENJI: Okay.

JESS: I don't mean to be rude.

BENJI: Sure.

JESS: Sorry about the HPV.

BENJI: Me too.

JESS: Condoms actually do reduce the risk of transmission, so you might be fine. But don't believe those tests. They're bullshit.

BENJI: Got it.

JESS: I saw *Lars and the Real Girl*. It was good.

BENJI: Yeah?

JESS: No, I don't know why I said that. It was bad. It was really terrible. So. Bye.

BENJI: Bye. Um... Good luck with everything.

JESS: Yeah. You too.

(*He goes to the door. He turns around.*)

BENJI: You're going to find a note I left on your dresser. Which will seem pretty embarrassing after this conversation. But. All my info's on there.

(*Lights.*)

END OF PLAY

THE CONTRACT

Theresa Rebeck

The Contract was originally produced at Naked Angels West in July 1996, Jerry Levine, director, with the following cast:

PHIL   Merrill Holtzman
TOM   Willy Gerson

CHARACTERS
PHIL: An agent.
TOM: An actor.

SET
An agent's office.

Two men sit in an office. PHIL *sits at a desk, reading* TOM*'s résumé.*

PHIL: Yeah, this is—

TOM: I also dance. Plus, I condensed. That's not everything.

PHIL: Oh—

TOM: I mean, it's representative. There's a ton more stuff, I just thought—

PHIL: No question. The thing is, your type—

TOM: I don't really see myself as a type. There's much more range, you know different—

PHIL: Character—

TOM: Yeah, character-type work, and, um, improvisation—

PHIL: This is what I'm saying. A character actor, what are you, mid-thirties—

TOM: Early. Early thirties, although I often read, last year, I played a twenty-three-year-old junkie, in an independent, and it was—

PHIL: (*Slightly impressed.*) A junkie? 'Cause there's maybe, they're hot this year—

TOM: You want tape on that? 'Cause I could get you that tape. The junkie tape—

PHIL: Yeah, I—

TOM: I mean, it was excellent, I didn't have a lot to do, but there's a great cameo of me nodding off, it's killer stuff—

PHIL: No, you know what you should do? All this, you do a lot of theater, right? This is mostly like stage stuff?

TOM: Yeah, a lot, my training is—

PHIL: Fantastic. I love the theater. Why don't you give us a call, next time you're in something, we'll stop by and take a look, OK?

(*He pushes the résumé toward* TOM. TOM *does not take it.*)

TOM: Well but isn't that why you called me in? 'Cause you saw the showcase and—

PHIL: It would just be great to see you in something bigger. Get more of a sense of what you can do.

TOM: Yeah but you called and asked me to come in and now—

PHIL: Hey can I be candid? (*Looks at résumé.*) Tom? I mean, this is a tough business, it's best to be candid, right?

TOM: Oh absolutely, that's—

PHIL: 'Cause I'm sort of not really getting your tone here. I mean I called you in 'cause I think you have talent, I might want to, you know, *represent* you someday and now I'm getting like a ton of attitude here.

TOM: No, you're not getting attitude. I just—

PHIL: I'm just saying. Don't talk to me like a jerk.

TOM: I'm not talking to you like a jerk. You're talking to me like— You call me in, I take time out of my schedule—

PHIL: Your very busy schedule— (*He waves the résumé, unimpressed.*)

TOM: I told you, that's not—besides, who cares what's on my— Harrison Ford was a *carpenter* for God's sake—

PHIL: If you were Harrison Ford, believe me, this conversation would be very different.

TOM: You called me. *You* called *me*—

PHIL: Yes, I called you and you jumped. You jumped at this. I mean, you want representation or not? You want it or not?

TOM: Of course I want it, I—

PHIL: All right. I am the representation. I am what you want. I am the object of desire in this town. Got that? It's not some fucking starlet tits out to here. It isn't a gold BMW. It's me. You want to work, you want to see your face on the big screen, the fucking tube, whatever—

TOM: Look, I—

PHIL: (*Very reasonable.*) I am what gets you that. I am what makes this town run. So when I say jump, you don't say why. I mean, what, you have a problem with authority? You didn't like your dad or something? Tell it to your shrink. Keep it out of my damn office and just do what I say.

TOM: Why are you yelling at me?

PHIL: Oh, now I'm—

TOM: Yes, you're not even representing me and you're, you're—

PHIL: I said I *might*.

TOM: Oh well that's—

PHIL: Look. I didn't invent the world. I didn't make up the rules. I'm giving you advice here. This is free! Do you know what you are? You're an actor! No one gives a shit about you! You're a total nobody! The fact that I'm even speaking to you is going to be the most significant thing that happens to you all year. You should be fucking genuflecting, and I mean literally hitting your knees when I say boo, and what do I get instead? What do I *get?* "You called me up and now you aren't being nice to me." This is show business, you moron! Nobody's nice to anybody! Especially actors. You guys are the lowest form of life. Oh yeah, I know everybody says that about agents, but they're wrong. I mean, we're slime, OK, I don't argue that, but we're slime that *you* need, and *you* want, so you are lower even than me, and that means I don't *have* to be nice to you. *You* have to be nice to me!

TOM: I just—I don't—that's nuts. You're nuts.

PHIL: I'm *what?*

TOM: I mean, I'm an actor. How can you— I'm an *artist*. Laurence

Olivier for God's sake—this is an art form and you're—
yeah, OK, I understand that it's not show friends, it's show
business, but—we're talking about telling *stories*, reaching in
and communicating our humanity, and if you can't even—
if decency means *nothing* anymore, then why—I just don't
accept that. I'm sorry, but I don't. I've given up everything
to do this work, my family thinks I'm completely—I've
maxed out all—I mean, I am fucking broke every second
of my life, and I know that I'm just another actor but that's
not—this is a *noble thing*. Do you understand that? We are
as puppets dancing for the gods. We spin meaning out of
nothing, out of oblivion we make *art*, and you—well. You're
not—I can't—you don't— No.

PHIL: Did you finish a sentence in there? I mean, did you actually say something?

TOM: I don't want you to represent me.

PHIL: You *what*?

TOM: You're a bad person. (TOM *takes his résumé and puts it in his
knapsack.*)

PHIL: Oh. Well. You cut me to the quick, Tom. I, I just don't
know what to say.

(TOM *is heading for the door.*)

Hey! What are you doing?

TOM: I'm leaving.

PHIL: Did I say you could go? 'Cause I don't remember saying that.

TOM: I, I didn't ask.

PHIL: Tom. This is really—sit down. Would you sit down? Come
on. I mean, I like you, Tom, would I be even talking to you
if I didn't—sit down. Come on.

(TOM *does.*)

TOM: I'm really confused.

PHIL: I don't see why.

TOM: I'm getting very mixed signals from you.

PHIL: How so, Tom? 'Cause I'm being as candid as I possibly
know how to be. I mean, most people in this town—some
of that stuff you said, you could've really pissed some people
off with that. And you know, someone like me, if I were
vindictive, I could call every casting agent I know and tell
them, you know, you're a difficult guy, and that would be it.
Your career would be over.

TOM: Is that a threat?

PHIL: It's just a fact. Nobody wants to deal with anybody who's
difficult. Life's too short, babe. You want to have a conversation about, what do you call it—

TOM: The work?

PHIL: "The work," people aren't gonna put up with that.
Humanity, noble, decency, art—Tom. People are not gonna
put up with it.

TOM: Why are you saying these things? I was going to leave. I
am leaving—

(*He stands.*)

PHIL: You leave when I tell you to leave!

(TOM *looks at him, confused.*)

I mean, there's something you're not getting here, Tom. I am your friend. I see an actor with talent, I ask him to come in, he's clearly confused about how the world works but I like him so I decide to teach him a few useful lessons. I am your friend. And if you ever want to work as an actor, get paid, actually have a real acting job instead of some stupid *theater* thing, then you will LEAVE when I SAY LEAVE.

(*They stare at each other.*)

TOM: You know, Nietzsche was not right.

PHIL: Oh, Jesus—

TOM: Yes, Nietzsche, the philosopher, said—

PHIL: I'm trying to tell you something, Tom—

TOM: And I'm trying to tell you, the guy was like obsessed—

PHIL: Yeah, that's fascinating, I'm so—

TOM: So we did this acting exercise in grad school, which was based on a Nietzschean model of humanity and basically the exercise was all about who's going to win the scene, because Nietzsche has this theory about the will to power but—

PHIL: DON'T YOU FUCKING TALK TO ME ABOUT NIETZSCHE!

TOM: (*Cowed but continuing.*) It's just that it's a very limited model of humanity. As an actor you have to draw on many aspects of...you know what? I can see that this is really important to you, so you know what I'm going to do? I'm going to let you win the scene. (*He sits back down.*)

PHIL: You're what?

TOM: Whatever you want, Phil. I'll do whatever you want. You want me to stay, leave, whatever. That's what I'll do.

PHIL: I want you to listen.

TOM: I'm listening.

PHIL: I want you to get with the picture.

TOM: That's what I'm doing.

PHIL: I mean, which one of us knows this town, you or me?

TOM: You.

PHIL: That's right.

TOM: That's right. And I really appreciate everything you've said to me. You really put me on the right path and I appreciate it.

PHIL: You should.

TOM: I do.

(TOM *looks at him.* PHIL *studies him, uncomfortable.*)

PHIL: What are you doing?

TOM: I'm letting you win the scene.

PHIL: You're *letting* me? What do you mean, you're—

TOM: I don't mean anything.

PHIL: You said "let."

TOM: That's not what I meant at all. What I meant was it just took me a while to understand what you were trying to tell me, and I'm just, I'm saying you're right. You are right. You're amazing. It's a thrill meeting you and thank you for your time.

PHIL: (*Suspicious.*) You're acting, aren't you?

TOM: Do you want me to be acting?

PHIL: Yeah, that's funny. I mean, you're a real comedian.

TOM: If that's what you want me to be.

(*He strikes a little shticky pose for him.* PHIL *laughs a little.* TOM *joins him. They have a good chuckle together.* PHIL *looks at him, liking him again.*)

PHIL: So... was this whole thing an act? One big mind-fuck? Nietzsche and art and humanity—you been putting the whole thing on, right? You're fucking with my head so I'll sign you. Am I right? I mean, 'cause that's kind of brilliant.

TOM: Well...

PHIL: I mean, I could work with that. 'Cause then we understand each other. You know, then we're on a wavelength.

TOM: (*Some growing concern.*) Oh... oh. Oh, oh, oh.

PHIL: (*Snapping again.*) Oh what? Are we understanding each other or not? I mean, am I winning this scene or not?

TOM: Yeah. Yeah, of course.

(PHIL *studies* TOM, *then points his finger at him and starts laughing.* TOM *laughs too, a bit uncomfortably.*)

PHIL: I like you. I like you. (*He thinks for a minute, then suddenly yells.*) Hey, SUZIE! Get me a set of standard contracts, will you?

(*Tom looks around, concerned.*)

TOM: Oh. You want to—

PHIL: I'm gonna sign you, Tom! Welcome to Hollywood.

(*He shakes his hand, laughing.* TOM *laughs too. The laughter goes on for quite a while.* TOM *ends up looking a little sick.*)

(*Blackout.*)

END OF PLAY

CURTAIN RAISER

Eric Lane

Curtain Raiser premiered under its original title, *Restoration*, at Live Theater Company (Melanie S. Armer, artistic director; Chance Muehleck, literary director) at Center Stage in New York City in November 2001. The play was directed by Jimmy Georgiades, with the following cast:

LORRAINE   Megan Hollingshead
OSCAR   Jim Ireland

It was named finalist for the Heideman Award in the Actors Theater of Louisville National Ten-Minute Play Contest.

CAST

OSCAR: Twenties to thirties. An overly intelligent, neurotic man who still manages to be likable. When it comes down to it, he'd give you the shirt off his back. Not fat, just obsessive.

LORRAINE: Twenties to thirties. Pretty, sweet, eternally optimistic. Often taking on more than most people could imagine, yet somehow manages to handle it all.

SETTING

An abandoned Woolworth's building. The place is pretty beaten up. It's a mess, but there's an innate charm if one can see beyond.

   The set should be pretty minimal. The two scene changes occur quickly. The transformation in the space should be conveyed mainly through lighting and the actors' reactions to their surroundings.

SCENE ONE

An abandoned Woolworth's building. Late afternoon. LORRAINE *enters and drinks in the space, becoming quietly excited.* OSCAR *enters, takes in the space, somewhat horrified.*

LORRAINE: It's beautiful.

OSCAR: Let's go.

LORRAINE: Can't you see it.

OSCAR: No.

LORRAINE: This is it.

OSCAR: This is what? It's a mess.

LORRAINE: Just look around.

OSCAR: I am. All I see's an abandoned Woolworth's building.

LORRAINE: The space.

OSCAR: Too much space.

LORRAINE: The light.

OSCAR: What light? We're turning it into a theater.

LORRAINE: The history.

OSCAR: The smell. Let's go.

LORRAINE: This is it.

OSCAR: Lorraine.

LORRAINE: I'm telling you, Oscar.

OSCAR: No.

LORRAINE: Yes.

OSCAR: No.

LORRAINE: Yes.

OSCAR: No . . .

LORRAINE: Yes.

OSCAR: You think?

LORRAINE: Trust me.

(*He looks around. A beat.*)

OSCAR: Oy.

SCENE TWO

Three months later. They are in the midst of cleaning. Have been cleaning. Need to clean more.

OSCAR: (*Offstage.*) There's a ghost in the bathroom.

LORRAINE: What are you talking about?

(OSCAR *enters, wearing yellow gloves, carrying a bucket and mop.*)

OSCAR: Well, something is making that smell and it is not human.

LORRAINE: You'll take care of it.

OSCAR: How do you know I'll take care of it?

LORRAINE: Because you always do. Whatever it is, you'll take care of.

OSCAR: What if it lingers?

LORRAINE: It's not going to linger.

OSCAR: But if it does.

LORRAINE: It won't.

OSCAR: Do you have to be so optimistic? Whatever I say, you
    disagree.

LORRAINE: I do not.

OSCAR: And you have to get the last word.

LORRAINE: No.

OSCAR: Yes.

LORRAINE: No.

OSCAR: Yes.

LORRAINE: No.

OSCAR: No...?

LORRAINE: No. Is something going on?

OSCAR: No.

LORRAINE: Yes.

OSCAR: Just everything. This place. My life. Everything. Why are we even doing this?

LORRAINE: What?

OSCAR: (*Gestures to entire place.*) This.

LORRAINE: You know why.

OSCAR: I don't.

LORRAINE: Why do you even say—?

OSCAR: I don't. (*Lorraine just looks at him.*) What?

LORRAINE: This is the story of a shy, quiet five-year-old boy—

OSCAR: Oh, jeez.

LORRAINE: ...who played Chicken Little in his kindergarten production. And suddenly he was transformed from—

OSCAR: OK, OK. You win. (*She stops.*) Thank you.

LORRAINE: I'm sure you made a very fine chicken.

OSCAR: I was brilliant.

LORRAINE: Show me.

OSCAR: What?

LORRAINE: Show me your chicken, Oscar. (*He rolls his eyes.*) You know you want to.

OSCAR: No.

LORRAINE: You know you do. Come on, Oscar.

(*Tentative but wanting to, he starts to show his chicken. She laughs. He quickly stops.*)

    (*Laughing.*) Oscar.

OSCAR: I'm glad I amuse you.

LORRAINE: You do. It's one of your most endearing characteristics.

OSCAR: Great.

LORRAINE: What about me?

OSCAR: What?

LORRAINE: What are mine?

OSCAR: Lorraine...

LORRAINE: Name five things you love about me.

OSCAR: Five?

LORRAINE: If it's too many...

OSCAR: I didn't say—

LORRAINE: OK. Five.

OSCAR: Five. (*He thinks.*)
You're smart.
You're sexy.
You're beautiful.
You're really patient.
And you make me laugh.

LORRAINE: And you know what you are?

OSCAR: What?

LORRAINE: Correct!

OSCAR: Thanks a lot.

LORRAINE: Oscar.

OSCAR: How could anyone name their child that?

LORRAINE: What? I love your name.

OSCAR: (*With disdain.*) Oscar.

LORRAINE: It's got a sexy "O" at the front.

OSCAR: You think I'm fat?

LORRAINE: I think you're sexy.

OSCAR: I can't believe you think I'm fat.

LORRAINE: (*If the actor is thin, include:*) You're the skinniest man I know. (*Thin or not, say:*) All I said was it has an "O."

OSCAR: (*Overlapping the end of her sentence.*) Round. That's what you said. All the way round. No beginning. No end. Just one big endless fat zero.

LORRAINE: It's just a vowel.

OSCAR: But it fits. That's what you said.

LORRAINE: This snaky ssss in the middle. Then this rrr at the end. Like a seductive growl. Rrrrrrr.

OSCAR: I'm fat and I snore. That's what you think.

LORRAINE: Are you done?

OSCAR: Now "Lorraine," that's another matter.

LORRAINE: I like my name. It's nice.

OSCAR: It is more than nice. With the name Lorraine, you are destined for a life that's charmed.

LORRAINE: How do you figure?

OSCAR: You got Sweet Lorraine. Laraine Day—very popular film star of the nineteen forties and fifties. Lorraine Hansberry, gifted African-American playwright of the sixties. Quiche Lorraine, a beloved brunch item on several continents.

LORRAINE: Too heavy. (*He shoots her a look.*) Not you.

OSCAR: Then we get to "Oscar."

LORRAINE: I knew this was coming.

OSCAR: Think. Who are the famous Oscars? You've got Oscar Madison. Oscar on Sesame Street. And Oscar Meyer. A slob. A grouch. And a very popular brand of wiener. Now, what kind of life is that to aspire to?

LORRAINE: Oscar Levant.

OSCAR: Fat dead pianist.

LORRAINE: Oscar De La Hoya.

OSCAR: Lightweight.

LORRAINE: Oscar. The Academy Award. A prize everyone in Hollywood aspires to.

OSCAR: A short bald guy with great posture and no genitals.

LORRAINE: You're not that short.

OSCAR: (*Sarcastically.*) Thank you.

LORRAINE: Oscar. (*She comes up from behind and holds him.*) Oscar. (*Kisses his ear.*) Ossscarrrrr. (*He relaxes for a moment.*) You OK? (*He nods yes.*) Good.

OSCAR: Why do you put up with me?

LORRAINE: Somebody's got to. Besides I like fat men. (*He looks at her.*) It's just a joke. Keep cleaning. (*They go back to work.*)

SCENE THREE

Three months later. OSCAR *pulls off a yellow glove and throws the pair in the bucket. They take in the space. It is clean.*

LORRAINE: It's beautiful.

OSCAR: It's nice.

LORRAINE: You like it?

OSCAR: I think it's nice.

LORRAINE: Smell's gone.

OSCAR: Pretty much.

LORRAINE: Almost entirely.

OSCAR: Almost.

LORRAINE: Yeah.
    "If you build it, they will come."

OSCAR: (*Realizing:*) Oh no. We were supposed to build a *baseball field.* (*She laughs.*)

LORRAINE: Close enough.

OSCAR: You think. That they'll come?

LORRAINE: Yeah. I do.

OSCAR: Yeah.

LORRAINE: Yeah.

(*He holds her. They look around for a moment.*)

OSCAR: Now what?

LORRAINE: Turn up the lights.

(OSCAR *and* LORRAINE *kiss. Sweet, sexy, passionate. Theater lights fade up bright.*

Blackout.

For the curtain call, the song "Sweet Lorraine" plays.)

END OF PLAY

DOUBLE DATE

Nina Shengold

Double Date was first performed during Actors & Writers' Shorts Festival at the Odd Fellows Theatre, Olivebridge, New York, on November 12, 2005. The cast was as follows, with the playwright directing:

MAX	David Smilow
MURRAY	Mikhail Horowitz
STELLA	Carol Morley
ADELAIDE	Sarah Chodoff
WAITRESS	Sophia Raab

SETTING
Minimal indication of Max and Murray's apartment, and a booth in a Mexican restaurant.

SCENE ONE

MURRAY, *dressed for a date and trembling with nervous excitement, leans out from behind the proscenium arch as he speaks to* MAX, *just offstage.*

MURRAY: Hurry up, I don't want her to wait at the restaurant.

MAX: (*Offstage.*) I'm shaving.

MURRAY: Your chin is a poem, come on.

MAX: (*Offstage.*) She's not going to like you.

MURRAY: Why not? I'm articulate, debonair, winsome...

MAX: (*Offstage.*) Murray.

MURRAY: What's not to like?

MAX: I am.

(*He bumps* MURRAY *onstage from the side, and we see that they're Siamese twins, joined at the hip in a slightly diagonal fashion, with their upper torsos rayed out like the arms of a* Y.)

MURRAY: Don't put yourself down, Max.

MAX: (*Darkly.*) They all say it isn't an issue, but wait till you go for that good-night kiss.

MURRAY: Well, maybe if you didn't grope them...

MAX: They're my hormones too!

MURRAY: I'll say. Anyway, this one is different.

MAX: They're all different, Murray. You always think—

MURRAY: Stella *is* different.

MAX: Stella? Is her sister named Blanche?

MURRAY: Adelaide. And she's looking forward to—

MAX: Wait, wait up. This is a *double* date??

MURRAY: Well, duh.

MAX: No, I mean, you set me up with her *sister*? (MAX *nods happily.*) This is one hell of a blind date.

MURRAY: We've been corresponding for weeks.

MAX: *When?*

MURRAY: You were, um, occupied.

MAX: Oh.

MURRAY: You shouldn't look at those Web sites.

MAX: They're safer than Cupid-dot-com. Did she send you her photo?

MURRAY: Her e-mails are fervent. She told me that I have panache.

MAX: (*Suspicious.*) Does she use emoticons?

MURRAY: Never.

MAX: The odd smiley face, on its side like a haddock? Semicolon winks?

MURRAY: No.

MAX: Frilly font?

MURRAY: Times New Roman.

MAX: Well, everyone lies on the Internet.

MURRAY: I don't.

MAX: You *told* her?

MURRAY: Of course.

MAX: And?

MURRAY: It wasn't an issue.

MAX: Oh God, she's a liberal. If she calls us "differently abled" or "separationally impaired," I will vomit.

MURRAY: She asked where we're joined.

MAX: And you answered.

MURRAY: Of course. Full disclosure.

MAX: You actually typed the word "scrotum"?

MURRAY: I mentioned the hip thing as well.

MAX: The hip thing is cake, little brother. The kinky ones might dig the hip thing. But nobody, nobody, goes for two brothers, three balls.

MURRAY: I may have omitted some details.

MAX: Omitted some details. Co-testicles are not details.

MURRAY: We're just having dinner.

MAX: Where?

MURRAY: El Conquistador.

MAX: Mexican?? We're eating *beans*?

MURRAY: Stella picked it. Come on, get your jacket, I'll hail us a cab.

(*He sidles for the door.* MAX *folds his arms, standing firm.*)

MAX: I think not.

MURRAY: You can't! (MAX *just smiles.*) We're meeting them there in ten minutes!

MAX: Be my guest.

MURRAY: Max, you can't do this to me! I'll hold my breath till we turn blue!

MAX: (*Serene.*) Go ahead, threaten.

(MURRAY *takes in a huge gulp of air, puffing his cheeks like a blowfish.* MAX *ignores him, then starts to redden and gasp.*)

Hey, come on. You know what this does to our blood pressure.

MURRAY: (*Spits the word out, gulps air again.*) Date!

MAX: Come on, it's not funny.

MURRAY: DATE!

MAX: Okay, fine, you can go!

(MURRAY *exhales and grins.* MAX *takes a deep breath.*)

But NO KARAOKE.

MURRAY: I promise.

(*They shuffle toward the door.* MURRAY *stops, peering at* MAX.)

MAX: . . . What?

MURRAY: You still got some shaving cream.

(*He reaches out a finger, swoops it off* MAX*'s nose. Exeunt omni. Blackout.*)

SCENE TWO

MURRAY *and* MAX *sit in a corner booth at El Conquistador.* MURRAY *is next to the empty seat, gazing eagerly at the door.*

MAX: Twenty minutes. She's not going to show.

MURRAY: Oh ye of little faith.

MAX: No faith. Not a jot.

MURRAY: There was traffic.

MAX: Right. That, and the detail.

(MURRAY *sulks into his drink.* STELLA *and* ADELAIDE *enter. They're Siamese twins, joined at the shoulder.* STELLA *bubbles over with eagerness.* ADELAIDE *looks like she'd rather eat gravel.*)

STELLA: There he is!

ADELAIDE: Stella, he's on that man's lap.

STELLA: No, he's not, Addie, they're—

(MURRAY *spots* STELLA *and rises, hauling* MAX *forcibly out of his seat.*)

MURRAY: Stella! Stella for star!

(*He lurches forward, again hauling* MAX, *to kiss* STELLA's *hand. She swoons, smitten, taking her seat with a thump that pulls* ADELAIDE *onto the bench.*)

STELLA: So continental.

MURRAY: It's so elegant. So intelligent—

STELLA: (*With him.*) OOOO that Shakespeherian rag!

MURRAY: Do you do the *Times* crossword?

STELLA: In ink. Proust or Ovid?

MURRAY: James Joyce. Your eyes, they're—they're luminous.

STELLA: Yours are lustrous.

MURRAY: Lambent.

STELLA: Refulgent.

MAX: Revolting.

ADELAIDE: You must be the brother.

MAX: How did you guess?

ADELAIDE: (*Eyeing him sourly.*) You don't *look* identical.

STELLA: (*Delighted at having so much in common.*) Neither do we!

MAX: You're not joined at the scrotum, either.

ADELAIDE: Don't be so sure.

(*They both look at her.*)

  Kidding. Joke. Ha. Ha. Ha.

MAX: I'm astral projecting. I'm not really here.

ADELAIDE: Thank God for small favors.

STELLA: (*"Private," to* MURRAY.) I'm glad you're the nice one.

MAX: Oh, this is too much.

ADELAIDE: You can say that again. That again. Joke. Ha. Ha. Ha.

(*A sexy, hard-bitten* WAITRESS *approaches their table.*)

WAITRESS: What can I get youse?

MAX: (*Still glaring at* ADELAIDE.) A really sharp cleaver.

WAITRESS: What?

(MAX *turns toward her. It's lust at first sight.* ADELAIDE *stares at her, smitten.*)

MAX: Um...a cleavage.

WAITRESS: A cabbage?

STELLA: (*Sotto voce.*) She's *deaf.*

WAITRESS: I can lip-read.

MAX: Read mine.

(*He puckers up, flicks his tongue.*)

MURRAY: Max! (*To* WAITRESS, *overarticulating each word.*) Can we
  see a menu?

WAITRESS: I *said*, I can lip-read.

(*She sashays off.* MAX's *eyes swivel with her hips.*)

MAX: Tie me down, boys, that waitress is *hot.*

ADELAIDE: I'll say.

STELLA: .... Adelaide??

ADELAIDE: What?

MURRAY: (*Agitated.*) Max. Are you ... Are we ...?

MAX: Twice the testosterone, Murray. You know how it goes.

STELLA: ... You mean you're a *lesbian*?

ADELAIDE: I didn't say that.

MAX: (*Presexual moaning.*) Um ... unngh ... Ohhhh boy ...

ADELAIDE: I'm a transgendered conjoined individual. A man in two women's bodies.

STELLA: Well, you picked a hell of a time to come out of the closet!

ADELAIDE: (*Shrugs.*) Hey, at least I'm pre-op.

MURRAY: (*Trying to maintain equilibrium as* MAX *groans and sways.*) Can we order some nachos?

MAX: Check, please!

(*He waves. The* WAITRESS *reappears instantly.*)

WAITRESS: What can I do for you?

ADELAIDE: Anything.

MAX: Everything.

STELLA: Leave.

MURRAY: We'll have four margaritas.

WAITRESS: With salt?

MAX: Yes.

MURRAY: No.

STELLA: Frozen.

ADELAIDE: Rocks.

WAITRESS: Coming right up.

(*She turns to go.*)

MAX AND ADELAIDE: WAIT!!!

(*She turns back.*)

MAX: Do you like older men?

ADELAIDE: Other women?

MURRAY: (*To* STELLA.) Je t'aime.

STELLA: (*To* MURRAY.) Te adoro.

MAX: (To WAITRESS.) You think you could go for a ménage à cinq?

WAITRESS: I'm into leather.

MAX/ADELAIDE/MURRAY/STELLA: Woo-hoo!/Ride 'em, cowgirl!/ STELLLLLLLA!!!/Yes I said yes yesyesyes YES!

(*They converge in a giant group hug.*)

THE END (OF ALL DIGNITY)

ERNESTO
THE MAGNIFICENT

Edwin Sánchez

A man in a tuxedo that has obviously seen better days takes center stage. He walks with a very stiff leg.

ERNESTO: Hello, my name is Ernesto the Magnificent! I said, "My name is Ernesto the Magnificent." Hold for applause. I'll wait. I have performed for presidents, crowned heads of state, and film stars from around the world. And yet, somehow tonight, I am here with you. What a thrill. Prepare to be amazed, for I am, drumroll please.

(There is no drumroll. He sighs.)

A FIRE-EATER!!!!! Now you are impressed, no? My remarkable feats of derring-do have astounded and confounded young and old alike. Fire is primal, fire is sexy, fire, she is dangerous. The heat. Enveloping you, swallowing you, until you—disappear. Having said that, however, my agent in his infinite wisdom has seen fit to book me in a club where even a match cannot be lit onstage without an overzealous fire marshal wrestling you to the ground so that he can beat you unconscious with a fire extinguisher. Charming, no? But not to worry, for tonight Ernesto the Magnificent becomes Ernesto the Stupendous going where no man has gone before. Behold!

(He pulls a sword out of his pant leg. After a moment he winces.)

I'm okay. Yes tonight, for your viewing pleasure, Ernesto will swallow this sword! Feel free to gasp. Go ahead.

(*He hisses.*)

Gasp!

(*After a beat, satisfied.*)

This is a real sword. Not some dummied-up prop where the blade disappears into the handle. Yesssss, even Ernesto is amazed. I have, once again, amazed myself.

(*He takes the sword, leans his head back, and positions the sword over his open mouth. Beat. He lowers the sword.*)

I should point out that Ernesto the Fearless has never actually done this act. But I have been cheating death my entire life, so I am not afraid.

(*He again lifts the sword, tilts his head back, and opens his mouth. Again he lowers the sword.*)

For what is there to fear, but fear itself. A very great man once said that. Yes, he did. A very, very great man.

(*He looks at the sword, runs his finger along the blade.*)

A sharp, great man.

(*He raises the sword, but stops midway, brings it down. He loses his accent.*)

My father was the one who did the fire-eater act, and his father before him and so on and so forth. This is my legacy.

No matter if I wanted it or not. Imagine being born and being given a book of matches and being told, that's it kid, that's your lot in life. Maybe I didn't like fire or maybe I wanted to be an arsonist, not as a career you know, but more like a hobby. But no, no choice for Ernesto. I hate that name! First time I did the act I was eight years old. The novelty of having a child fire-eater, what won't they think of next? It was a beauty pageant. First my grandfather came out, then my father. I was saved for last. Onstage with fifty of the most beautiful girls from the United States. I brought the flame up to my lips, sweat pouring off me, hand shaking, and at the worst possible moment I get a sneezing attack. I didn't swallow the fire, I spit it out and all of a sudden all these girls with their oversprayed, moussed and gelled hair are going up like Roman candles. It was like *Dante's Inferno*, if *Dante's Inferno* had an evening-gown competition. Red and blue states running amok, crashing into each other, while I continued, unable to control my sneezing. Until like an asthmatic dragon, only faint sparks remained to punctuate my fiery debacle. My father and grandfather were finally able to get close enough to me and began beating me right onstage. "It's fire-eating, NOT fire-breathing! You've ruined us! Ruined us!" And all I'm thinking is I'm sorry, I'm sorry, I'm sorry....But tonight Ernesto the Failure gets to carve out a new identity for himself. One where he is not the source of disappointment to a fire-breathing father but rather a rebel, capable of a greatness his father could only dream of, could only hope to attain. Could only aspire to if he were half the fucking man I am! Who stands here with a motherfucking sword while he and every other lame-o man in my family coat their lips with enough flame retardant for an Alaskan oil spill, but hey, somehow I'm the loser, I'm the wannabe, I'm the nothing!!!!

(*Pause. He resumes his accent.*)

Please forgive Ernesto. Sometimes I am reminded of why I envy orphans. So please welcome Ernesto, His Own Man.

(*He lifts the sword, tilts his head back, the sword poised over his mouth. He turns to face the audience while holding his pose.*)

Remember, whatever doesn't kill us only makes us stronger. Or is that, whatever doesn't kill us leaves us scarred for life? No matter.

(*He again faces the point of the sword.*)

Okay, Dad, top this.

(*He slowly begins to lower the sword. Blackout.*)

END OF PLAY

FRIENDSHIP

Peter Handy

An old man, FRANK KADJANSKI, *sits in a chair in the living room of his house somewhere in Ohio. He is seated in front of the television set and there is a chessboard in front of him (with the white pieces on his side of the board) and an old telephone on a little table at his side. There is a knock at the door.* FRANK *looks at the door. There is another knock at the door.* FRANK *reaches for the remote control and turns down the volume on the television.*

FRANK: Hello? (*Pause.*) Hello? (*Pause.*) Is there someone there?

(FRANK *struggles to get out of his chair and hobbles to the door. He opens it. In the doorway stands another old man,* NICK WODJANISKI. NICK *is holding a gift-wrapped blue box in his hands.*)

NICK: Hello. (*Pause.*)

(FRANK *doesn't respond.*)

    Frank? (*Pause.*)

FRANK: Yeah?

NICK: Frank?

FRANK: Yeah.

NICK: How's it hanging?

FRANK: It's all right...I guess.

(*Beat.*)

NICK: Why'd you miss the game?

FRANK: The game? (*Pause.*) What game?

NICK: What game? The play-offs...the ah...you know...the play-offs.

FRANK: I've been busy.

NICK: Busy? (*Pause.*) What have you been so busy with?

(*Pause.*)

FRANK: Business.

NICK: What kind of business?

FRANK: What kind of business? (*Pause.*) Who wants to know?

NICK: I do.

FRANK: You do?

NICK: Yeah.

FRANK: What business is it of yours?

NICK: I'm making it my business.

FRANK: Okay. You're making it your business. So...who the fuck cares?

NICK: I do.

(*Pause.*)

FRANK: Okay...I've been seeing a...lady friend. She's only free on Thursday nights.

NICK: A lady friend?

FRANK: Yeah, a lady friend. I haven't had a minute to spare to call you about it.

(*Pause.*)

NICK: A lady friend?

FRANK: Yeah.

NICK: What's her name?

FRANK: None of your...beeswax. I don't kiss and tell.

NICK: You got a hell of a...an attitude...that's what you've got.

FRANK: Think what you want.

NICK: Frank? Are you pissed off or something?

FRANK: Am I pissed off? What makes you say that?

NICK: The way you've been acting.

FRANK: Yeah? How've I been acting?

NICK: Kinda moody, if you know what I mean?

FRANK: Nick, you haven't seen me in over a month. Why you acting like this is a different situation all of a sudden?

NICK: Frank. Are we friends or what?

FRANK: We were friends, Nick. I thought we were friends, but I have to say…you've been no friend to me, Nick. No friend at all.

NICK: What are you talking about? I invited you along to go fishing. I take you in…to my circle of friends.

FRANK: You know, Nick, your friends ain't so nice to me no more.

NICK: What are you talking about?

FRANK: I said your friends ain't so nice to me no more.

NICK: How's that?

FRANK: Nick, they laughin' at me behind my back. They snicker every time I open my mouth.

NICK: Aw…they just kidding you, Franky. They don't mean nothing by it.

FRANK: Nick. The last time I was there they asked me about my son? You remember?

NICK: No. What about it?

FRANK: They asked me how come he lives in San Francisco?

NICK: So?

FRANK: Nick. How come they know he lives in San Francisco? Huh? How much you tell them? Huh?

NICK: Aw geez. Come off it, Frank, what's the big deal, huh?

FRANK: What's the big deal? I tell you something ... personal ... a family secret ... and you blab to your friends about it. What's the big deal? Come on, Nick. You know I ...

NICK: All right, Frank, whatever you say. You got all the answers. I'm real sorry.

FRANK: Thanks, Nick. I appreciate it. That's all you got to say, huh?

NICK: What do you want me to say? That you're too thin-skinned, Frank. No wonder your son turned out like he did.

FRANK: What?

NICK: You heard me.

FRANK: All right, so you came to insult me more. Are you finished?

NICK: Yeah, I'm finished. How about you? Are you finished?

FRANK: Yeah, I'm finished, Nick. Have a good night.

(FRANK *starts to close the door.*)

NICK: Listen. Frank. Maybe we ... can ...

(FRANK *has closed the door all the way.*)

FRANK: Son of a bitch.

(*More knocking at the door.* FRANK *goes back to his chair and sits down. There is more knocking at the door.* NICK *yells through the door.*)

NICK: Happy birthday, you son of a bitch!

FRANK: What?

NICK: I said... "Happy birthday, you son of a bitch!"

(FRANK *gets out of his chair and walks over and opens the door again.* NICK *holds out the blue box with a ribbon around it. Pause.*)

NICK: Like I said, I'm sorry, Frank.

(*Beat.*)

FRANK: Thanks, Nick.

NICK: Don't mention it.

(*Pause.*)

FRANK: Can I have my present now, Nick?

NICK: Sure, Frank.

(NICK *hands the box to* FRANK. FRANK *holds it in his hand. Beat.*)

FRANK: What is it, Nick?

NICK: You gotta open it, Frank.

FRANK: Yeah, I know I just... What did ya get me, Metamucil?

NICK: Na, Frank, come on, what d'ya think I am, huh? You gotta open it!

(FRANK *takes off the ribbon and opens the box. He takes out a singing bass.*)

FRANK: Thanks, Nick.

NICK: It sings too, Frank.

(NICK *presses the button and the fish sings "Don't Worry, Be Happy."*)

FRANK: That's a neat little trick, Nick.

NICK: Isn't it?

FRANK: Where'd you get it?

NICK: You can put it on your wall there.

FRANK: Where'd you get it?

(*Beat.*)

NICK: Downtown. I got it downtown after we went fishing
    last week.

FRANK: Oh?

NICK: Happy birthday.

FRANK: Thanks. (*Beat.*) Well, I'd ask you to sit down, but...

NICK: Oh, don't worry about it. I gotta go soon, anyway.

FRANK: Oh... You gotta go.

NICK: Yeah sorry. I got plans.

FRANK: Huh... Plans with whom?

NICK: Some of the guys.

FRANK: Which guys?

NICK: The guys...You know...Tony Boyd, Jimmy T Bone...
the fellas.

FRANK: Is that who you went fishing with?

NICK: Yeah, that's who I went fishing with.

FRANK: Good. Did you have fun?

NICK: Yeah, Frank. Yeah, we had...fun. Wish you'd been there.
Everybody did. We ah...yeah we...missed you, man.
(*Beat.*) What were you doing? Were you tied up with your
lady friend?

FRANK: Yeah, we were ah...indisposed at the time.

(NICK *notices the chessboard.*)

NICK: You been playing chess with someone?

FRANK: Yeah, I got a new friend. He, ah...plays with me over
the phone.

NICK: Sounds nice, Frank.

FRANK: Yeah, it's a lot of fun.

(*Pause.*)

NICK: Well...if you're not doing anything later on...feel free
to stop by...we gotta card game tonight.

FRANK: Yeah, thanks, maybe I will.

NICK: Yeah, you should. It would be good for you.

FRANK: What does that mean?

NICK: It doesn't mean nothing, just...you know...we'd like to see you.

FRANK: Yeah. Well...I'm supposed to talk to my son pretty soon...he's...

NICK: Not a problem. Maybe next time, Frank.

FRANK: I wasn't finished, Nick. What I'm saying is maybe I could be there around eight-thirty or so.

NICK: Yeah we can deal you in late...I suppose.

FRANK: Good.

NICK: How is your son?

FRANK: He's doing okay...He's got a new...friend...So, I guess he's excited about that.

NICK: Oh, a new friend, well that's...nice.

FRANK: Yeah.

(*Pause.*)

NICK: How's his health?

(*Beat.*)

FRANK: Better. He's doing better...Got a...new...medication or something...Yeah...

NICK: Glad to hear it.

FRANK: Yeah, I was too. (FRANK *looks at his watch*.) All right, well, I'll see you a little later...

NICK: You bet ya...See you at the game...

(NICK *turns to go and walks to the door to leave*.)

You're a good father, Frank.

FRANK: Thanks, Nick. You're a good friend.

NICK: Thanks. Happy birthday, you son of a bitch.

(FRANK *laughs and closes the door. He goes back to his chair and is about to sit down, but decides to get a glass of water. He walks over to the sink, gets a glass, and fills it with water, goes back to his chair, and picks up the phone and dials a long-distance number. He waits as the phone rings a few times until somebody picks it up*.)

FRANK: Michael? (*Beat.*) This a good time? (*Beat.*) Yeah, thanks. I'm doing great.

(FRANK *looks down at the chessboard*.)

Yeah, I got it last night. Beautiful... (*Beat.*) What? (*Beat.*) Yeah, I threw out the old one. (*Beat.*) How are you feeling? (*Beat.*) Good. (*Beat.*) Yeah, of course, I'm ready. (*Beat.*) Okay... Queen Knight...to Queen Bishop file... (*Beat.*) You got it? (*Beat.*) Good.

(FRANK *reaches to move the black pieces*.)

King Knight to King Bishop file.

END OF PLAY

FUNERAL PARLOR

Christopher Durang

ORIGINAL PRODUCTION

Funeral Parlor was included in the TV special *Carol, Carl, Whoopi and Robin*, which originally aired February 10, 1987. Marcy Carsey and Tom Werner, executive producers. Stephanie Sills, Dick Clair, and Jenna McMahon, producers. Writing supervised by Dick Clair and Jenna McMahon. Directed by Harvey Korman and Roger Beatty. Written by Chris Durang, Jim Evering, Ken Welch, Mitzi Welch, Dick Clair, and Jenna McMahon. Musical material by Ken Welch and Mitzi Welch. The cast was as follows:

SUSAN	Carol Burnett
MARCUS	Robin Williams

CHARACTERS
SUSAN
MARCUS

Interior: A funeral parlor. Quiet, grave (sorry) setting. Perhaps a bit of casket shows. Certainly lots of flowers. Hushed atmosphere. SUSAN, *the mourning widow, is dressed in black, with pearls. She is sedate, proper, formal. A few people are in line, offering their condolences, shaking her hand. She acknowledges them with a little nod and little smile, and a whispered "Thank you." As we begin, at the end of the line to see* SUSAN *is a man named* MARCUS. MARCUS *is dressed in a nice suit, but it's kind of a light color and his tie and shirt are kind of flowery, not really right for a funeral, but maybe he had to come straight from work (or Hawaii). Otherwise he looks appropriate enough. The person before* MARCUS *makes quiet sounds of condolences, and leaves.* MARCUS *reaches* SUSAN. *He is sincere and genuine, it's just that he's, well, odd.*

MARCUS: Susan, I'm so sorry. My deepest condolences.

SUSAN: Yes, thank you . . . (??) (*She doesn't know who* MARCUS *is.*)

MARCUS: Marcus.

SUSAN: (*Still doesn't know him, but is gracious.*) Yes, Marcus. Thank you for coming.

MARCUS: We'll all miss him terribly.

SUSAN: Yes. It's a great loss.

MARCUS: We'll all miss him.

SUSAN: Yes.

MARCUS: You must feel terrible.

SUSAN: Well...I don't feel good. It was a terrible shock.

MARCUS: Death is always a shock. You're sitting home doing nothing, and then suddenly death goes "Boo!" and somebody falls down dead.

SUSAN: Yes. (*Looks around, hopes someone else will come over.*)

MARCUS: What were his last words? Were they "Boo"?

SUSAN: What? "Boo"? No. He didn't really have any last words.

MARCUS: Did he make any last noises?

SUSAN: Noises? What?

MARCUS: Guttural sorts of noises? Or high-pitched-shrieking ones? (*Makes high-pitched sounds.*) Eeeeeeeek! Eeeeeeeeeek! Awooooga! Awoooooga!

SUSAN: Just noises, I don't know. They were lower than that. Don't do that anymore.

MARCUS: (*Sympathetically.*) Oh, Susan, you poor, poor thing. (*Turns to someone who's gotten in line behind him.*) I wouldn't wait if I were you, I'm going to be a while.

(*The person in line looks surprised but goes away;* SUSAN *looks alarmed.*)

All alone in the house now. Alone in the kitchen. Alone in the dining room. Alone in the living room—living room, that's a mocking phrase now, isn't it? Alone, alone, alone. All alone. Alone, alone, alone.

SUSAN: Please don't go on.

MARCUS: Yes, but you have to mourn, Susan, to *mourn*. I always thought the Irish were right to do all that keening. Do you want to keen, Susan?

SUSAN: Not really. Thank you anyway.

MARCUS: How about singing a Negro spiritual?

SUSAN: I don't think so. (*Looks about madly for people.*)

MARCUS: (*Sings.*)
Swing low, sweet chariot,
Comin' for to carry me home...

SUSAN: Thank you for coming.

MARCUS: Don't you want to sing?

SUSAN: I don't want to keen or sing. I'm an Episcopalian. I'll cry quietly in my room later this evening. Now I must attend to the other mourners.

MARCUS: Susan, you're avoiding the sadness, I can't let you do that.

SUSAN: Please, please let me do that. It's been a terrible day. I have to bury my husband.

MARCUS: Is he in the casket? It's a closed casket, he's not actually in some other room, propped up in some stuffed chair or other, waiting there to startle someone, is he?

SUSAN: Certainly not. Thank you so much for coming.

MARCUS: That would give someone quite a fright. They'd be standing by this chair making conversation and then realize they were talking to him, only he was stark, stone dead! Ahahahahaha, that would be a good one!

SUSAN: Yes, very good. (*Calls.*) Oh, David! (*No luck.*)

MARCUS: I'm going to miss him too, you know.

SUSAN: Ah, how nice. Or rather, how sad. Well, time heals everything.

MARCUS: You're not the only one with sorrow written on your forehead.

SUSAN: What?

MARCUS: I should say not. (*Shows his forehead, previously covered with bangs; it has "sorrow" written on it.*) Magic Marker. Doesn't wash off. We're going to miss him on the commuter train. We used to exchange morning pleasantries. "Nice morning," or "Cold enough for you?" or "The train seems to be on time today for a change."

SUSAN: I see. Excuse me. I think the mortician is signaling me.

MARCUS: You know, your husband was the only person on that whole damn train who was even willing to speak to me.

SUSAN: (*Very much at a loss.*) How interesting.

MARCUS: The other people would get panic in their eyes if I even started to walk in their direction, and they'd move away or pretend to be sleeping. But they didn't fool me, I'm no dope. *You can't sleep standing up!*

SUSAN: (*Trying to make small talk.*) Well, if you're tired enough maybe you can.

MARCUS: Your husband, though, was always very friendly to me. Not like my father. Nowadays my father won't even return my phone calls, I went to a séance and everything.

SUSAN: What?

MARCUS: Well he's dead, but I have this medium friend who gave me this special 800 number that lets you call the dead. Maybe you'd like the number to try to reach your husband on the other side.

SUSAN: I don't think so. Well, *que será, será.* Ah me. La dee dah. Well, thank you so much for coming.

MARCUS: (*Warmly.*) Well, you're welcome. I just feel so terrible about your husband being gone, and I don't know what I'm going to do on the train in the morning.

SUSAN: Yes. Well—why don't you read a book?

MARCUS: That's an idea. Do you have any suggestions?

SUSAN: Oh my, I don't know. *The Thorn Birds, Great Expectations.* Any book, I don't care.

MARCUS: My favorite book is *Babar the Elephant.*

SUSAN: Yes, that is excellent.

MARCUS: Have you read it?

SUSAN: No, but I hear wonderful things. Ah me. My, my. Well, thank you for coming. Good-bye.

MARCUS: (*Surprised.*) Are you leaving?

SUSAN: (*Losing her temper.*) No, I'm not leaving. I want *you* to leave. You're making me hysterical. Can't you take a hint? When I say "Thank you for coming," that's code for "Go away now." Don't you understand that?

MARCUS: (*Terribly abashed, a bit hurt.*) Oh. I'm sorry. I thought it just meant "Thank you for coming." I'm sorry. I didn't realize. I . . . Is there anything else you've said in code I haven't understood?

SUSAN: No. Nothing. I don't think so.

MARCUS: (*Still a little thrown.*) Oh good. (*He looks very abashed and embarrassed.*)

SUSAN: It's . . . just . . . well . . . (*Feeling bad for him.*) Oh dear, now I feel terribly guilty about having expressed my emotions.

MARCUS: (*Friendly again, thinking of her.*) Oh don't feel guilty about expressing emotions. That's a *good* thing to do. You've had a terrible loss.

SUSAN: (*Somewhat seriously, realizing.*) Yes, I have.

MARCUS: Are you sure you don't want to keen yet? I'm not Irish, but I think it's a very appropriate thing to do at a wake.

SUSAN: Oh I don't know. Maybe another time.

MARCUS: This would be the most likely time.

SUSAN: Well, I don't know. (*A little interested.*) What does keening sound like exactly?

MARCUS: Oh, it's real interesting. It's sort of like this.

(MARCUS *makes an enormously strange, low, sustained moan-whine that goes up and down the scale. The rest of the people present come to a dead halt and stare.*)

SUSAN: (*To crowd; slightly annoyed.*) Please stop staring. Go back to your conversational buzz.

(*The crowd goes back to its hum.*)

MARCUS: Did I do something wrong again?

SUSAN: Well, it was a very startling sound.

MARCUS: It's just like crying, but more dramatic. I love to cry. You loved your husband, didn't you?

SUSAN: (*Genuine.*) Yes.

MARCUS: Well, then, don't you want to keen just a little?

SUSAN: Well, I see your point a little but... I don't know that I really could.

MARCUS: You could do it softer than I did.

SUSAN: I don't think so.

MARCUS: Oh please, I'm sure it would make you feel better.

SUSAN: (*Wanting to feel better.*) Would it? (*Starts to, but freezes.*)

This is difficult to do in public. Couldn't I call you later this evening, and do it on the phone?

MARCUS: No, it's much more healing to keen at the funeral. You shouldn't do it on the phone.

SUSAN: Oh, I don't know.

MARCUS: Come on. It'll help.

SUSAN: (*Hesitates, but then.*) Ooooooooo. (*It's very soft. Sounds like a ghost sound, or a person imitating the wind.*)

MARCUS: That's good.

SUSAN: Oooooooo.

MARCUS: That's good.

SUSAN: Oooooooo.

MARCUS: That's good. AAAAAAOOOOWWWWWOOOO-OOOO!!!!

(*SUSAN looks aghast for a moment. The crowd stops and stares again. Momentary silence. After a beat, SUSAN gives in to some odd combination of grief and having fun, and makes extremely loud keening sounds simultaneously with MARCUS.*)

BOTH: AAAAAAAAAAOOOOOOOOOOOOOOOOOOOWWW-WWWOOOOOOOOOOOOOOOOOOO!!!!!!!

(*From out of these very satisfying, if shocking noises, SUSAN starts to cry loudly and uninhibitedly. MARCUS pats her on the back in a comforting manner, looking out at the crowd a bit proudly as if to say, "See what I did?"* SUSAN's *crying subsides, and her breathing returns more to normal.*)

MARCUS: There, that's better.

SUSAN: (*Drying her eyes.*) Thank you so much for coming. (*Just as* MARCUS *begins to wonder.*) No, no, not code. Thank you. I feel much better.

MARCUS: Oh good. Well, you're welcome.

(MARCUS *and* SUSAN *shake hands warmly. Marcus smiles at her, moves aside, as other mourners come over to speak to* SUSAN. *Quick fade.*)

END OF PLAY

GABRIELLE

Liz Ellison

GABRIELLE: Mr. Katzander. I guarantee I will be the friendliest, most dedicated greeter this Walmart has ever seen. I am such a people person. I worked with people all the time at my last job—well, I had my own business actually. Designing alternative wedding dresses. I've just decided it's time for a change. Well—there was sort of a misunderstanding. With my last client. A real bridezilla. Everybody gets a difficult customer once in a while, right? This girl's daddy was paying for everything, so she wanted me to go all out. I made her the most gorgeous gothic ball gown you have ever seen. Fifteen yards of taffeta. It was a dress for a queen. She wanted it in burgundy. Now, do you know what burgundy looks like? Because I sure do. And when she comes in to pick it up, you know what she says? "What is this? I can't get married in purple!" I was completely professional. I told her it was what she asked for. I told her, sweetie, this is burgundy. And she starts using foul language. She says I ruined her wedding day and she's gonna tell everyone she knows that they should never get a dress from me, and blah blah blah blah. But she already paid and the wedding's in three days, so she has to take it. She's about to leave. And something just comes over me. Who the hell does she think she is? Some people really need to be put in their place, you know what I mean? I had a venti café Americano on the counter, hadn't even taken a sip yet, and I just—! All over that damn dress. And then—wouldn't you know—it turns out her daddy's a lawyer. Apparently I caused her "severe emotional distress."

And the little twit must know a lot of people, because business has been in the toilet. But I don't have any regrets. It
felt so goddamn good seeing the look on that hussy's face.
She had it coming. You know, Mr. Katzander, people just
piss me off. They really, really do.

(*She thinks.*)

Maybe you have an opening in the warehouse or
something.

END OF PLAY

GETTING HOME

Anton Dudley

Getting Home was originally produced off-Broadway by Second Stage Theatre, New York. It was directed by David Schweizer, with the following cast:

TRISTAN	Brian Henderson
CABDRIVER	Manu Narayan

CHARACTERS
TRISTAN: White male, late twenties.
CABDRIVER: Indian male, late twenties.

SETTING
A bare stage. Characters flow freely between direct address and being in a scene. Lighting and sound effects, perhaps a chair or two, should be used to create physical space.

TRISTAN *alone on a bare stage.*

TRISTAN: I'm thinking I'm going to start charging—oh, God no, don't jump to any conclusions just because I'm standing on this street corner looking like I am: I meant charging for advice.

I just seem to be far better at dispensing relationship advice to my friends than I do to myself. Take my friend Josie, whom I met accidentally this one time I really had to go to the bathroom in the women's section of Bloomingdale's. She calls the other day from her new apartment in Jackson Heights—why? I couldn't tell you—crying about how all the best men are back in the Midwest. Determined, I take her to gay bingo, because there's always a small handful of attractive straight Jewish men there for some reason and—bam!—one week later they're talking about moving in. Then there's my token heterosexual friend Laser—he's from Reykjavik, I think his real name is Lars or something, but he's a semiprofessional skateboarder and Laser's what we call him—anyway, Laser calls me 'cause he's lonely and looking for a little "village to pillage"—it's a Viking thing, don't ask—so I take him shopping and get him all gussied up so he *doesn't* look like he just discovered Greenland...next thing I know, Laser's got more villages than Epcot Center and I haven't heard from him since.

All this to say, that after dispensing my wisdom, I am now left here on this street corner alone, all by my pathetic self, while the people I would normally be hanging out with on a night like this are off living happily ever after in the Dating Kingdom.

(*His cell phone rings.*)

Oh my God—how rude: who forgot to turn off their—?

(*Rings again.*)

Oh—that's mine—how embarrassing. Sorry.

(*He turns it off.*)

It's probably just my mom: she was gonna call with a recipe or something—anyway. Relationships. Complicated.

    I had a close call the other week, though. I had just started taking this continuing-ed class at NYU called "Fairy Tales and Their Contemporary Urban Parallels in Reality." Please, it meets on Wednesday, and I'm so over *Project Runway*. Anyway, that weekend, I found myself on the street corner—I know, it's a theme—drunk off my face and—uh-huh—alone. I had been out clubbing—and following the ubiquitous Gaga and what I think, God forbid, was a Hannah Montana remix—*something happened*. The flows came on and I'm the only one there: it's like the world has vanished. I walk outside and suck in my breath, it's four a.m. and I'm going to face the subway.

    Look at me. The state I'm in now, no one would ever guess my pedigree. I look like I've been working all night in the *former* Times Square and then was mugged of everything I got for it. I'm walking on, and out of my peripheral vision—a yellow car has stopped—ah, a cab! The driver is looking at me—now, yes I do have a full-time job and a rather respectable apartment in one of the already up-and-came sections of Brooklyn—but at "ce moment,"

as Juliette Binoche would say: "Je suis broke"—"Sorry"—I
smile goofily and keep walking. Five steps down the cab
pulls up again. He's still looking at me. How desperate—I
know that no one in his right mind is on the street right
now and this guy's just trying to make an honest buck like
everyone else, but really, cabdrivers who idle outside gay
bars when they're closing are something akin to ambulance
chasers and I just won't support their misconceptions of my
people—at least not in this specific instance.

I smile very friendlical—then shrug "sorry" once
more, and I am walking on. Subway, subway, subway. I am
a supporter of public transportation—I love getting down
and dirty with "the people"—I support my right to travel
this city twenty-four hours a day and—oh my God!—he's
driven up like half a block and stopped and his window is
rolling down.

(*Suddenly, the* CABDRIVER *appears.*)

CABDRIVER: Hello.

TRISTAN: Dude! That is so more interesting than just listening to
me tell the whole thing—how cool is live theater?

CABDRIVER: Where do you live?

TRISTAN: Brooklyn.

CABDRIVER: Where in Brooklyn?

TRISTAN: The good part.
Well, I tell *him* the address, but please—I don't know
who any of you are, I'm not going to freely give out my
address in a place like *this*. If you really want to know then
friend-request me on Facebook, okay?

CABDRIVER: Get in.

TRISTAN: I don't have any money.

CABDRIVER: That's okay.

TRISTAN: . . . I have *lived* enough movies to know where this is headed. But, God, he's Indian—and beautiful. His skin sort of glows—like really expensive peanut butter—that's probably not a great analogy, but the sort of honey-golden-mousse tone of his skin framed by the blackest hair you've ever seen—hair so black it's practically violet as it shines in the moonlight and these soft eyes—like—like you just want to go to American Apparel and get you some hot little stretchy made-in-America swimmies and dive on into those eyes and never come up for air ever again—they're like that— they're glistening pools.

CABDRIVER: Yes?

TRISTAN: He has a really thick accent that makes it hard not to just think he is the sweetest thing in the world.
    Should I get in the front seat or the back?
    Oh my God—who am I? Did I really just ask—?

CABDRIVER: You can get in the front.

TRISTAN: Hold that question. (TRISTAN *gets in "the car."*) Wow, you're beautiful.

CABDRIVER: Thank you.

TRISTAN: You have beautiful eyes.

CABDRIVER: Thank you.

TRISTAN: And beautiful hair.

CABDRIVER: Thank you.

TRISTAN: Beautiful, glowing skin.

CABDRIVER: Thank you.

TRISTAN: And a beautiful...cab.

CABDRIVER: Thank you.

TRISTAN: No, really, you do—I have been in a lot of cabs and this one is immaculate. Wow.

CABDRIVER: Thank you.

TRISTAN: Lord, this guy's polite. Clearly new to the city. But his cab? No joke: it's like another world in here: even the air seems different: like I've stepped into the pages of a...well, if you were enrolled in the class at NYU you'd think the same thing.
        Long night?

CABDRIVER: Yes.

TRISTAN: Yeah, me, too.

CABDRIVER: *Fun* long night?

TRISTAN: Maybe.

CABDRIVER: I have been working long night.

TRISTAN: Please! Back-to-back remixes of "Seasons of Love" and the Shangri-La mix of Rihanna's new single isn't work?
        Maybe this guy is straight after all. No, there's a hand on my thigh. He plays for the home team!

CABDRIVER: This is nice.

TRISTAN: Yes. It is. Us sitting here in this immaculate cab, like it's some Italian sofa we bought together on that trip to Milan we took after we got married in Boston and took some time off to see the world. And we did that sort of pilgrimage thing to India and visited the town where you were born. Rode the elephants and lit candles at the shrine of that one with all the arms and you laughed 'cause I said about the arm coming out of his face and it's actually his trunk and well, that was funny, I guess; but us sitting here, like it's Sunday morning and I've just made you breakfast and we're watching the water roll up on our beachfront property because we moved to the Hamptons to get away from it all is *really nice.*

CABDRIVER: You work out?

TRISTAN: Oh, you meant my thigh. Yeah, it's nice I guess. I was a bike messenger before landing my full-time job—but no one needs to know that.

　　He splits his attention between the road and me and he's ever so calm. I feel exceptionally safe and there's a history here. An entire history we share in some strange way.

　　We pass over one of the bridges, I don't really notice which: all I see are the lit suspension wires dance behind his head like strands of shooting stars. There's not much traffic and we're moving at a good pace, which normally would be cause for a backseat cell phone call to News of the Weird, but right now, at four whatever on this Sunday morning, it isn't fair, 'cause I want this moment to last forever.

CABDRIVER: I turn here?

TRISTAN: Hm?

CABDRIVER: Here, I turn?

TRISTAN: Oh yeah. And then like five blocks down—I'm across

the street from the Shop 'n Save, but I promise I never go in there to do either.

CABDRIVER: Can I park on the street?

TRISTAN: It's only then that I realize that I have never seen a Yellow Cab parked *anywhere*. I mean cabs are like...and cabdrivers?...what happens to a cabdriver when he gets out of his cab? Is it like a character in a play when he exits the stage? Does he just vanish? Disintegrate? Become something else entirely? Or is it like a fairy tale and does he turn into a prince?

These are the questions you ask yourself when you are enrolled in a continuing-ed class at NYU called "Fairy Tales and Their Contemporary Urban Parallels in Reality."

CABDRIVER: You have a beautiful apartment.

TRISTAN: And then we're in bed. And it's glorious. He is glorious. I am glorious. All of it. Just glorious. And oddly silent. Whispered almost. But large. Heavy. Overwhelming and soft all at the same time. But very very silent. Like a secret.

Don't keep me a secret. Please?

CABDRIVER: There is a fairy tale from Firozpur in India that tells of a young princess who was to marry a mysterious prince. When they had wed, she refused to speak until he revealed the secret of his birth. "Tell me your secret" were the only words she would say. He answered that if he did, she would regret it until the end of her life. She took no heed of his warnings, simply repeating the only words she would say: "Tell me your secret. Tell me your secret. Tell me your secret." Finally, he said, "At midnight you shall have your wish. But I warn you, you will regret it."

TRISTAN: Good for her: I've come to realize that secrets kill.

CABDRIVER: Secrets are often a great source of safety.

TRISTAN: But he told her anyway?

CABDRIVER: Yes. He turned to his wife, whom he loved very much, and said, "Know that I am the son of the king of a far-off country who was turned by enchantment into a..." And right as the prince said that fateful word, he turned *back* into a snake and slid into the river. From that day on, the pair could only see each other at midnight, when the serpent would sneak into the house of black stone where the princess lived alone.

TRISTAN: Would she speak to him there?

CABDRIVER: She did not recognize him. She saw only a snake. She said to it, "Who are you? What do you want?" The snake replied, "I am your husband. Did I not tell you that if you forced my secret from me, you would regret it?"

TRISTAN: ...So what does all that mean?

CABDRIVER: I have to go.

TRISTAN: No! Give me a break, no.

CABDRIVER: Give me your phone number.

TRISTAN: (*Quickly.*) Yeah, sure, here!

CABDRIVER: Give me your cell number, too.

TRISTAN: Here. Can I have yours?

CABDRIVER: I call you.

TRISTAN: And in silence he got dressed. I stared at him. In silence. I opened the door—in silence—and he slithered out. He

was halfway down the hall and I was closing the door when
I heard him say . . .

CABDRIVER: I love you.

(CABDRIVER *vanishes.*)

TRISTAN: And then he was gone.

Josie says he's probably married with children and that
she would be the one to know: living in Jackson Heights
and all. And that I shouldn't keep my hopes up, that dash-
ing Indian princes don't just roll up in cabs, sweep you
off your feet, and live happily ever after no matter what
the Contemporary Urban Parallels in Reality say. Tosh!
I wanted to know how the story ends. The story of the
Snake Prince and the Princess. I couldn't buy that that was
the whole ending. I mean, who says that—don't ask people
their secrets, the end. I didn't buy it. My friend Nilesh, who
works in this cool Indian boutique in Brooklyn where
desperately hip white people buy ethnic things to decorate
their apartments with, knew the end to the story. He said
that the princess lures all the river snakes into her house
and then captures the queen snake and says, without even
a flinch of fear, "Queen of snakes, Queen of snakes, give
me back my husband." And that the queen sways her head
to and fro, fixing the princess with her wicked, beady eyes,
but the princess does not flinch, she just repeats, "Queen of
snakes, Queen of snakes, give me back my husband." And
the queen—*accepting* the *courage* of the princess—simply
says, "Tomorrow. Tomorrow." And the very next night, at
midnight, the prince appears. And there were never any
secrets between them again. Nilesh says, "You see, my friend,
it takes *courage* to be in love."

Still, the answer wasn't enough for me. I mean. The guy
said he loved me. And screw courage! I mean: *love.* Doesn't
that count for anything: secrets, truth, whatever. Laser says

that my superhero power is the ability to turn everything into a love story. That this Indian cabdriver experience was really just a one-night thing and I shouldn't look at it like some fairy tale. But I have to think that fairy tales, like stereotypes, have their foundations in truth. They reflect something of our collective human experience—all of us, in some way, can not only understand but *relate* to them. And if that is so, then a love story *can* bloom from a simple, immediate, human connection. And if this connection wasn't what I thought it was—well, then . . . I traded my dignity for a fifteen-dollar cab ride home.

And so here I am: no dignity, no lover, no courage: I may as well end it all here. Ah look: headlights! I'll show you, Nilesh; I'll show you, Love; and I will show all of you that an NYU education *is* relevant to contemporary urban life!

(*Emboldened,* TRISTAN *steps out in front of the car, which is racing toward him. We hear beeping, over which* TRISTAN *chants with his eyes closed . . .*)

Queen of cabs, queen of cabs: give me back my husband!
Queen of cabs, queen of cabs: give me back my husband!
Queen of cabs, queen of cabs—

(*The screeching of tires. The car stops.* TRISTAN *is a doe in the headlights.* CABDRIVER *enters.*)

CABDRIVER: Tristan?

TRISTAN: Huh?

CABDRIVER: It's you.

TRISTAN: Hey . . . why didn't you call?

CABDRIVER: I did. Twice. You didn't answer your phone.

TRISTAN: Oh—well—I've . . . been at the theater—a lot of theater lately.

CABDRIVER: I thought the wrong number was not right so I am going to your apartment to leave you this.

(*A note.*)

TRISTAN: It's warm.

CABDRIVER: (*Touching his heart.*) It has been in my shirt pocket for a few days. Fear keeps me small, I think.

TRISTAN: But that night, you left so quickly. I thought—

CABDRIVER: I was still working. I had to return the car. How many of us can actually afford a medallion?

TRISTAN: . . . Wow. How did I miss that?

CABDRIVER: It takes courage to trust others . . . and ourselves.

TRISTAN: What was your secret?

CABDRIVER: You.

TRISTAN: But I don't want to be someone's secret.

CABDRIVER: No, neither do I.

(*Pause.*)

TRISTAN: You're not married are you?

CABDRIVER: Not since I came here. (*They laugh.*) I am sorry I was afraid.

TRISTAN: Yeah. I am sorry I was too.

CABDRIVER: So. Now?

TRISTAN: . . . Dinner?

CABDRIVER: There is a very good place over across there. We walk?

TRISTAN: Why don't we take your cab?

CABDRIVER: Please, there is more to me than that.

TRISTAN: . . . I think I'm going to enjoy taking the subway home tonight.

(*They walk off together.*)

END OF PLAY

H.R.

Eric Coble

H.R. was commissioned by Dobama Theatre, Cleveland, Ohio, and premiered March 13, 2009, directed by Joe Verciglio. The cast was as follows:

FRANK	Michael Regnier
KRISTEN	Jennifer Klika
CHIP	Tom Woodward
MARGARET	Lissy Gulick

CHARACTERS
KRISTEN: An department chief, thirties.
FRANK: An office administrator, fifties.
CHIP: A sales rep, thirties.
MARGARET: A vice president, fifties.

TIME
Now.

PLACE
An office.

SETTING
A receptionist's desk in an office.

At rise: FRANK, *fifties, in shirt and tie, sits behind the desk, on the phone.*

FRANK: (*Into phone.*)...thank you.

(*He hangs up, concerned, as* KRISTEN, *thirties, also in business attire, walks in with a file. She glances behind the desk.*)

KRISTEN: Hey, Frank. Is the fax machine broken?

FRANK: No, ma'am.

KRISTEN: 'Cause the Peterson people were supposed to fax me an invoice.

FRANK: Yes, ma'am.

KRISTEN: You're sure it's plugged in and everything?

FRANK: Yes, ma'am.

KRISTEN: They said by ten o'clock.

FRANK: We got nothin'.

KRISTEN: Well, screw them.

(*She grabs a candy from the little bowl on* FRANK's *desk.*)

FRANK: Yes, ma'am.

(*Kristen starts out.*)

You should know, H.R. called.

(*Kristen stops.*)

KRISTEN: From corporate?

FRANK: Yes, ma'am.

KRISTEN: When?

FRANK: Just now, I just hung up the phone, I was about to tell Margaret.

KRISTEN: So what did they want?

FRANK: They're coming.

(*Beat.*)

KRISTEN: Today?

FRANK: This afternoon.

KRISTEN: And this is the first we hear about it?

FRANK: We're just employees, why should they tell us?

KRISTEN: Why are they coming?

FRANK: They didn't say.

KRISTEN: Didn't say or wouldn't say?

FRANK: Is there a difference?

KRISTEN: All the difference in the world, Frank.

(CHIP *enters, a good-looking guy in his thirties in collar T-shirt, jeans, and flip-flops.*)

CHIP: Hey, Kristen-McGisten. (*Kisses her cheek.*) Morning, Franker. (*Shakes his hand, glances behind the desk.*) Is the fax machine broken?

FRANK: No, sir.

CHIP: I should have gotten a fax from the Brownsteins.

FRANK: Yes, sir.

CHIP: But no faxy-taxy, huh?

(*Taking a candy from* FRANK'*s bowl.*)

KRISTEN: Chip, H.R. called.

CHIP: Who's H.R.?

KRISTEN: Human resources, Chip.

CHIP: Right! Absolutely! Yeah, no, I was thinking like *H.R.*, like *H.R. Pufnstuf.*

FRANK: No, this would be human resources.

KRISTEN: From corporate. They're coming.

CHIP: Where.

KRISTEN: Here, Chip, they're coming here to our office.

CHIP: Why?

KRISTEN: We don't know.

CHIP: Well, why don't we know?

KRISTEN: Because they won't tell us.

FRANK: "Didn't" tell us.

(MARGARET, *fifties, enters in a business outfit with papers.*)

MARGARET: Frank, is the fax machine broken, because— (*Sees the others.*) Oh. Did I call a meeting and forget to CC myself?

KRISTEN, FRANK, CHIP: H.R. is coming.

MARGARET: What?

FRANK: I was going to tell you, I just got off the phone with them, I tried to tell you, but these, these, these (*gestures to* KRISTEN *and* CHIP) hindrances hindered me.

MARGARET: When are they coming?

FRANK AND KRISTEN: Today.

MARGARET AND CHIP: What??

CHIP: They can't come today! Today is casual day!

KRISTEN: For you anyway.

CHIP: I wasn't seeing anyone today—Margaret, you said on days when there was no face-to-face I'd be Mr. Phoner Man, I could dress down, you said they wouldn't know how I looked over the phone, you said so!

MARGARET: Well, I didn't know H.R. was coming, did I?

CHIP: Oh, Christ, I gotta, they're gonna see me, I'm not, they're gonna totally—

KRISTEN: Didn't you used to keep a shirt and tie in your office just in case?

CHIP: (*Slaps his forehead.*) Duh! Yes! Emergencies! If this isn't an emergency I don't know what is, right? Thank you!

(*He grabs another candy and charges off.*)

MARGARET: It's not an emergency, it's just H.R.

KRISTEN: But they didn't call you?

MARGARET: No. Which is sort of... Frank, why are they coming?

FRANK: They didn't say.

MARGARET: Didn't say or wouldn't say?

KRISTEN: (*To* FRANK.) You see?

FRANK: I was as surprised as anyone, but I played it cool, like you always told me to do, I asked, "Oh, really?" very calm, very like, "Hmm. What's the occasion?" and they said they just needed to meet with the staff and they'd be here this afternoon.

KRISTEN: "Meet with the staff..."

MARGARET: Was that exactly what they said?

FRANK: "We just need to meet with the staff." That's what they said.

MARGARET: "Meet with the staff."

KRISTEN: "We need to meet with the staff."

MARGARET: (*Checking her PDA.*) We're not due for another town hall meeting until next month.

KRISTEN: (*Checking her PDA.*) Self-evaluations are due in May...

MARGARET: And the confessional retreat is in June...

KRISTEN: "Dreaming Outside the Box" is in July...

MARGARET: (*To* FRANK.) Do you have anything on your calendar?

FRANK: (*Looks at his desk calendar.*) Mmmm... Tomorrow is Tina's birthday.

MARGARET: They aren't coming for Tina's birthday.

KRISTEN: Them and me both.

MARGARET: You're not still mad about the refrigerator thing?

KRISTEN: I'm not mad. I'm just disappointed.

MARGARET: It was two months ago, Kristen.

KRISTEN: And the Oreo pie was clearly labeled as mine, it was from *my* party, it was on the left side of the second shelf which is *my* side of the second shelf—

FRANK: (*Reading calendar.*) This is National Blood Pressure Awareness Week.

KRISTEN: Oh, I'm aware.

MARGARET: They wouldn't—

FRANK: (*Reading.*) My cat has a vet appointment on Thursday. I
   think they're gonna give her one of those big white collar
   things—

MARGARET: You're sure they said "meet with the staff."

KRISTEN: Maybe they just need to meet with sales again.

MARGARET: Then Chip damn well better have a tie in his office.

(*And* CHIP *trots on buttoning the most wrinkled dress shirt you've ever
seen, over incredibly wrinkled dress pants, a tie in his hands, but still
wearing flip-flops.*)

CHIP: Okay, no worries, the Chip machine is powered up,
   people.

(*He makes a "clicking on" motion.*)

KRISTEN: Jesus, Chip, where do you keep that suit, in your desk
   drawer?

CHIP: . . . yeah.

(*He takes another candy from the bowl.*)

MARGARET: Okay, look, people, H.R. could be coming for any
   number of reasons. To discuss new benefits packages or go
   over new evaluation forms, talk about the needs of each
   department—

KRISTEN: Or they could be coming to ax someone.

(*Beat. They look at each other.*)

MARGARET: We have no reason to believe that.

KRISTEN: Then why are they coming? Why no notice? Any of that other stuff, they could do in e-mails—

CHIP: But it's Monday. They don't fire people on Monday.

KRISTEN: Tell that to Howard and Laneesha.

MARGARET: And Gregory. Don't forget Gregory.

CHIP: Oh, God. Gregory.

FRANK: I don't care what they do, I'm not going down like Gregory.

KRISTEN: My point is the day makes no difference.

MARGARET: But it does matter who's coming. (*Dials her cell phone.*) Hang on.

CHIP: But we know who's coming.

FRANK: We don't know names. If it's Mr. Hickenlooper, we're all probably all right.

CHIP: As in Mr. CEO?

KRISTEN: You know another Hickenlooper?

FRANK: The big boss won't be anywhere near a firing. Wherever he goes there's this protective bubble. Like you're fine until he walks out of the room.

CHIP: I want to be in that bubble. I need to be in that bubble.

MARGARET: (*Into phone.*) Uh, hi, Francie, this is Margaret in

Cleveland, just got word about the impending visit and wanted to check on who exactly we should expect. Call me back, okay? Thanks. Bye.

(*She hangs up, looks at the rest of them. They look at her.*)

I left a message.

KRISTEN: They didn't take your call?

MARGARET: Well, no ... but ...

(*They all take a step back from her.*)

Oh, come on! I'm sure she was just on the other line.

CHIP: Not taking your calls. That's like the first sign.

KRISTEN: (*Nodding.*) They're sending H.R. From corporate. They don't do that for little people. They only do that for higher-ups.

FRANK: No, little people they fire over the phone. Remember Henry?

CHIP: They got him over the phone?

FRANK: Whenever he hears a ring tone now? He wets himself.

KRISTEN: They're sending someone in person ...

CHIP: Margaret ...

MARGARET: This is ridiculous. They're not— I haven't even— If they were going to terminate anyone, they'd be scheduling a survivor's guilt workshop for next week. We're all fine.

FRANK: Unless they were sending H.R. *because* they want us to think it's for someone higher-up, and it's really for one of us.

CHIP: ... or multiple ones of us.

KRISTEN: Unless they think we think they *think* we'll think they're thinking of a manager, so they can actually think about one of us, but they're *really* thinking about a manager.

MARGARET: ... They're not that smart.

KRISTEN: Or they want you to *think* they're not that smart.

MARGARET: These are the people who made Frank count out spoonfuls of creamer to see if we were actually getting what the container said we were getting.

CHIP: And were we?

FRANK: The jar said there were 150 servings, I counted 137.

CHIP: Maybe you counted wrong. Maybe that's why they're coming.

KRISTEN: No. You know what. I bet it's Tina.

FRANK: Won't be Tina.

KRISTEN: Why?

FRANK: She filed a complaint against Leon last year, remember? For inappropriate behavior. There'd be lawyers all over them if she got fired.

KRISTEN: Then maybe it's Leon?

FRANK: Won't be Leon. He's African-American. There'd be lawyers all over them if he got fired.

KRISTEN: Dammit! I wish I'd filed a complaint.

CHIP: I wish I was African-American!

MARGARET: We've got to let the rest of the office know they're
coming. Frank, send out a memo—

KRISTEN: No!

MARGARET AND FRANK: What?

KRISTEN: What about Desmond?

MARGARET: In I.T.?

KRISTEN: He's dug in in his little spider hole back there. He's an
ex-marine.

CHIP: He collects guns.

KRISTEN: If he gets advance word H.R. is coming? It's gonna
make Waco look like a freakin' doll party.

MARGARET: Oh, for God's sake.

CHIP: But the rest of the crew should probably know. They
might need to change their clothes too.

FRANK: Who knows? The rest of 'em might even have shoes.

(CHIP *looks down at his flip-flops.*)

CHIP: Shit!

(*He charges off.*)

KRISTEN: It's me, isn't it, Margaret?

MARGARET: What?

KRISTEN: Frank's right. They're coming for the little people. I'm the last one standing in my department, they're just gonna shut down my whole operation, aren't they?

MARGARET: Kristen, I haven't heard any such—

KRISTEN: At that luncheon two years ago! I sat next to what's-his-name—that V.P. for development. I told him about my grandmother's Alzheimer's. Dammit, dammit, dammit!!

MARGARET: But you don't have Alzheimer's—

KRISTEN: Yet! They're cutting me now before their coverage has to cover me—

(CHIP *runs back on, still in his suit but now barefoot.*)

CHIP: I don't have any shoes!! I wore 'em home last time I had to change! Frank! Do you have an extra pair of dress shoes with you?

FRANK: I don't know, Chip, let me look. No. No, I don't seem to have brought an extra pair of dress shoes with me today.

CHIP: (*To* MARGARET *and* KRISTEN.) Did either or you guys?

KRISTEN: Not that'd fit you.

CHIP: Crap. Crap crap crap. I'll just...

(*He crowds in to stand beside* FRANK *behind the desk.*)

FRANK: What are you doing??

CHIP: I'm hiding my feet. When they come in I'll just stand back
here and smile.

(*He gives a little wink and a cocky "finger gun" click.*)

FRANK: Not beside me you won't.

CHIP: Oh, come on!

FRANK: You've got your own desk, go smile behind it.

CHIP: (*Not leaving the desk, reaching for another candy.*) You're such
a jerk, you know that?

(FRANK *slaps his hand and* CHIP *drops the candy.*)

    Hey!

FRANK: I'd rather be a jerk than a mooch! You always got your
goddamn paws in my candy bowl—

CHIP: I thought it was for everybody!

FRANK: It is! But have you ever, EVER brought in any food for
the office?

CHIP: I don't know, probably not—

FRANK: No, the answer is definitely not, because you're a mooch!
A big old moocher mooch!

CHIP: Yeah, well, at least I'm not...screwing the boss!

(*Beat. They all stare at him.*)

I'm bettin' there's some kind of rules against *that* one, Mr. Smarty Man.

FRANK: I don't—

MARGARET: We don't—

FRANK: Margaret!

MARGARET: I mean, it's ridiculous, Frank!

CHIP: Oh, please, everyone knows!

FRANK: ...they do?

MARGARET: There's nothing to know!

FRANK: (*To* KRISTEN.) Do you know what he's talking about, Kristen?

(*Beat. She nods sheepishly.*)

MARGARET: Oh my God.

KRISTEN: Pretty much everyone in the office pretty much knows.

FRANK: But we were so careful...

MARGARET: There's nothing to be careful about! Nothing happened!

FRANK: How can you say that?

MARGARET: Because it's true! Tell them it's true that it's not true, Frank.

FRANK: ...I thought the things you told me were true...

KRISTEN: I mean, it's cool with us, it's none of our business.

MARGARET: Exactly.

KRISTEN: But I think it's kind of against company policy.

FRANK: (*Head in hands.*) Oh God oh God oh God...

KRISTEN: But I mean, so are your naps, Margaret, and we're not reporting those!

MARGARET: My what?

KRISTEN: Every day at 2:13 when you close your office door.

MARGARET: I'm not sleeping!

CHIP: (*Sheepishly.*) You do kind of snore pretty loud.

(*Beat.*)

MARGARET: I snore?

CHIP: If the air conditioner is off, you can pretty much hear it through the whole office.

FRANK: All those walls and cubicles. It bounces. Like a canyon.

(MARGARET *sits on the desk, dazed.*)

MARGARET: ...I'm dead.

FRANK: Maybe they don't know.

MARGARET: They know. They always know. I just...I haven't been sleeping well, the second and third quarters were lousy...

FRANK: I know.

CHIP: Of course you've got your reasons—

MARGARET: I do!

FRANK: Like I'm sure Chip has reasons for downloading all that porn.

CHIP: WHAT??

FRANK: I mean, it's totally your business.

CHIP: I never...I don't...

(*They all stare at him. Pause.*)

Does everybody know?

(*They all nod.*)

Even Desmond?

KRISTEN: Desmond's the one who pointed it out.

FRANK: And please, you're in sales. Sales departments are what keep Internet porn alive.

CHIP: ...I'm dead.

KRISTEN: The nuns with the Saint Bernard was a little off-putting...

CHIP: That site was an accident! It just popped up! It was a, a cookie—

KRISTEN: I never saw it, I just heard about it.

MARGARET: (*To* KRISTEN.) Exactly. Like we just heard about you in the storage closet.

KRISTEN: ...what?

MARGARET: Oh, come on, Kristen.

KRISTEN: I don't know what you're talking about.

FRANK: The storage closet, Kristen. You've been huffing the toner cartridges in the closet.

KRISTEN: I never...!

CHIP: Pretty much everyone in the office knows about it, Kristen.

KRISTEN: I don't... I mean, accidentally, it's a small room, I might have inhaled once or twice—

MARGARET: I'm pretty sure there's a company policy on that one.

KRISTEN: Do you think they know?

FRANK: They know. They always know.

KRISTEN: I'm so dead. (*To* MARGARET.) You're dead. (*To* FRANK.) You're dead. (*To* CHIP.) You...

CHIP: I wore my fucking flip-flops on the wrong fucking day!!

KRISTEN: Excuse me.

(*She walks out.*)

FRANK: (*To* MARGARET.) I just need to know that we had something, Margaret.

MARGARET: What do you think I was losing sleep over?

FRANK: It wasn't just third-quarter losses?

MARGARET: The third quarter can go to hell. Every quarter can all go to hell, as long as I have you.

FRANK: Do you mean it?

MARGARET: If I'm going down I'm going down like a grown woman. On my terms.

(*They're now behind the desk, crowding* CHIP, *who is increasingly uncomfortable, but unable to leave . . .*)

FRANK: And I'm going down as the best damn office administrator this crap shack has ever known.

(*And they kiss passionately inches from* CHIP.)

CHIP: Um. Excuse me . . .

(*And in stumbles* KRISTEN, *black ink smudges over her nose and mouth, clutching her files and a toner cartridge.*)

KRISTEN: THERE IS NOTHING HUMANE . . . OR RESOURCEFUL . . . ABOUT HUMAN RESOURCES!!

(FRANK *and* MARGARET *continue kissing.*)

CHIP: Kristen!

(KRISTEN *staggers back toward the door.*)

Where are you going?

KRISTEN: I am taking the Vanguard supple-leather-armrest, quadri-rolling, ergonomic chair from Margaret's corner office twenty-six stories up and I am chucking that sucker straight through her floor-to-ceiling sun-tint window and I am then chucking myself down all twenty-six stories onto the goddamn smokers bitterly huddling around the front door! I am making my own final parking place all over the freakin' curb and sidewalk!!

(*She staggers out.*)

CHIP: Kristen! Somebody! Somebody should stop her, she needs to be stopped—

FRANK: (*In mid-kiss, now on the desk, writhing with* MARGARET.) You stop her.

CHIP: I can't! I'm barefoot! If H.R. walks in that door right now and I'm running around barefoot... (*Calling out.*) Someone? Kristen's going off the reservation!

MARGARET: (*To* FRANK.) I love you so much.

FRANK: I love *you* so much.

CHIP: Anyone?? We're about to have a serious P.R. challenge!

(FRANK*'s phone rings.*)

FRANK: (*To* MARGARET.) I have never, never loved any of my supe-
riors like I love you.

MARGARET: No one is your superior, Frank Dilford.

CHIP: (*Calling out.*) Leon? Tina??

(*Phone rings.*)

FRANK: Oh, dammit.

MARGARET: Don't answer it.

FRANK: Habit. (*He grabs the phone.*) Good morning, Wilkeson
Midwest... (*They stare at him.*) Yes. Yes. Of course not. No.
Thank you.

(*He hangs up as* KRISTEN *staggers back on in a stupor, dragging a rolling
chair behind her...*)

MARGARET: What.

FRANK: That was H.R. From corporate. They aren't coming
today after all. They said they'd call back when they're coming to town. Maybe tomorrow.

(*They all look at each other... total wrecks...*)

MARGARET: Ah.

CHIP: Oh.

KRISTEN: ... huh ...

MARGARET: I'll just... take my chair back, Kristen. Thank you.

(*She pries the chair from* KRISTEN*'s grip and wheels it off.*)

CHIP: I should go call the Brownsteins and see where that fax is.

(*He grabs a candy and hurries off.* KRISTEN *and* FRANK *look blankly at one another.*)

KRISTEN: I'm gonna take a little break.

(*She turns and stumbles off. An offstage thud as she collapses.*

FRANK *stands alone. Sits at his desk. Straightens his tie. Pause. His phone rings. He jumps. It rings again. He stares at it . . .*

Blackout.)

END OF PLAY

I LOVE NEIL LABUTE

Gary Winter

I Love Neil LaBute premiered in Sticky at Belly Bar, on August 23, 2004. The play was directed by Ali Ayala, with Libby Emmons, Brett England, Matthew Korahais, and David Marcus.

I Love Neil LaBute was produced in Big Sticky at the Flea Theater in October 2004. The play was directed by Ali Ayala, with Jim Boyle, Matthew Korahais, Ana Valle, and Matt Wells.

CHARACTERS
NEIL LABUTE #1
NEIL LABUTE #2
NEIL LABUTE #3
JOSEPH SMITH: Played by a woman.

SETTING
A bar.

SCENE ONE

NEIL LABUTE #1 *sits at a bar table with a drink.* NEIL LABUTE #2 *enters with drink and sits.*

NL #2: Hi Neil LaBute

NL #1: Hi Neil LaBute.

NL #2: Hi Neil LaBute.

(NL #3 *walks in with a drink.*)

NL #3: Hi Neil LaBute.

NL #1: Hi Neil LaBute

NL #2: Hi Neil LaBute.

NL #1: Blackout.

(*There is no blackout.* NL #1, #2, #3, *all just stare at their beer bottles.*)

NL #3: Lights up.

(*They all drink.*)

NL #1: Okay. What do you want to do now?

NL #2: I don't know if I should write a play, a film or a poem.

NL #3: A poem. Hey! That's a swell idea.

(*They all look serious for a moment. Then they all start cracking up laughing.*)

NL #1: Hey—you're funny Neil LaBute.

NL #3: Hey thanks, Neil LaBute.

NL #2: Hey let's make a film.

NL #1: We're out of money.

NL #3: Money? What're you fucking stupid?
     We just rob the bar and we'll have money.
     How do you think any film gets financed?

NL #1: I didn't know that.

NL #2: Just watch, asshole.

NL #1: Hey bartender! Yeah you bitch! Empty the cash register
     and toss over a wad of cash or I'll come over there and shove
     this beer bottle up your armpits. Then we'll work on your
     other orifices.

(*Nothing.*)

NL #3: Please, bitch.

(*A roll of money comes flying over the bar and into their booth.*)

See. You gotta know how to talk to people, fuck face.

NL #2: So look, Neil LaBute. I want to make this film about three guys who are married. They hate their wives and pain-in-the-ass kids. They hate their jobs. Their bosses are assholes. Their coworkers are like shit-eating mole rats. So these guys get together one night and get shit-faced. They sign a contract in blood on a napkin.

NL #1: They all agree to fuck each other's wives!

NL #3: And make each wife not tell anyone else!

NL #2: Then they agree to fuck each other's daughters!

NL #1: And the daughters can't tell anyone or the fathers stop supplying them with crack.

NL #3: And they won't pay for their high school graduation breast implants.

NL #2: And they'll cut off their boyfriends' balls on prom night!

NL #1: They should do that anyway!

NL #3: We are fucking geniuses.

(*They drink and high-five.*)

NL #2: Blackout!

(*They stare at their beer bottles.*)

NL #1: Lights up.

NL #2: I'm not sure if this is a film or a play.

NL #3: Well, Neil LaBute, a fucking play is language-driven.

NL #2: And a film is visual-driven.

NL #1: (*Snooty British accent.*) Is this a language-driven story or visual?

(*They all contemplate this very, very seriously.*

Then they all look at each other and crack up.)

ALL: Ahhhhh! It's a fucking movie. We're fucking geniuses.

NL #3: Blackout.

(*They stare at their beers.*)

NL #1: Lights up.

(*They all have legal pads in front of them.*)

NL #2: Okay! Let's write a scene.

NL #1: We got three couples. John and Betty. Alice and Peter. Mark and Sarah.

NL #3: This is fucking amazing! We're not even sticking with our original idea.

NL #2: John is having a midlife crisis, even though he's only twenty-six.
Peter and Alice throw a barbecue, where all the couples meet.
John gets trashed, and Betty is embarrassed. They fight.
John storms into Peter and Alice's bedroom, where he sulks about his miserable life.

Then Sarah walks in. She tells John not to sulk, that Betty
is an uptight asshole.
John agrees and rapes Sarah. Sarah is pissed, but says, what
the fuck. Turns out she too is having a midlife crisis. So
they agree to meet every other night at a motel and fuck.
John and Sarah seem rejuvenated.

(*Pause. They think.*)

NL #1: What next?

NL #3: Mark suspects Sarah is fucking John, but he's a wimp and
doesn't say anything.
But Peter has been arrested for molesting one of his eight-
year-old students, and Alice knows Sarah is screwing
John.

NL #2: Alice shouldn't know. She's too stupid.

NL #3: Okay. Alice just decides to have an affair with Mark, but
John finds out and cuts off Mark's balls.

NL #1: Why should John cut off Mark's balls when John is
screwing Mark's wife?

(*Silence.*)

NL #3: Then Betty should cut off John's balls and fuck Peter.

NL #2: How can she fuck Peter if he's in jail?

NL #1: Yeah, and we already established that Peter only likes
little girls.

NL #3: What if Peter got out of jail and got counseling?

NL #2: Betty has to remain sweet and naive. That way everyone else can look like complete assholes.

NL #1: Way to go, Neil LaBute.

NL #3: Good thinking, Neil LaBute. That's why we're like a fucking modern-day Shakespeare.

NL #2: Thank you, I agree Neil LaBute. We have a window unto the human soul.

(*Joseph Smith, founder of the Mormon Church, appears.*)

NL #1: Who the fuck are you?

NL #2: Who the fuck are you?

NL #3: Who the fuck are you?

NL #2: The whorehouse is on Clinton Street.

NL #1: Hand jobs outside the Lincoln Tunnel, bitch!

JOSEPH SMITH (JS): I am Joseph Smith, founder of the Church of Jesus Christ of Latter-day Saints.

(*NL #1, #2, #3 think about this a second, then all crack up laughing.*)

NL #3: Hey, asshole. I'm a Mormon. I know what Joseph Smith looks like.

JS: What does he look like, Neil LaBute the Mormon?

NL #1: He's six feet eight inches, is two hundred years old and has a white beard.

JS: Is that so, Neil LaBute the Mormon?

NL #2: Yeah I'm Mormon I should know!!! Don't you read *Entertainment Weekly*? If you did you wouldn't be asking such stupid questions.

JS: Well I'm Joseph Smith you idiot.

NL #3: Prove it, asshole!

(JOSEPH SMITH *waves her hands around.* NEIL LABUTE #1, #2, #3 *look on in awe.*)

NL #1: Whoa. That was incredible.

NL #2: I never seen anything like it. Deep shit.

NL #3: Only Joseph Smith, our beloved founder, could do that.

JS: Now Neil LaBute, are you going to stop embarrassing Mormons? I don't care if you make porn-slasher films with Mel Gibson, as long as you say you're an atheist.

NL #2: Oh, we couldn't do that.

JS: Why not?

NL #1: We'd lose all our credibility.

NL #3: By saying we're Mormon we can do whatever we want and people believe we're sincere.

NL #2: Without any religious affiliation we're fucked.

JS: I don't care! All you have to say about people is that they fuck their neighbor's husbands and wives. And that's it! That's all you have to say?

(*Silence. All the* NLs *look at each other.*)

NL #1 , #2, #3: Yeah.

JS: Don't you think that's fucked-up?

NL #1: No.

NL #2: It's real life.

NL #3: It has deep meaning. People screw each other. We're like, reporters of the human condition.

NL #2: Like, hey Joseph Smith, we just added child molestation.

NL #1: How about that?

JS: I'm excommunicating you from the Mormon Church, Neil LaBute.

NL #2: Why don't you join us, Joseph Smith?

NL #1: Wouldn't you like to be a screenwriter and playwright, Joseph Smith?

NL #3: Sure you would. People will think you're so cool.

(*Pause.* JOSEPH SMITH *contemplates this.*)

JS: Really?

(NLs *nod.*)

Blackout!

(JS *sits at the table. Takes out a white pad.*)

Lights up!

So I think Betty is pretending all along to be sweet and naive, but at the end of the film she ties Alice up and fucks her in the butt with a riding whip.

NL #1: Way to go Joseph Smith!

JS: Hey! I can write a movie!

NL #2: And you are exposing the underbelly of human nature!

NL #3: Just wait until you try and write a play!

(*Blackout—this time, for real.*)

END OF PLAY

LIFE WITHOUT SUBTEXT

Michael Mitnick

Outside of the restroom.

Park Avenue Armory. New York City.

A blond, slight, young girl of seventeen, DELLY, *leans against a wall opposite . . .*

BEN, *also seventeen, in a blue blazer and tie.*

BEN: In terms of punch, I think this is tremendous punch.
Or if I'm actually talking in punch terms, this is the
    punchiest punch in the oh my God I hate myself.
Your hair is really straight.

(DELLY *doesn't respond.*)

I should probably apologize.
I'm sorry.
I'm sorry.

(*Silence.*)

I don't know why I'm apologizing. I don't know why
    I'm talking. When I planned this—
None of this would . . .
I'm sorry I asked you to talk near the bathrooms. I
    should have said "on the veranda" but I honestly

don't know if there's a veranda door that's open. Plus
  what the hell. I should have said "hall" but that's not
  very...the band is so loud, but I just needed to...
Who knew a trumpet could be so loud.
OK I'm Ben.

(*Silence.*)

Oh God is that creepy? I hope not. Oh shit. When I
  said "creepy" did it first bring it to your mind? The
  notion that this might be—
You probably want to be getting back...

(*Silence.*)

You are so, soooo pretty.

(*Silence.*)

Is that creepy? I don't care. I honestly don't care if it is
  creepy.
And fuck you if you honestly have a problem with
  honesty.
I'M NOT IN CONTROL OF THE TRUTH.
If this is the world I'm in. And if I can't be honest about
  what I feel deeply inside of me, then fuck it. Can
  I say "fuck" around you? Do you care about things
  like—

(*Silence.*)

What I mean is that if I can't be honest, and put
  everything I feel out on the proverbial table then I
  don't even care about anything anymore...
You are so, so pretty.
That sounds shallow but it's not. I don't know you.

Except to know that I feel things that I thought were
hooey and balderdash and other words that expired
like sour milk in 1944.

(*Silence.*)

I understand if you want to walk away. I'm Ben.
I don't go here.
Or to your school. Is what I mean. Soooooo. Oh God
if I heard myself right now. If I were you. In that
white dress and. Your hair is so straight. Did you.
You probably spent like hours on that. Probably. I'm
wasting your evening. I'm sorry. No actually. No.
I'm not sorry. I'm a human being. This is how great
things happen. This is how amazing things in life
happen. If you could recognize how great stories
start, this would be it. I'm sorry.
I don't go here. I go to public school.

(*Silence.*)

I'm sure you get this all the time but. Listen. Um. I'm
Ben.
The only way that I can convince you of anything is to
say that I'm a VERY CYNICAL PERSON.

(*Silence.*)

That should tell you everything.
What I mean to say is that I don't believe in love. I
don't. I honestly don't.
I believe in self-delusion.
I don't believe in God.
I believe in some miracle of physics that spawned life
and I believe in the miracle that I was born when
I was and you were born when you were born,

after microbes and caves; through religious hatred
and early science. Through dark ages, renaissance,
restoration, and gilded age. Through all that B.S. and
wars and shit so that we could stand in a hallway and
I could say that...
Urgh. OK. Here goes:
I JUST DON'T CARE.
I fucking. Excuse me. I honestly fucking don't. You've
awakened something in me oh my God I sound like
a fuckin.
Excuse me.
I don't go here.
I go to P.S. 122 and I saw you walk into a Duane Reade
and then I did and then I saw you buy a Reese's
Peanut Butter Cup and shampoo and my connection
to you from that moment OK there is no way for
me to convey this without sounding like someone I
would like to murder slash report to the—
I'm Ben.
This is going to sound like. Urg. OK. So I love you.
I do. I honestly fucking do and I don't care. Why aren't
you walking away? I had all these plans of things to say
if you were going to walk away. But you're not so...
I don't believe in love. My parents married because they
met each other in the three years where you better
meet someone or else you're not gonna have your
own kids.
I don't believe in "meant to be." I honestly believed
there are like one hundred people. No. Like. Four
hundred people out there who you'd honestly marry.
And you just sort of fall in love slash settle. But when
I saw you. I dunno.
You made me feel things that I didn't think it was
possible in life to actually feel. Honestly. You
awakened something in me. Something I thought
only happened in fiction.

I saw you and life came to life this sounds sooooo
    stupid.
So stupid.
I'm Ben.
If someone told me that I'd have to run through a field for
    days and days and never stop. If someone said I'd have to
    run in order to see you one last time or just pass away
    immediately, I'd run. I swear to...whoever. I'd run.
I feel something and it is weird and I'm honestly
    looking at it like a science experiment because it
    makes NO SENSE. But...I'll just say it.
When I saw you something clicked ON inside me that
    I never, *NEVER*, felt.
Never.
And I honestly don't care. I honestly don't give a fuck if
    you walk away. Excuse me. I don't give a. OK. I don't
    give a SHIT if you walk away because I'm being
    Honest.
You gave me reason to feel like I'm alive. That my
    eighty-six years or whatever were worth it because I
    felt like there was something more than what comes
    from me. Something I can't control that moves my
    emotions.
I love you.
Boom. I said it.
OK. URGH.
You can go. Honestly, you can walk away and I'd not
    judge you whatso...
I DON'T CARE IF I'M CRAZY. I HONESTLY
    DON'T CARE IN THE VERY CORE OF ME.
    EVERY PRIORITY I EVER HAD—
Why do you keep getting prettier?

(*Silence.*)

I'm not profound. I know it.
And if I'd honestly taken three minutes to sit on

the steps and smoke a cigarette and plan out
something slick to say then maybe this would be
different but I INTENTIONALLY didn't. OK? I
INTENTIONALLY didn't because this is as much
about my future happiness as it is about my faith in
the universe.
I'm not religious.
I saw you buy shampoo and I fell apart.
I'm Ben.

(*Silence.*)

I'm pretty stupid. I'm not going to a fancy college like
you. I'm a third-tier kinda person. And you know
what. I'm FINE with that. Because instead of your
rat-race existence. Instead of being like... "Oh. I
didn't go to DUKE." I'm gonna feel like shit just
because a bunch of assholes who lived before me
established a hierarchy. OK listen. There's this guy
who lives in my building who used to be associate
manager at the Strand. He didn't go to *college*. I'm
pretty sure he didn't graduate from high school
but if he did who cares. He's read so many books
and he's so much smarter than that assfuck who
teaches economics at my high school who graduated
Harvard class of '68 and is sadder than a Sacajawea
dollar coin.
I'm not creative and I'll probably do, like, eight jobs
before I realize what I want.
I bet my grandfather saw my grandmother and had
all these same cynical thoughts. All the stupid like
supercomputer—oh—we're at the apex of technology
everything that can be invented has been invented.
I'm just a jerky poor kid from Brooklyn who doesn't
want do anything but sneak into Garrick Gaieties and
draw naked pictures of showgirls and throw a baseball
around and everything's cynical and I was born too

late and old people are a real intrusion on my epic
thoughts but...
I feel like I'm part of something bigger now.
And I'm sure your dad owns, like, the Discovery
Channel but...
I NEED TO STOP TALKING.
I'm Ben. I don't believe in religion. But I believe in
you.

(*Silence.*)

If I were you and someone said that line to me I'd not
only walk away, but I'd honestly devote my life to
humiliating him.
I will honestly take a photo of myself with my cell
camera and post it on a Web site devoted to morons
who mess up potentially and devastatingly romantic
situations.

(*Silence.*)

I delivered groceries for four weeks to old ladies on the
Upper East Side to pay for this blue blazer.
I don't have very much money.
But.
I think you're so pretty and you make me feel
something I didn't know wasn't fictional.
You made me believe there's order. Or disorder.
    Or... something more than selfish discontent.

DELLY: I'm Delly.

(BEN *smiles.*)

BEN: I'm Ben.

(*Silence.*)

Do you want to dance?

(DELLY *shrugs.*)

I'm worried you won't live up to what I thought you were.

DELLY: Don't worry.
I'm better.

(*They clasp hands and exit.*)

END OF PLAY

LONG DISTANCE

Jane Shepard

Long Distance was first seen at Vital Theatre in New York City on February 17, 2000, written for and featuring Stewart Clark, and directed by Sir Frank Pisco.

A seedy little apartment. Can be represented by an old armchair and side table.

ROY *enters, high energy, and talks to audience as he puts down his things, takes off his coat, and dons an old bathrobe . . .*

ROY: Do you know what happened today? Oh! I couldn't wait to tell you! You will die! Do you know who I saw? Fatima Farterweigh! From the third grade, the one in the class picture caught for all eternity touching her tongue to her nose?!—Oh! I cannot get over that! Not for a thousand years and all the yen in yigamoo! Can you imagine the humiliation?! I combed my hair at least twelve times for that picture, not a pasty hair out of place! I lived in terror a tweak would have fallen down, and Momma would point and Alvin would scoff and I would live a condemned life!

But Fatima! Fat Fatima! Oh, not fat, I shouldn't say fat, that's mean, um . . . Pudgy—no, not pudgy—plump! Generous. No! Rubenesque. Okay, that's not it but let's pretend it is so we can get on with it, okay? Okay! *Rubenesque* Fatima Farterweigh, embedded into that picture with Brillo hair and her tongue up her nose, one eye going this way and one eye going that! Oh! It frightens me, it chills me, *burned* into my memory!

So! I am walking across the plaza this afternoon, and this, this petrified photographic image is transformed before memory's eye into a living, breathing, grown-up Fatima

Farterweigh! Standing before me, frowning, just like she was in third grade, all pimply—ew, do third graders even have pimples?!—and do you know what she did? She pointed at me and shouted, "*You!*" And I tried to pretend that I hadn't seen her, but it didn't work very well because I was so surprised I was just staring, and she shouted, "*Roy!*"

And, I have to tell you, I said, "*Me? No!*" And she absolutely screamed, "*Roy Gannoy!*" And—what could I do? She chased me across the plaza screaming, "*Roy Gannoy the Bubble Boy!*" I shouted back, "*I don't know you, and for God's sake, Fatima, stop screaming!*" Oh! Can you believe it? I am so lame! But I was absolutely cornered!

And Fatima Farterweigh goes, "*You're Roy Gannoy, that boy who talked to himself and blew bubbles all alone on the playground!*"

Well. I just turned to her and said, "*And you're Fat Fatima who's going to fart-her-way to fourth grade!*"

And she stopped, and said, "*But that was mean.*"

And I said, "*So were all of you!*" Yes I did. I said that. That put a crimp in her bonnet.

She says, "*I remember you now, you were always mean.*"

And I said, "*No, I was witty.*" This is a common misconception. If you're a man you can be witty, but if you have ironic insight as an eight-year-old, you're mean.—Although, apparently, if you blow bubbles or talk to yourself at any age, no one will ever, *ever* forget it!

And do you know what Fatima said then?

She smiles and goes, "*Do you still talk to what's-his-name?*"

"*No, Fatima, I don't see anyone from third grade, I don't know what you're talking about.*"

"*No, not a student! That thing you did, your little playground friend!*"

I said, "*I don't talk to anyone.*"

"*No, your special friend.*"

I did not know what to say. I do not know what to say

to people like that, to this day, I don't, period, good night. She leers and says, "*The one you always talked to on the playground. You're the one who had an invisible friend.*"

Okay, fat girl, the cat is out of the bag! Do you still pick your pimples?! Do you still eat your boogers?! Are you still inflated with enough hot air to blow yourself to fourth grade?! Yes, apparently you are! Well, of course I didn't say that. I didn't say, "Fat Fatima Fart-her-way to fourth grade hair like a Brillo pad sucking snot out of her sinuses in the school picture, eyes doing this: ga ga ga!" No! I didn't say that!

And then she, she who has to shop for clothes at the *Hindenburg* factory, says, "*I was mean too. I just didn't know how to tell anybody I liked them. Did you?*"

Fatima Farterweigh . . . I shrugged. I said, "*I never liked anybody.*"

She says, "*Oh, that's sad.*"

Can you imagine? I said, "*No. It's not. It's witty.*"

And she said, "*No, Roy, that's sadder than me.*"

I said, "*But, you're Fat Fatima Fart-her-way to the fourth grade, walleyed and licked your nose in the picture and everybody hated you, even me.*"

"*I know,*" she said. "*But I liked you.*"

(*Silence for a bit, as he noogles around, not sure how to respond.*)

Well . . . I could have told her I guess. I could have told her about you. I could have said, Fatima, girl who turned out to actually like me . . . I don't *need* to be liked. Because I no longer have that invisible friend that I talked to. Now I go home, and put on my robe, and talk to an entire *room* full of them!

I have *masses* at my disposal whenever I need them!— I've made up more people than you will ever know in your life, I've talked to more different kinds of people— Oh, I talk with friends, family, me and Momma gab up a storm!

She loves gossip now the way she never did when she was alive! Sometimes I sit Alvin down right here and read him the riot act about the way he treated me and Momma and, let me tell you, in *this* house, *this* time around, he's sorry! And how he and Momma should have had a little brother for me, even a sickly one, I would have watched out for him. And I talk with my little brother.

Mm-hm! It's not everyone who gets to decide whether or not they have a baby brother. Sure, he can be a pest— when he's in his teens, he's unbearable! Doesn't listen to a thing I say. I tell him. But he's a good boy basically. And when he's not, I make him a neurosurgeon! Yes!

And I am so not a jealous big brother. I'm the kind that attends his medical graduation and gives the talk!

(*Behind chair, as podium.*)

"No brother could be more proud than I, to look upon the young man sitting here today, and know that that little hand, that I taught to tie shoes, will be used in the service of mankind. Congratulations, Gary." Gary, after Gary Cooper.

When Gary's not around I hold salons! Oh yes, right here in my room! In my robe! People love to gather here, excellent meals, always casual. Henry Kissinger, Truman Capote, Dorothy Parker, Britney Spears— Don't laugh, Britney is very much underrated. And cute as a button! I admit, Truman and Dorothy make merciless fun when she's out of the room. I smooth things over.

(*Looking out over all the audience.*)

Debutantes, dilettantes, dignitaries. Common hairdressers, businessmen, poets, those with hard traveling. All of you. There is no lack of a listening ear in this room! Is there? I could have told her all of that.

And for a moment, for a fleeting moment, it passed

through my mind to do it. To tell her everything! Just...let it all rip, even bring her home, introduce her around! It was funny, I must say, the urge, the funniest sort of...bubble. I suppose I might have told her that I had sort of liked her too.

All I said was, "I have to go now."

To her, you understand, I will always be Roy Gannoy the Bubble Boy. The kid who talks to himself and has no friends. A product of their limited minds.

So! Fatima, in her coat—she had this horrendous, oh-dear-God-what-did-you-hit-with-the-truck, dead fur thing on! Yes. And this, this slightly crooked front tooth when she smiled. And pudgy hands. Very soft. Pudgy, quite soft hands, that shook yours firmly, not mean, just firm. And she said, "Well, I have to go back to the stand anyhow, we're selling long-distance cards, because it's a better deal than Verizon, you don't need a long-distance card do you?" And I told her I didn't.

She said, "Good-bye, Roy." And she walked away across the plaza. A waddling wave of green and yellow muumuu. Soft green. And soft yellow. Back to her long-distance cards.

So! That was my day! I absolutely had to tell you before I popped! Oh! What a weird, weird venture! *Never* touch your tongue to your nose when a camera is anywhere in the vicinity, that's all. You will never escape it. I am so glad to be home. With you. All comfy.

I still...I feel...the funniest kind of twinge still. Curiosity I think. Which is natural. Ironic, really, for me. In passing. I just...I wonder, in retrospect is all, what exactly the cost of long distance is these days.

(*He sits staring vaguely into space. Lights fade.*)

END OF PLAY

MARY JUST BROKE UP WITH THIS GUY

Garth Wingfield

Mary Just Broke Up with This Guy was originally produced as part of *Dating Games* (an evening of Garth Wingfield's one-act plays) by Winged Angel Productions at Theatre Row Studio Theatre in New York City on June 10, 2003. It was directed by Laura Josepher. The set design was by Sarah Lambert. The lighting design was by Susan Hamburger. Sierra Marcks was the stage manager. The cast was as follows:

MARY	Karin Sibrava
HER DATES	Michael Anderson

CHARACTERS
MARY: Twenties or thirties.
HER DATE: Roughly the same age as Mary.

TIME
Current day.

PLACE
A coffeehouse.

PRODUCTION NOTE: The man should use no costumes or props (hats, glasses, etc.) to distinguish between each of the various characters. They should all be realized as simply and theatrically as possible.

"De do do do, de da da da,
is all I want to say to you."
—The Police

A woman sitting alone on a chair in a coffeehouse. She glances around occasionally, fidgets, sips from a latte. On a table in front of her is a buzzer like you'd find on a game show.
A man enters, looks around, then approaches her.

DATE #1: Are you Mary?

MARY: I am. It's nice to meet you... Alex.

DATE #1: Likewise.

MARY: You want a coffee?

DATE #1: I grabbed the waitress when I came in. She's getting me a latte.

MARY: (*Smiles.*) Oh, that's what I'm having.

DATE #1: (*Smiles, sits.*) Oh.
(*A little awkward.*)
So. Here we are.

MARY: Uh-huh.

(*A little beat.*)

I've got to admit I'm a little nervous.

DATE #1: Actually, me too.

MARY: I just broke up with this guy I'd been seeing for a while. Tony. Was his name. But you don't want to hear about him. I'm kind of rusty at the whole dating thing is all.

DATE #1: Yeah, Sally mentioned something about that when she called. So you and this guy were together for what...?

MARY: Six years.

DATE #1: Wow.

MARY: Yeah.

DATE #1: That's a long time.

MARY: I know. But enough about him. He's ancient history. You know Sally from Cornell?

DATE #1: Yep, we met the first day of freshman year, if you can believe that. She's great, isn't she?

MARY: The best. Everyone at work adores her. And it's kind of funny, actually, because she'd mentioned you a while ago, months ago, I think. She announced at lunch that she had this great single friend named Alex she was just *dying* to fix someone up with. Of course, I was with Tony at the time so I didn't pay much attention. But now...here we are.

DATE #1: Life's weird like that, isn't it?

MARY: It is.

DATE #1: So how long ago did you and Tony break up?

MARY: Tuesday.

(*A little beat.*)

DATE #1: Sorry?

MARY: This past Tuesday. But it's okay, it's not like I'm on the rebound or anything.

(*He shoots her a strange look.*)

That must sound insane. I mean, yes, on some level, I probably am on the rebound, but... (*Trying to sound very sincere.*) It was over for a very long time before we actually ended it.

(*He starts to laugh.*)

What?

DATE #1: I appreciate your attempt to... you're adorable.

MARY: Well, okay... thanks.
   (*Then.*) Y'know, this is so much easier than I thought it would be.

DATE #1: What do you mean?

MARY: You just seem so... normal.

DATE #1: I guess that's a good thing.

MARY: Are you kidding? You hear these stories. And I *am* sort of picky.
   (*Faux serious.*) Please tell me you don't smoke.

DATE #1: I don't smoke.

MARY: Thank God. Because I could never date a smoker. I mean, I smoked. For years. Never gonna go there again.

DATE #1: Good for you.

MARY: (*Winces, expectantly.*) And I'm hoping...you like dogs...because I have one.

DATE #1: I haven't petted a dog in weeks. I can't wait to meet yours.

MARY: And I really like going to the theater. Mostly off-Broadway stuff.

DATE #1: Oh, then you should see the new John Patrick Shanley.

MARY: I saw it! I loved it!

DATE #1: Oh my God, so did I!

MARY: You're kidding?!

DATE #1: I'm not!

MARY: What a coincidence!

DATE #1: (*Blurts, almost over her last line.*) I'm gay!

(*Beat.*)

MARY: I'm sorry...?

DATE #1: (*All in one breath.*) Sally has no idea—it would kill her if she knew. She was completely in love with me in college, before she met George and he became an orthodontist and they fell into their loveless marriage in Hackensack. Promise me you won't say a word.

MARY: Uh-huh...

DATE #1: But you seem really fun. We should go to the theater!

(*A beat; then Mary reaches over and presses the buzzer: BUUUUUUZZZZZ! The man stands.*)

DATE #2: (*More assertive.*) You must be Mary!

MARY: I am. It's nice to meet you... Tom.

DATE #2: Yeah.

MARY: You want a coffee?

DATE #2: I just grabbed the waitress. She's whipping me up a chai.

MARY: A what?

DATE #2: A chai. It's like this infused tea thing.

MARY: (*Not as comfortable with this.*) Oh... I'm having a latte.

DATE #2: (*Equally unsettled, sits.*) Oh...

(*A little beat. She relaxes a bit.*)

MARY: (*Less nervous than last time.*) I've got to admit I'm a little nervous. I just broke up with this guy I'd been seeing for a while. Tony. Was his name. But you don't want to hear about him.

DATE #2: Yeah, you mentioned something about that when you answered my personal ad. So you and this guy were together for what...?

MARY: Six years.

DATE #2: Wow, that's significant.

MARY: I know.

DATE #2: And when did you break up?

MARY: Like...a while ago...

DATE #2: Gimme a ballpark.

MARY: Um...three months?

DATE #2: (*Fast.*) Damn, so you're totally on the rebound.

(*A little beat.*)

MARY: No, I'm not. At all. And maybe it was more like four or five months, it's hard to remember.

DATE #2: Wait, you can't remember when you broke up?

MARY: Not specifically.

DATE #2: And you were together six years?

MARY: That's right.

DATE #2: Something's not tracking here.

MARY: You asked me to give you a ballpark...

DATE #2: I remember *exactly* when I broke up with my last girlfriend, Tanya, and we were only together for like—

MARY: (*Overlapping, embarrassed.*) It was last Tuesday, okay? Two Tuesdays ago. And I'm really... gonna go kill myself or something now.

(*BUUUUUUZZZZZ!*)

DATE #3: (*Smoother.*) I'm guessing you're Mary.

MARY: That's me. It's nice to meet you... Darren?

DATE #3: Yep.

MARY: You want a coffee?

DATE #3: I just grabbed the waitress. She's whipping me up some pasta.

MARY: (*Not understanding his order.*) I'm having a latte.

DATE #3: That works for me.

(*A little beat. He sits.*)

MARY: (*Bored, slow, as if saying a script for the zillionth time; not nervous at all.*) I've got to admit I'm a little nervous. I just broke up with this guy I'd been seeing. Tony was his name, and *blah, blah, blah*...

DATE #3: (*Eyes her askance.*) You don't seem nervous.

MARY: (*Snaps out of it.*) What?

DATE #3: At all.

MARY: (*Covers.*) Well, I . . . hide it well, I guess.

DATE #3: Apparently. (*Then.*)
So yeah, you mentioned your ex on the phone. You and this guy were together for what, six years?

MARY: Right.

DATE #3: And when did you break up?

MARY: (*Without missing a beat.*) Months ago. I could give you a specific date, if you want. October eighteenth—there. I'm *so* not on the rebound.

DATE #3: I didn't say you were . . .

MARY: I've moved beyond him. Completely.

DATE #3: Great.
So . . . you wanna fuck?

(*BUUUUUUZZZZZ!*)

DATE #4: (*More intense.*) Your personal ad. What you wrote was really cool.

MARY: You thought so?

DATE #4: Yeah, especially the part about rats.

MARY: Aren't they somehow repellent and exhilarating at the same time?

DATE #4: Totally. (*Very fast and dark.*) This one time I had a rat in my apartment—and it was a big fucker too—and it tormented me, man, landing with a *boom* on the floor in the middle of the night and making me do somersaults of fear off my futon at two a.m. So what I did was, I cornered it and trapped it and called my friend Edgar, and I was all, "You've gotta come over here, man." And he was all, "But why?" And I was all, "Just get your ass *over* here." So he did, and I doused the little furball in gasoline, and we kicked back and drank beers and watched that motherfucker *BUUUUUUUUUUUUURN*!! (*Then, completely normal.*) So your ad said you liked sushi.

(*BUUUUUUUZZZZZ!*)

DATE #5: (*More earnest.*) I've seen your personal ad on Nerve-dot-com for *weeks* now, and I've always meant to respond.

MARY: It hasn't been there *that* many weeks…

DATE #5: You wrote some nice things.

MARY: Oh. Thanks.

DATE #5: Especially the part about God.

MARY: Um…I didn't write about God.

DATE #5: And I think that's a problem, don't you?

(*BUUUUUUUZZZZZ!*)

DATE #6: (*More bookish.*) So how many times have you gone to Date Bait?

MARY: That was my first time. I've never done *anything* like that before.

DATE #6: They all say that.

MARY: No, really, it's true.

DATE #6: (*Not believing her.*) Uh-huh . . .

MARY: Standing up in front of all those people. It was horrifying.

DATE #6: It gets easier.
And why did you write down my number?

MARY: I don't know . . . I thought you were cute. You've got great eyes. A very piercing green.

DATE #6: Yeah? I thought you were cute too.

MARY: (*Smile.*) Thanks.
(*Then.*) Also, you said you like dogs.

DATE #6: Right.

MARY: I love dogs.

DATE #6: Oh, I was just saying that.

MARY: What?

DATE #6: Gets 'em every time. Women love guys who love dogs. I mean, it's not like I *hate* dogs or anything. I'm just more of a cat person.
(*Then, afraid he's offended her.*) Do you have a dog?

MARY: (*Covers.*) No ...
   (*Then.*) Do you have a cat?

DATE #6: A couple. Well, seventeen. Mind if I smoke?
   (*As he pulls out a pack of cigarettes.*) I really hate when people
   give other people shit, for smoking in public. If I wanna
   smoke, I'll smoke. Besides, it's sexy!

MARY: I feel like I should be giving you the benefit of the doubt
   here, but ...

(*BUUUUUUZZZZZ!*)

DATE #7: (*More suave, off the cigarettes.*) Would this bother you?

MARY: Well, a little ...

DATE #7: Oh, then I don't have to. I'm trying to quit anyway. It's
   such a disgusting habit.

MARY: *Isn't* it?

(*Before he puts away the cigarettes he pulls a Ziploc bag from his jacket
pocket—it's filled with something we can't quite make out.*)

DATE #7: Quick question: How do you feel about that?

MARY: What's that?

DATE #7: My own hair. I've been collecting it since 1986. I have
   sixty-seven jars. Is *that* a disgusting habit too?

(*BUZZZZZ!*)

DATE #8: (*Picks up the cigarettes again.*) Oh my God, you hate I'm
   a smoker!

MARY: That's okay.

DATE #8: No, seriously...

MARY: It's really okay...

(*He puts away the cigarettes.*)

DATE #8: I smoke. It's so gross. Is that a deal breaker?

MARY: (*Weak smile.*) No...

DATE #8: Thank God. So tell me what you do.

MARY: I'm an editor. At *Time Out.*

DATE #8: Fun.

MARY: Yeah, but it pays nothing. And you?

DATE #8: (*Sexy leer.*) Certified public accountant.

MARY: (*To herself.*) *That's* a deal breaker.

(*BUUUUUUZZZZZ!*)

DATE #9: (*More upbeat.*) Wow, you're an editor at *Time Out!*

MARY: It's okay. It pays nothing, but I get to go to a lot of free
      screenings and stuff.

DATE #9: That's a nice perk.

MARY: And what do you do?

DATE #9: I'm a sex worker. (*Off her look.*) I'm kidding.

MARY: (*Hugely relieved.*) Oh, thank God!

DATE #9: Come on, look at me, like I could be a ho! (*Then, fast.*) Well, I *am* sort of in the industry. I'm in marketing. Sales and marketing. Of videos. Mostly girl-on-girl. Girl-on-guy. Girl-on-just-about-anything–*human*.
   (*Then, considers.*) Actually, *that's* not entirely true.

(*BUUUUUUUZZZZZ!*)

DATE #10: (*Overly bright.*) I'm a kindergarten teacher—you should see my kids!

(*BUUUUUUUZZZZZ!*)

DATE #11: I'm a massage therapist for birds and reptiles.

(*BUUUUUUUZZZZZ!*)

DATE #12: I'm a lawyer.

(*BUUUUUUUZZZZZ!*)

DATE #13: Lawyer.

(*BUUUUUUUZZZZZ!*)

DATE #14: Lawyer.

(*BUUUUUUUZZZZZ!*)

DATE #15: Entertainment lawyer.

MARY: Oh, that sounds interesting. What kind of stuff?

DATE #15: Making deals. Negotiating contracts. Alec Baldwin's a client.

MARY: (*Very fast, babbles.*) Oh my God, I met him at a party once! He seemed like *such a nice guy*! I went to this screening of a movie. He wasn't in the movie, but he was there. So at the party afterwards—at Chelsea Piers—he was about to eat this gloppy curry shrimp-ball thing, and I just *walked into him*! *Splat!* All over my blouse. And he made this huge deal, calling over the waiter and getting seltzer and apologizing profusely even though it wasn't his fault *at all*!

(*Silence.*)

(*More awkward.*) And then, um...he went back to Kim Basinger. And I went back to my friends. From work. And it...it didn't stain...in case you were wondering...

(*A beat.*)

(*Re: the buzzer.*) So, um...like, I don't know, if you wanna...?

(*He presses the buzzer: BUUUUUUUZZZZZ!*)

DATE #16: (*With a British accent.*) And I really just adore the Upper West Side.

MARY: (*A little unsettled.*) It's nice up there...

DATE #16: The stores, the park, the well-scrubbed young couples pushing babies in their prams.

MARY: I lived up there for a while when I first moved to the city...

DATE #16: And you should come back and visit us again, Mary. We'd welcome you with open arms!

MARY: Um, Gordon...

DATE #16: Yes?

MARY: It's...the thing is...all those times we chatted online, I had no idea you were British.

DATE #16: Really?

MARY: No, you never mentioned it.

DATE #16: Well, I was born in London but came stateside when I was a child.

MARY: Okay, see, I thought you said you were from New Jersey.

DATE #16: Well, we moved to New Jersey when I was twelve. Then I went to university here.

MARY: Really.
(*Smiles.*) It's such a funny thing. I had this, this...image of you after our chats. A very specific image. And I never once thought of you as having an accent.

DATE #16: (*Drops the accent.*) That's probably because I don't have one.

(*A little beat.*)

MARY: Sorry?

DATE #16: I was just putting you on.

MARY: You were...?

DATE #16: You got it.

MARY: Why?

DATE #16: Because I'm just really good at accents is the thing.

MARY: Uh-huh...

DATE #16: And you believed me, didn't you? I love that you believed me. God, you're so great!

(*BUUUUUUZZZZZ! Mary pulls out a pack of cigarettes. She's got more of an edge now.*)

MARY: Christ, am I dying for a cigarette! I would *kill* for a cigarette, actually—I *would*!

DATE #17: I really liked your Web site.

MARY: Uh-huh. So what's your story?

DATE #17: I'm a carpenter.

MARY: What's that supposed to mean?

DATE #17: That I build stuff. Like cabinets and benches. Recently, I've been working on this chair with hard-carved legs. It's pine, and it's...beautiful...it's a total labor of—

(*BUUUUUUZZZZZ!*)

MARY: Talk to me.

DATE #18: What can I say? I'm just a regular guy. I love holding hands, and spooning in bed at night, and waking up and having sex before breakfast...

MARY: Could you speak in anything *but* clichés?

(*BUUUUUUZZZZZ!*)

DATE #19: I'm very spiritual. Do you know Marianne
   Williamson?

(*BUUUUUUUZZZZZ!*)

DATE #20: I can bench-press my body weight.

(*BUUUUUUUZZZZZ!*)

DATE #21: I knit.

(*BUUUUUUUZZZZZ!*)

DATE #22: I...uh...

(*She reaches for the buzzer.*)

   Jesus, lady, I haven't even *said* anything yet!

MARY: You're right, I'm sorry. Go on.

(*She places her hand inches above the buzzer, her eyes trained on her
hand, ready to buzz away.*)

DATE #22: (*Hesitates, then.*) I...like children...?

MARY: Look, pal, I don't know what you mean by that, but I'm
   sure it's totally icky.

(*BUUUUUUUZZZZZ!*)

DATE #23: I thought your Web site was really great.

MARY: What about it?

DATE #23: I don't know, the way it was designed. All the photos.

MARY: (*Jumps on him.*) And I *look* like my photos. They're *recent* photos.

DATE #23: (*Recoils a bit.*) You look just like your photos...

MARY: I hate it when people e-mail you their photos, and then you meet them at Sbarro's, and it turns out the photos were from fucking 1991!

DATE #23: You've done a good job with the photos...

MARY: You got that right.
(*Re: the cigarettes.*) I'm gonna light one up. Let 'em stop me. Fuck 'em!

DATE #23: Um, would you mind not doing that? I'm kind of...asthmatic...and I didn't realize you smoked actually.

MARY: Fine.

(*She puts down the cigarettes.*)

DATE #23: I guess I should tell you...I've never done this before, met someone through the Internet.

MARY: They all say that.

DATE #23: No. But it's true...So tell me about your job.

MARY: I don't want to talk about that. That's boring.

DATE #23: Okay. So you like Italian food?

MARY: I used to. Too many carbs.

DATE #23: You like the Bronx Zoo, right? I *love* the Bronx Zoo. The gorilla exhibit made me cry.

MARY: Yeah, but have you been recently? The lines are just awful.

(*A beat. He stands.*)

DATE #23: Look, Mary. I should go.

MARY: Just like that?

DATE #23: I think so.

MARY: This is perfect—I don't even know your name. Well, one less thing to remember.

DATE #23: It's just…you're not at all what I was expecting from your Web site. Look, maybe I'm new to this, but you seemed like this really funny, madcap sort of…I mean, those photos of you on the Cyclone laughing your head off were great. And the picture of you with your dog. And then I meet you in person and you're…
    Anyway, it was nice sharing half a latte with you.

(*He starts to go.*)

MARY: Wait…just…
    What's your name?

DATE #23: Charlie. My name is Charlie.

MARY: Look, Charlie…it's been a rough year. A really rough year. Why don't you stay and at least finish your latte?

DATE #23: I'm sorry, I don't think so.

(*A little beat.*)

MARY: Okay, I respect that. Well. Have a nice evening, Charlie.

(*He starts to go, but stops.*)

DATE #23: Look...I have no business being here in the first place. The thing is, I just broke up with this girl.

MARY: Really. How long ago?

DATE #23: I don't know, like...three months ago.
(*Admits.*) One month ago.
(*Admits.*) Tuesday.

MARY: (*Smiles a little.*) I think it's kinda perfect that you're here.

DATE #23: But I don't even know what I want.

MARY: You'll figure that out.

DATE #23: I'm probably totally on the rebound.

MARY: Or maybe not.

DATE #23: I brought pictures of my dog.

MARY: You did?

(*He moves to her, pulls the photos from his jacket pocket, and sits next to her.*)

DATE #23: Her name's Venus. She's a cocker-Lab mix.

MARY: Oh my God, mutts are the best!

DATE #23: Aren't they?
(*Then, as they look at the photos.*) You should see how she

sleeps. On her back with all four legs straight up in the air. It's completely ridiculous. Wait, I have a picture of it. (*He finds it.*) Here.

(*Mary looks at the picture, and then starts to laugh. Mary is laughing her head off . . . as the lights slowly fade to black.*)

END OF PLAY

MEN IN HEAT

Dana Yeaton

Men in Heat premiered at Emerson Stage, where Steven Yakutis
directed the following cast:

Murray	Alexander Albregts
Mike	Dennis Starr
Steve	Hans K. Hauge

CHARACTERS
murray: thirty-nine.
mike: thirty-two.
steve: Late twenties.

SCENE
The sauna of a health club.

At rise: A sizzling sound. Dim light comes up on MURRAY, *who sits, hunched forward, staring at the electric heater. He squirts his water bottle on the heater—sizzle, steam. The door opens and* MIKE *pops his head in.*

MIKE: You comin' out, or what?

(MURRAY *shakes his head.*)

Look it's too long man, you're gonna melt.

(MURRAY *sprays the heater.*)

How can you breathe in here?

(MIKE *flips on the overhead light, steps in. He is fully dressed, hair wet from the shower.*)

MURRAY: I like it dark.

MIKE: Look, Murray, it's a game.

MURRAY: I know it's a game.

MIKE: You've got tendinitis for Christ's sake.

MURRAY: You beat me before the tendinitis. I'm used to it.

MIKE: You won the last game.

MURRAY: You threw the last game.

MIKE: I did not throw—that would be totally opposite, everything.

MURRAY: You always throw the last game.

MIKE: I play to win, Murray, you know that. I'm a competitor.

MURRAY: And I'm not.

MIKE: What is wrong with you?

MURRAY: I'm thirty-nine years old, Mike. Already I've got no wrist, what's next?

MIKE: I'm thirty-two, already I'm losing night vision, so what?

MURRAY: Sit down.

(MIKE *remains standing.*)

I want to have a kid, Mike.

MIKE: A kid.

MURRAY: You know how they're doing these artificial insemina-tions now, with like test-tube babies?

MIKE: Yeah.

MURRAY: And they don't even need real mothers anymore, it's all done in the lab.

MIKE: You want a kid.

MURRAY: Sit down.

MIKE: You want a kid.

MURRAY: Yes. And I want it to be ours. I'd keep it and everything, you wouldn't have to do anything. But it would be ours. We'd be the parents.

(MIKE *sits.*)

MIKE: . . . What?

MURRAY: We wouldn't have to have sex, Mike. Jesus. It would be done for us, by doctors. Artificially.

MIKE: Have you told anyone this?

MURRAY: Of course not . . . You probably want to think about it.

MIKE: No.

MURRAY: I'm just saying, I've had a long time to think about this.

MIKE: Well stop thinking about it. Jesus.

MURRAY: Mike, just because I want to have your baby—

MIKE: Don't say that!

MURRAY: It doesn't mean that we're attracted—

MIKE: Shut up!

(MIKE *is standing over* MURRAY, *threatening to punch him.*)

Just . . . no more.

(MIKE *grabs the bottle, takes a drink.*)

MURRAY: So the answer's no.

MIKE: The answer is shut up.

MURRAY: There's nobody listening, Mike.

MIKE: *I'm* listening, okay? I don't want to hear this. I'm in here with some... This is not what I want to be talking about.

MURRAY: I figured you'd freak.

MIKE: I'm not freaking, okay.

MURRAY: You threatened to hit me, Mike.

MIKE: When have I ever hit you? Huh?

(MIKE *squirts* MURRAY *with water.* MURRAY *doesn't react.*)

Asshole.

(*Squirts* MURRAY *again. No reaction.*)

Hey...

(MIKE *offers his hand.* MURRAY *shakes it.*)

... Water?

MURRAY: Nah.

(MIKE *drinks.*)

MIKE: ... What about Steve?

MURRAY: Huh?

MIKE: I mean he's the big triathlete and everything, big champion, in the paper. Why'n't ya ask him?

MURRAY: We're not supposed to talk about this.

MIKE: No I'm askin'.

MURRAY: Steve shaves his body.

MIKE: For resistance! The guy's built like a brick, Murray, plus he can move. He's like point nothing percent body fat.

MURRAY: I'm not shopping, Mike. It's not just something I want to do with anybody. Forget about it, okay?

MIKE: There's nobody else...?

MURRAY: No.

MIKE: I'm...thanks.

MURRAY: It's not a compliment.

MIKE: It's not a compliment you want to bring a child into the world like me? The combination of you and me? That's a put-down?

MURRAY: I didn't *mean* it as a compliment, okay. It's just, this idea of a kid with everything, he's got my math and science, my thing with computers, right? But he's got your power-tool skills, he's tough. Like you said, he's a competitor.

MIKE: I'm okay with math.

MURRAY: That's not the point, the point is, no woman genes.

MIKE: Shaving your body doesn't make you a woman.

MURRAY: He would be a guy, through and through.

MIKE: No woman stuff.

MURRAY: No weaknesses.

MIKE: And this is possible?

MURRAY: Biotechnology, Mike.

MIKE: Geez...

(*Takes a drink.*)

What if it's a girl?

MURRAY: Huh?

MIKE: What if this baby, by some mathematical twist of fate, turns out to be female?

MURRAY: That couldn't happen. Two guys could not make a girl..

MIKE: Like two wrongs.

MURRAY: Exactly.

MIKE: ...So you figured I'd freak, huh?

MURRAY: Mike...

MIKE: No I'm just curious, you think, what, I'm uncool about stuff?

MURRAY: It's just some of your opinions, like capital punishment and, I don't know, immigration.

MIKE: What's that got to do with—

MURRAY: We're not discussing—

MIKE: No, what has this got to do with capital punishment, Murray? We're talking about a human being here.

MURRAY: Forget it.

MIKE: You think I'm just some jock, I don't think about what *I'm* gonna leave on this earth, what's *my* contribution? I have a philosophy too, Murray; you're not the only one who can sit around with his head up his ass thinking.

MURRAY: Shouldn't have brought it up.

MIKE: "You get the kid you deserve, man," that's what I say. You want a tough kid—smart, shrewd, whatever—you gotta be tougher, smarter, you gotta challenge that little son of a bitch every day so that one night when he says he's goin' out and you tell him no—he reaches back and BAM! An hour later you wake up, he is *gone*.

MURRAY: I'm not sure I—

MIKE: It's about *desire*, Murray, the instillation of desire. Got nothing to do with genes. I mean sure, I can sit around complaining about my eyes or maybe, *maybe* what I need to do is one night I get behind the wheel, go for a little ride around the neighborhood *whether I can see or not*. Otherwise,

I walk out of a restaurant some night, I get blown away by some guy with superior night vision, whose fault is that? Now intelligence, I don't know maybe that's different, IQ and stuff, maybe that's something you just get a certain amount of at birth and you're stuck, but I tell you one thing, I don't care how big, how strong, how fast: my kid is going to make his living with this.

(*He taps his temple.*)

MURRAY: I didn't know you wanted kids, Mike.

MIKE: Course I want kids, that's the human function. Reproduce yourself. Now you look at Steve.

MURRAY: He has no kids.

MIKE: No I'm saying look at Steve, physically, he's got it all. And that wasn't just some gift, the guy works out like four times a day, right? But what do you think he does the *rest* of the day?

MURRAY: Eats?

MIKE: Murray.

MURRAY: Sleeps?

MIKE: Makes money. He runs a profitable health club business by using his head. He's a nonquitter when he runs, he's a nonquitter when he's, whatever, making money. *That* is Steve... Fact, if you're really serious about this thing...

MURRAY: No.

MIKE: You should ask. He's perfect.

MURRAY: No.

MIKE: Steve has got DNA that would make any man proud. You should walk out there right now, what've you got to lose?

MURRAY: (*Overlapping.*) I'm not going to do that.

MIKE: Because you're not serious.

MURRAY: No.

MIKE: Because it's too embarrassing, you're worried about—

MURRAY: That's not it.

MIKE: What people will say.

MURRAY: No!

MIKE: Why not then?!

MURRAY: He said no.

MIKE: . . . You already . . .

MURRAY: Yeah . . . he said no.

MIKE: Who else?

MURRAY: Nobody.

MIKE: Come on, who else besides Steve turned ya down?

MURRAY: Nobody!

MIKE: You must have asked Tom—he presses 280.

MURRAY: Look, I'm sorry, it's just that—

MIKE: Hey, I understand: Steve is an obvious first choice.

MURRAY: No, it's just that—

MIKE: You know what does bother me though, and this is something I've noticed about you, is the way you just assume that you're the one with all the human instincts.

MURRAY: Can we just drop—

MIKE: Like I wouldn't know how to hold a kid or something. I'd break it, I'd lose it or something. A kid needs more than a shoulder to cry on, Murray, he needs more than a little mouse pad and computer lessons to know how to *compete* in that global fucking slime pit out there. Truth is, I think *I'm* the one who should raise this kid and I will tell you why.

(MURRAY *stands to go.*)

No wait a minute.

MURRAY: Mike, I wouldn't have a kid with you if you were the last man on earth.

(MURRAY *turns off the overhead light, exits.*)

MIKE: (*Fumbling after him.*) You—hey, come back here. HEY! You fucking loser! I wouldn't have your kid if you fucking—

(MIKE *burns his hand on the heater.*)

Ow, shit shit shit shit shit SHIT!...Limp-wristed son of a...FUCK-ING LOSER!

(*Door opens, figure enters, flips the light on.*)

... Steve.

STEVE: (*Fresh from the pool, wearing a racing suit.*) Hey, Mike. You want the light off?

MIKE: (*Hiding his burned hand.*) No, that's okay, I'm just, I'm done.

(STEVE *sidles past.* MIKE *watches from behind as* STEVE *spreads out his towel and prepares to sit.* MIKE *gets an idea.*)

Hey, Steve...

STEVE: Yeah?

MIKE: You ever have any trouble at night? You know, seeing?

END OF PLAY

MERE VESSELS

Mikhail Horowitz

Mere Vessels was first performed as a staged reading on November 13, 2004, at Actors & Writers, the Odd Fellows Theatre, Olivebridge, New York, as part of the Actors & Writers Fall Shorts Festival 2004. The cast was as follows:

MANNY	David Smilow
SHORTY	Brian MacReady
ZEKE	John Seidman
ZEB	Sarah Chodoff

The play received its first Equity production on May 8, 2005, as part of the Stageworks/Hudson Play-by-Play Festival in Hudson, New York. Directed by Deena Pewtherer, the cast included:

MANNY	Terry Rabine
SHORTY	Justin Gibbs
ZEKE	Eileen Schuyler
ZEB	Sandra Blaney

CHARACTERS
ZEKE: A Christian ventriloquist.
ZEB: Zeke's dummy.
MANNY: A Jewish ventriloquist.
SHORTY: Manny's dummy.

NOTE TO THE ACTORS
ZEKE speaks in a bright, neighborly, confident voice; ZEB has a goofy, aw-shucks-folks voice; MANNY has a jaded, quintessentially New

York flavor to his voice; SHORTY is a quick, sarcastic little smart aleck.

Both ZEKE and MANNY should manipulate the actors playing ZEB and SHORTY in ways appropriate to the action when the dummies are speaking.

The characters are male, but ZEB may be played by a female actor and called ZEBINA.

Backstage, such as it is, at a rural community center. ZEKE *is sitting with* ZEB *on his knee as* MANNY *enters, carrying* SHORTY, *whom he places on his knee.*

ZEKE: (*Beaming.*) Greetings, brother!

MANNY: Uh, yeah. Hi. How ya doin'.

ZEKE: (*After an expectant pause.*) Here for the benefit?

MANNY: Well, I'm not here for the climate or the cuisine.

SHORTY: Hey, there's always the wooden conversation!

ZEKE: (*To* SHORTY, *chuckling good-naturedly.*) And greetings to *you*, little brother! Zeke's the name, short for Ezekiel. And this here's Zeb...

ZEB: ...awwwww, short for Zebedee.

ZEKE: And who, pray tell, do we have the pleasure of addressing?

MANNY: I'm Manny, short for cash, and this is Shorty, short for...

239

SHORTY: (*Using a W. C. Fields voice for the first two words.*) ...longitudinally attenuated. But never upstaged—not by *this* chip-off-the-old-lip-mover, anyway.

ZEKE: Well, Zeb and I think it's right neighborly of y'all to pitch in for this benefit.

ZEB: Eee-yup. We shore do appreci—

SHORTY: (*Interrupting.*) Zip it, Zeb. (*To* MANNY.) Hey, boss, we've been here two minutes and that's the second time I've heard the "B" word. What's the deal? We got a religious prohibition against getting paid?

MANNY: (*To* ZEKE.) You'll have to excuse my curmudgeon homunculus over here. He has a woodpecker in his pants and it keeps him up at night.

SHORTY: Hey, that's *my* material!

MANNY: (*Ignoring him.*) So, uhhh, Zeke, right? Listen, Zeke: Shorty and I have had a pretty hectic touring schedule this month and we're pretty much flying blind here... Y'see, we let our agent do the booking and she doesn't always hip us to which gigs are which or to the specific requirements of each venue. We just show up on time, wherever the tour itinerary happens to stipulate. So, according to you...

ZEKE: (*Chuckling.*) And Zeb—don't forget Zeb!

MANNY: Yeah, Zeb. So, uhh, you said this gig is a benefit?

ZEKE: For the Suffer the Little Children Bible School. *You* know why it's called that, don't ya, Zeb?

ZEB: Ahh shore do, Zeke, because Jee-sus said, "Suffer the little children to come unto me, and forbid them not; for of such is the kingdom of God."

(Pause, as both MANNY *and* SHORTY *look on speechlessly, with dropped jaws.)*

Awww, Mark, 10:14.

SHORTY: Earth to Manny! Earth to Manny! A little bird, possibly the woodpecker in my pants, just told me it's time for a new agent!

MANNY: *(To* ZEKE.*)* So, this is a fund-raiser? For a fundamentalist school?

ZEKE: *(Beaming.)* Bringing the Full Gospel to the little angels of Waxahachie County. See, Zeb and I have been doing the Lord's work on the Christian vent circuit for nine years now, ever since Zeb got saved. Why don't you testify to these good folks about the healing power of belief in Jesus, Zeb?

SHORTY: *(To* MANNY.*)* Listen, boss, the *least* you can do is put me back in my case.

ZEB: Awwww, yuh see, I wuz like to be dyin' of termites, and it was Brother Howell up to Willimotchee Falls who put the holy spirit on me and cast 'em out, ah-huh, ah-huh! And awwww, ever since that happy day, I've been filled with the Lord's Word, awwwwww, as it comes through Brother Zeke.

ZEKE: A-men!

MANNY: *(Aside.)* Christ on a crepe!

SHORTY: *(Aside.)* Halle-fuckin'-lujah.

ZEKE: That's why we're so happy to meet y'all: why up until today Zeb and I never *did* hear tell of any vents from New York who spread the Good News.

ZEB: Aw-yup, for it is written, "Not in bread alone doth man live, but in every word that proceedeth from the mouth of God, aww, through Brother Zeke." Awwww, Matthew, 4:4.

SHORTY: (*To* MANNY.) Well, Brother Onan, are you gonna tell him or am I?

MANNY: Look, Zeke. I don't know how we're billed on this program, but someone has been misinformed. With all due respect, I am *not* a Christian ventriloquist, and Shorty is *not* a Christian dummy.

SHORTY: I'm not a dummy, period—I'm a mahogany American.

MANNY: And I'm Jewish. OK, barely so, I grant you, because I'm a Reconstructionist. And Shorty, truth be told, is an atheist.

(*At the mention of the "A" word,* ZEB *audibly gasps and drops his jaw.*)

So obviously, this is all a mistake on the part of our agent. To put it as kindly and gently as possible, the act that Shorty and I do would be eminently unsuitable for this crowd.

ZEB: Aww ... aww ... what did you say that Shorty was?

ZEKE: Yes, we'd like to hear it from his own lips.

MANNY: Very well. Shorty?

SHORTY: A-hcm. I, Shorty McGorty, am an atheist. An unbeliever.

A person completely unswayed by any argument for the reality of a Creator. There is no God, and neither Jesus, Moses, Mohammed, or Joseph Smith is his prophet—*especially* Joseph Smith. Moreover, I am a polynotheist, in that I entertain a profound lack of belief in *many* gods—Allah, Brahma, Rama, Lama, Dingdong, Jehovah, Yahweh, Hisweh, Herweh—none of them exist, never have, never will, and the show would go on with a lot less grief if we gave 'em all the hook!

ZEB: (*Beginning to sneeze.*) Heh . . . hehhh . . . HEHHHH . . .

ZEKE: Lookee here. Y'all got Zeb so rattled, he's like to sneeze.

ZEB: HEHHHHHH-*CHOOOO!*

SHORTY: Great. Not only is God dead, but apparently, whatever he died of was contagious.

ZEB: (*Becoming irate.*) Awwww, you *shush up*, you . . . you . . . do you know what the Lord does to those who don't believe in him?

SHORTY: No, but it can't be any worse than having to follow a troop of flag-waving poodles at a matinee in Branson, Missouri.

ZEB: Awwww, it's a *lot* worse than that, ahhh-yup! "And whosoever was not found written in the book of life was cast into the pool of fire." Awwww, Revelation, 20:15.

MANNY: (*To* ZEKE.) Hey, Zeke, let's cut the crap, OK? Let's leave the little guys out of this. If you have something to say to me and, by extension, to Shorty—whose opinions, I might add, are not necessarily those of his manipulator—I would appreciate it if you said it directly to my face, and not through the medium of your mannikin.

ZEKE: (*Calm, measured.*) Well, sir, I'll say this. Although you, as a poor, lost sinner who has not yet opened his heart to Jesus, might think otherwise, the truth is that little Zeb here is no more my "medium" than I am his "manipulator." No, Zeb and I are both mere vessels for the Living Word. Verily, Lord Prince Jesus is the greatest and truest ventriloquist of us all, and I am unto Him as Zeb is unto me, and it is *His* voice, not mine, that animates us both.

ZEB: Awww, yuh took the words right out of my mouth.

MANNY: OK. Let's see if I've got this right. Essentially, what you're telling me is that you, Zeke, have a direct line to God. And that whenever... Woody Two-shoes over there opens his mouth it is not you, Zeke, who speaks, but God Himself—the Lord of Creation, the Master of the Universe, who has given to us his beloved son, Pinocchio.

ZEKE: Take good care, brother. God shall not be mocked.

SHORTY: Hey, it's a tough job, but somebody has to do it.

MANNY: Zeke, ol' buddy, it's been, well, revelatory. But considering that we are but a moment's sunlight, fading in the grass—Jesse Colin Young, 4:14—it's time to bid you both a fond fondue. Let's go, Shorty. We got a flaming chariot to catch.

SHORTY: *Thank*, if you'll pardon the expression, *God*. Hey, Zeb, there's a library leaving at five o'clock—be under it.

ZEB: (*Growing very agitated.*) Awwww, awwww...

(*He suddenly begins to shake and speak gibberish.*)

HAGGAMAGGACHAGGANOOKACHAGGA-
NOOKAMAGGAWALLYMAGGAWALLYWALLY (*etc.*).

(MANNY *and* SHORTY, *who have been exiting, stop and turn.* ZEB *continues to speak gibberish for the duration of the following exchange, fading out briefly when* ZEKE *speaks and then resuming his glossolalia, shaking violently the whole time.*)

MANNY: (*After a pause.*) Uh, what's with Zeb?

ZEKE: Brother Zebedee, my friends, has been possessed by the Holy Spirit. He is speaking in tongues.

SHORTY: (*Looks at his watch.*) Gee, I don't know what's keeping that retarded kid with the banjo.

ZEB: (*Raising his voice and shouting out the last words.*) GOLATCHAMATCHAWATCHA!

(*He collapses.*)

SHORTY: Holy shit.

MANNY: Is, uhh, is he all right?

ZEKE: He is *more* than all right. He has been blessed.

ZEB: (*Who from this point on speaks normally.*) O glory, glory, glory be to Jesus! He has cured me of my speech impediment! He has performed this miracle to show the way for the godless brother among us! Let us pray for Brother Shorty, that he may renounce the crown of Satan!

ZEKE: He has called you, Brother Shorty! Would you stop your ears and harden your heart to the pleas of Jesus?

MANNY: His ears are *already* stopped, you moron—they're *wood*.

SHORTY: Hang on a sec, boss. I've got to admit that I'm strangely... *moved* by what I've just seen. I mean, how did Zeb suddenly lose his goofy speech pattern?

MANNY: Shorty, don't *do* this to me! You know as well as I do that Zeb never *had* any speech patterns, goofy or otherwise, that weren't Zeke's! It's just a stupid trick! I can do the *same thing*, OK? I can make you sound just as brain-dead as Zeb:

SHORTY: (*Assuming* ZEB's *old voice.*) Awwww, shoot, folks, I reckon I'm just a little ol' stoopid country bumpkin who's just bumpkining along with sawdust in mah cerebellum... oops, didn't mean to use a word of more than three syllables, awww, ah-yup, ah-yup...

(*He suddenly reverts, angrily, to his old voice.*)

Hey, knock it off, boss! I'm serious, here! I'm feeling really... weird... look, I'm getting goose bumps!

MANNY: Those are knots in the wood and you *know* it, Shorty!

ZEKE: Cast him out, Brother Shorty! Renounce the servant of Satan who keeps the praise of Jesus from thy lips!

ZEB: Come, Brother Zeke! Let us do a laying on of hands!

(ZEKE *and* ZEB *each place a hand upon Shorty.*)

MANNY: GET YOUR HANDS OFF MY DUMMY, YOU IDIOTS!

(SHORTY *begins to shake.*)

ZEKE AND ZEB: (*Chanting simultaneously.*) OUT DEMONS OUT! OUT DEMONS OUT! OUT DEMONS OUT! OUT DEMONS OUT!

(SHORTY *suddenly stops shaking and gasps as if he's coming up for air. A goofy smile begins to spread across his face.*)

MANNY: (*Flabbergasted.*) How in the hell did you do *that*? How did you both speak at once?

ZEKE: O ye of little faith. The Lord moves His lips in mysterious ways His wonders to perform.

MANNY: (*Hissing, to* SHORTY.) Goddamn it, Shorty, it's a trick!

SHORTY: (*In* ZEB's *old voice.*) Awwww, nopey-nope, Manny. It's a miracle!

ZEKE, ZEB, AND SHORTY: PRAISE JEE-SUS!

ZEKE: Showtime, brothers! Let's all mosey out there and share this miracle with the kids.

SHORTY: (*Indicating* MANNY *with his thumb.*) Awww, not tuh mention the Yids, ah-huh, ah-huh!

(*As* MANNY *sits dumbfounded,* ZEKE, ZEB, *and* SHORTY *begin to exit, in that order.*)

ZEKE, ZEB, AND SHORTY: (*Singing.*) BRING-ING IN THE SHEAVES, BRING-ING IN THE SHEAVES, WE WILL COME RE-JOI-CING BRING-ING IN THE SHEAVES!
       BRING-ING IN THE SHEAVES, BRING-ING IN THE SHEAVES, WE WILL COME RE-JOI-CING...

(*At this point all three are offstage, but* SHORTY *pops his head back into view to sing the last line solo.*)

SHORTY: (*In his old smart-alecky voice.*) SCHLEPPING IN THE SHEAVES!

(*He leeringly winks to the audience while making a circle with his thumb and index finger, and pops his head back offstage.*)

END OF PLAY

MURDERERS

"MATCH WITS WITH MINKA LUPINO"

Jeffrey Hatcher

Murderers consists of three monologues and was designed to be performed on a bare stage. "Match Wits with Minka Lupino" is the play's third piece.

Murderers was commissioned by and premiered at Illusion Theater (Michael H. Robins and Bonnie Morris, producing directors) in Minneapolis, Minnesota, in February 2005. It was directed by Sarah Gioia; the set design was by Dean Holzman; and the stage manager was Matthew Dawson. The cast was as follows:

GERALD	Bob Davis
LUCY	Barbara June Patterson
MINKA	Phyllis Wright

Murderers was subsequently produced by Philadelphia Theatre Company (Sara Garonzik, producing artistic director) in Philadelphia, Pennsylvania, opening on October 11, 2006. It was directed by Michael Bush; the set design was by Jim Noone; the lighting design was by Traci Klainer; the costume design was by Karen Ann Ledger; and the sound design and original music were by Ryan Rumery. The cast was as follows:

GERALD	Brent Landon
LUCY	Marylouise Burke
MINKA	Kristine Nielsen

For Elizabeth Holmberg Stevens
"Toots"

MINKA: I am a murderer. Many times over. I do not like the term "serial killer," which, to my mind, suggests an emphasis on the numerical followed by too much time spent on the interstate highway system. My murders all took place in one locality.

Now, I should say right here at the beginning, I am not ashamed of having committed murder. You see, I believe in what is right. In justice. And every murder I ever planned— save one—was planned in that spirit of rightness, fairness and justice, the kind of murder planning that I like to think our forefathers would have approved of.

Besides, I was not always a murderer. Murderers are not born that way. The works of Jay G. Garland have taught me that. Jay G. Garland is my favorite author, the greatest mystery writer of all time, whose detective, gay Broadway impresario Jolly St. Holly, is always stumbling onto murders along the Great White Way. Jay G. Garland is the author of *Murder with the Lunts*, *Murder with Carol Channing*, and his magnum opus, *Murder with the Cast of* A Chorus Line *at Sardi's After the Show*.

He taught me that murderers have their reasons— usually splashy and interesting reasons with a lot of diabolical planning that is nonetheless foiled when Jolly sees through their one big mistake.

Not that Jay G. Garland is limited to his Broadway milieu. Under his pseudonym, "Maevis Marvella Pearl," he writes about Sister Angelicadore, the blind lesbian novice who solves convent crimes in sixteenth-century Venice; as well as his hard-core police procedurals written under the apt *nom de plume* "Peter Dick Johnson."

I've been reading this man since I was in high school. And the day he came down to live at the Riddle Key Luxury Senior Retirement Living Center and Golf Course...well, you can imagine.

I wanted to tell him how exciting it was he was taking one of the new villas, how I was such a fan, how whenever there was a lull in the members' office and Mr. Finn was out showing a prospective couple around, I'd sneak out a copy of *Pippin Must Die* or *Nine Novenas to Death* or *Cock My Gun Slowly*.

All in paperback of course. I can't afford the hardback copies. But I never said a word to him. For someone of his stature, Mr. Finn handled all of the details himself. I'd never even heard Mr. Garland's voice over the phone.

At least that's the way it was before. Before I ever thought I'd meet him. Before I became...a murderer.

It started with Mrs. Moses. Her name wasn't Mrs. Moses, of course. I was the only one who called her Mrs. Moses, and just to myself.

Her real name was Mrs. Westland from Sherrodsville, Pennsylvania. And she became Mrs. Moses to me because when I met her, she talked on and on about how her son and his wife had adopted a little Korean baby, and for the longest time she'd never been allowed to visit. Never seen her own grandson, just seen his pictures.

Mrs. Westland would say, "And I just felt like Moses in the Promised Land, yes, I did, I thought I'd never see that little baby, I was just like Moses in the Promised Land, just like him, just like Moses looking down on the land he was promised but he knew he'd never see, just like Moses!"

The reason she hadn't seen the baby was because she was in a war with her son and his wife. They wanted her to move down to Florida, where they could quote look after her, unquote, which is code for, "We don't want to have to fly up to that hick town in Pennsylvania anymore to make sure you aren't dead or eating cat food."

Mrs. Moses didn't want to move to Florida, of course, she liked it in that hick town, that's where her friends were, that's where she'd met her husband, Phil, that's where Phil was buried. And Phil had left her well-off, so she could afford help if she needed it, thank you very much, and was not interested in becoming part of any old folks' home.

Well, Mrs. Moses' only son, Young Phil, and his wife, Suzy, didn't see it that way. And so, when they adopted the baby, known as Young-Young Phil, they said, "You can't come down to see him, unless you agree to at least LOOK at Riddle Key."

So there was a standoff. And it lasted eight months, which is a long time for an eighty-four-year-old woman and this is your only grandchild.

"Why it's like Moses in the…"

So she gave in. Just a visit. After all, she'd get to see that grandchild of hers. She'd even ordered him a Korean War G.I. Joe doll, not quite understanding that it didn't mean the doll was Korean.

When Mrs. Moses came through the gates, she didn't know what hit her. The idea was they'd bring her in to "take a look" at the facilities—the restaurants, the shops, the pharmacy, the clinic, the basement storage rooms with hurricane protection—then, at the end of the visit, they'd take her up to a sample villa, just for a peek, go inside… and there would be her whole life from back home, hijacked, shipped by Mayflower, and plopped down where it was more convenient for THEM.

I was there when they showed her the villa—how nicely her breakfront fit the dining room, how well the upright piano looked near the window…

Mrs. Moses wanted to bolt right back to Sherrodsville, of course, but it was too late. Why, Young Phil had already done all that work, the expense of moving things, closing up

the house, having her stocks and bank accounts reassigned
to his power of attorney. And him not the success in wholesale scuba gear that his father had been in coal.

She moved in that night. She'd put up her pictures of
Young-Young on the living room wall, make some new
friends, make the best of it.

She was dead three months later.

Young Phil and his wife were on vacation in Bermuda
with Young Phil's new investment pals when I called them
with the news.

Phil said: "Geez, we're only two days into our vacation,
would you mind putting Mom on ice for a week till we get
back? I mean, she'll keep, right?"

I checked Mrs. Moses' living will, her special requests,
what she wanted to be buried with—wedding ring, yes,
engagement ring, no—she wanted to be buried next to
her husband back in Sherrodsville, so when Young Phil and
Suzy came into the office—Young-Young was with the new
nanny—I assumed it was to arrange transport up north.

"Cremation," Young Phil said. "You do that here on the
grounds, right?"

"... Yes ..."

"Well," he said, "let's do that!"

"But the request here says..."

Mr. Finn cleared his throat.

"I believe the crematorium is available at five, Ms.
Lupino. Friday is never very busy."

I tried not to show my reaction. "As for the service," I
said—

"No service," said Suzy. "She didn't have any friends
here anyway."

I nodded. Very professional. "Will you be coming by to
pick up the cremains?"

"No," said Young Phil. "Just..." And he made a gesture—(*does flip-wrist gesture*)—that either meant "whisk it
away" or "I'm really effeminate."

Mr. Finn stepped in. "Ms. Lupino will take you to the

storage room where your mother's things have been preserved. Anything of value we can ship."

I take them across the lot to the storage rooms, a
big cement block set three stories into the mud. It's
brand-new—not fully open yet—the cooling and ventila-
tion system isn't even working.

We reach Mrs. Moses' room. I unlock the door. Suzy
turns to me.

"You may go, Miss Lupino."

I nod, servile, eyes downcast.

I leave the room, filled with old furniture and pictures
of what I'm sure Mrs. Moses would have called her "loved
ones."

But I do not go away. I stand just outside the door. And
listen.

"Well, she went faster than I thought," says the bereaved
daughter-in-law.

"Not fast enough," replies the loving son. "Two years
ago, the portfolio would have been worth a quarter more
and I coulda bought six more waterfront lots."

"Can we use any of this crap?" asks his blushing bride.

"Nah. Cheap veneer and Naugahyde."

Suzy is getting all soft: "Shouldn't we save some of these
things for Young-Young?"

"What're we gonna give him, this needlepoint sign that
says 'With God All Things Are Possible?' Bad enough he's
got that kimchee G.I. Joe thing."

I move closer to the door. The edges have rubber seals.

I take a moment and recall all the Mrs. Moseses I've
seen, hustled into a beige wall-to-wall coffin at twelve hundred a month. All the sons and daughters who've asked Mr.
Finn, "How long, on average, do they last once they're in
here?" The grandkids who have to be bribed to visit, give
Grandma a kiss, pretend not to look bored and sullen while
they watch their parents do to their grandparents what
they'll do to their parents someday.

Inside, I hear Young Phil:

"Hey, look, my Cub Scouts cap——"

The door makes no sound, just a whisper of a pneumatic whoosh.

I don't hear the pounding until I'm well up the steel stairs to the floor above.

When I meet Mr. Finn at the crematorium, I tell him the family wanted some time with the mementos of their loss.

"No skin off my honker," he says, wittily. "See you Monday."

Monday is, of course, not much fun. One of the Cuban fellas who's supposed to clear out the room finds the bodies. He says the couple was found hugging a needlepoint sign that read "With God All Things Are Possible." Even though it's impossible to open the door.

The bodies are buried in Sherrodsville, Pennsylvania, which I think is a nifty touch. The money will eventually snake its way to Young-Young, who is adopted again, this time by a Korean couple. They name him Kevin.

Did I feel guilty? No.

Did I feel good? No. But I felt just.

I didn't kill again for almost a year.

Mr. James was a favorite of mine. When he and his wife had moved into an efficiency apartment—no fancy villas or condos for him—he'd made a point of dropping by the members' office a couple times a day.

One day he dropped in and asked to see some information on deep-sea fishing and as I handed him the brochures he bit my arm. And left his teeth there.

"What are you doing?!"

"You've heard of Jaws? I'm Jaws."

I kept his teeth for the rest of the day and after that we got on fine.

That year Mrs. James went through a couple of nurses— one was too young, one was too fat, one was a Holy Roller who was always trying to get them to donate money to her "tabernacle," which I think was run out of the back of her Dodge Dart. Finally they settled on Muff.

Muffalda was her real name, and she was the type of woman who had not given up on capri pants long past her legs' sell-by date. She had Bozo the Clown red hair and a nose the size of my head.

But Mr. James liked her. And Mrs. James... well, by that time, it was hard to tell what Mrs. James liked or didn't like, and two months after Muff was hired, Mrs. James was dead.

After the burial, Mr. James's daughters figured their father would let Muff go. But Mr. James, who had been independent all his life, decided he needed someone now. His eyesight, his walk, the lonely nights...

The daughters were not pleased. Especially when they couldn't find some of the jewelry their mother had promised them. Nor were they pleased when they saw the way Muff joked with Mr. James and tickled him while they watched *Diagnosis: Murder*. They particularly didn't like it when Mr. James decided to renegotiate his contract with Mr. Finn and move from his one-bedroom efficiency apartment to a two-bedroom condo with all the amenities.

"You wouldn't spend that much on Mother!" the daughters spat.

And they were right. They were also right that he didn't buy his late wife a new Cadillac, or new clothes or any of the other accessories Muff seemed to grow once she and Mr. James were ensconced in the expensively redecorated condo.

I hadn't seen Mr. James in a while. He'd stopped dropping by the way he used to, and one night I was at the Applebee's on Route 19, after work, having a Cherry Herring at the bar when who walks in but Muff. She sees me and smiles, sidles onto the bar stool next to me.

"Fancy seein' you here," she barks. She sounds like Rose Marie after having swallowed a cheese grater. "Gimme a boilermaker!"

"Night off?" I ask.

"Sorta. The old guy was wearin' me out so..."

She takes out a prescription bottle from her purse.

"...I popped a couple Valium into his Metamucil. He'll be out for the night. He thinks he's such an old bull...let me tell you: I'm breakin' my wrist just to hoist the weenie!"

Muff downs her boilermaker. I notice she's wearing a diamond wristwatch.

"That's a pretty watch," I say.

"Got it from Mrs. James." She coughs up some tobacco phlegm to make her even prettier.

"Fell off her wrist as the chill set in."

Now, I do not know what it is that makes people like Muff want to confide in me, but I do not disabuse them of this misplaced trust.

For the next three hours, she regales me with tales of tricking Mr. James out of money, out of jewelry, and how a lawyer is coming next week to look at Mr. James's old will that really needs to be rewritten.

"He can't live forever," she snorts. "Not with the workouts I'm givin' him."

By midnight, Muff is pretty drunk. Slathering on her orange lipstick she confides she came to Applebee's to get laid, but I note there are no blind penitentiary escapees to be had. Besides, she has to go back to Mr. James.

"There's his sheets gotta go in the dryer. And I hafta make sure he's still breathing."

She slips off her stool right to the floor.

"You're in no shape to drive," I say.

Which is true, I've pumped her boilermakers with the contents of her Valium bottle for three hours now.

I drive her back to Riddle Key in the Cadillac, use her key card to go through the gates. I get her into the condo. No one sees.

Mr. James is dead to the world, snoring the way a seventy-nine-year-old man on sleeping pills snores.

Muff stumbles into the utility room and leans over the clothes washer...

"Gotta get these sheets in the dryer or they'll mildew..."

Which are her last words, unless you count, "Hey!"

—As I swing the full bottle of heavy-duty economy-size Tide at her head.

Once she's out, I take the wet sheets and make sure they're caught tight on the steel tumbler. Then I take the other wet end and tie it around Muff's neck.

Set to spin. And push.

I regret the shock to Mr. James when he finds her, but I know I've made the right decision when he moves back the next week to his old efficiency apartment, and his round-the-clock care is a two-hundred-and-fifty-pound Samoan man named Tondaleyo.

I'd like to say that was the end of my murder spree. But after you've done it once or twice, it just gets easier and easier. Like bicycle riding or sex, which to me is the same thing.

After Muff was Mr. Dofferman, the undertaker who liked to take things off the deceased before the family got there.

And then there was Officer Getz, who arrested the seniors on trumped-up driving infractions and threatened them with losing their licenses unless they gave him half their Social Security checks every month.

And Nurse Vigesmond, and the Manzano brothers of Manzano Bros. Construction, and the checkout girl at the Holiday Inn. All the ones who took advantage and knew they shouldn't have.

And then...last week...

Mr. Finn comes into the office. And smiles. I know that smile. It's the smile Mr. Finn has when he's found a couple on their last legs and he's gotten them to sign a five-year fully loaded deluxe package lease he knows they're never gonna live long enough to enjoy. It's the smile he has when he's tricked the Cuban boys to work another hour because he didn't tell them about daylight savings. Mr. Finn is smiling that smile at me.

"Hi, there, killer."

I pretend I think he's come up with a clever nickname for me.

But he hasn't. He has a letter in his hand. And reads.

"'There is a murderer among us. A murderer who has committed at least six killings in the last four years. And that murderer spends each working hour within the members' office of Riddle Key.'"

I swallow. "That's it?"

"Isn't that enough? I'm not saying I NEVER suspected you. I mean, the way Dr. Vasquez and his girlfriend got fried in that sitz bath. And when the Reverend Chuck got drowned during Mrs. Peshke's 'Jesus Loves Jews' baptism? I've been looking through the files all weekend: suffocations, electrocutions...strangulation by sheets?! And one constant factor: Miss Minka Lupino."

I am sweating. I have killed so many people for such a long time now without fearing anyone that it is the mere newness of the concept that frightens me.

"Are you going to call the police?"

"And ruin a winning streak? No, Miss Lupino. I don't know who sent this, but I am afraid this office has overlooked your talents for too long. I want you to keep doing what you're doing. But with some guidance. We have a problem the front office is concerned about. As you know, our five-year plan almost always works to our advantage. But there is one who has overstayed his welcome, and due to a loophole in the original contract, is paying only the absolute minimum on a valuable villa that could garner millions on the open market...unless you kill him.

"His name is Jay G. Garland."

My heart has stopped.

"But he's my favorite author."

"Well, then, Minka...this will give you a chance to meet him."

Three days later...

It's Saturday night.

There's a dance up at the club. Big-band swing music drifts over the lawns as I drive the cart up the cul-de-sac to Mr. Garland's villa.

The plan is not mine, the plan is Mr. Finn's. I'm to ring the doorbell and tell Mr. Garland I have some documents for him to sign, and then hit him on the head with a lead pipe.

It's so pedestrian. Murdering a man like Jay G. Garland that way. It's like serving KFC to Julia Child.

When I reach the front steps, I halt.

There's music inside.

"You'll be swell.

"You'll be great.

"Gonna have the whole world on a plate."

I raise my hand to knock.

And the door opens.

Standing before me is a man of indeterminate age. His hair, what's left of it, is the color of squid ink and barbecue sauce. He has a mustache and goatee, half-glasses, jowly cheeks, pale, he never goes out in the sun. He wears a green brocade dressing gown, a white dress shirt, and a dress bow tie. He holds a brandy snifter.

"Enter."

I go inside where I am immediately transported into a world that is the exact opposite of the world people who like sports inhabit. Red flock wallpaper, lamps with tassels, Persian carpets, antiques.

Jay G. Garland is limping, leaning on a cane with a huge ivory head shaped like snake.

"Have you ever noticed that women seldom get gout?"

I have noticed this, but this is not the time to brag.

I look at his foot. It's gigantic. A whole extra human at the end of his leg.

"Would you like a drink? What do we have? Vodka, brandy . . . Cherry Herring?"

What did he say? No one offers anyone Cherry Herring.

"I can't touch the stuff. Dr. Nagangupta says if I do, my whole body will explode but I'll still have to hang around to clean up the mess. I'm a goddamned wreck, but they can't kill me. Sit. Now, before you do what you have to do, let me try out a story on you. You like mystery stories?"

Uh-huh.

"I've been noodling for a while, but I'm kinda rusty and I could use a sounding board. A killer. Let's call her a her. For fun. Starts to knock off the rotters in a town or village. They're stinkers and she's an avenging angel type. Gets in Dutch though, blackmailer has the goods on her, tells her she has to kill someone she doesn't have in the ledger, someone she likes . . . or the blackmailer gives her the shiv. This hooking you?"

Yeah, I'm hooked.

"Now. She could kill the blackmailer. But he's on his guard. So she has no choice but to go through with the deal. But she doesn't want to kill the guy. She'd like to put paid the blackmailer too. What's a girl to do?"

Jay G. Garland opens his hooded eyes.

"Question is—what kind of person is she? Is she a murderer? Really? In the sense that she is defined by her murder? A person who becomes a murderer and never really goes back to what she was kind of murderer? Or. Is she a very nice, very pleasant, very moral woman who *just happens to have committed a couple of murders?*"

"I think it's the latter."

"And frankly, she's pretty much run the table on all the creeps in the town, so there's no one left to bump off . . . save one."

He manages to lean forward, a big physical move. He makes Nero Wolfe look like Ben Vereen.

"Who do you think lets in all those bums anyway? Who turns a blind eye to the Young Phils and the Muffs and the rest of them?"

"The blackmailer?"

"Bingo. And by now . . ." He glances at a grandfather clock with the face of Noël Coward and I don't even want to tell you what the big hand and the little hand were. ". . . By now our friends should have him taken care of."

I stare at my idol.

"You're wondering how I knew it was you. Your last three murders were from my own books—*Murder Gotta Gimmick*, *A Little Night Murder* and *Murder at Jules Feiffer's Little Murders*. And who here at Riddle Key would know my books as well as Ms. Minka Lupino, who has purchased more cheesy paperback copies of my books than any other buyer on Amazon-dot-com."

I had left an e-trail!

"And now . . . since we understand each other . . . go."

"Go where?"

"To the club. There are people there who owe you a debt of gratitude. And they are waiting to show you their thanks."

So I go. As I do, I hear sirens. Two ambulances are shooting through the streets, one going up, one going down. Busy night in Riddle Key.

When I arrive at the club where Mr. Finn is to wait for me, the darkened ballroom is filled with figures, white hair, blue hair, toupees, bald pates . . . dancing in the dark to "Stardust." But there is no Mr. Finn.

I look down at the dance floor. There is a fine dusting of white sand on the parquet. And as I look at the dancers, I could swear I see the odd smile, hear the odd giggle, a whispered but buoyant "Shush!"

I look out through the ballroom windows to the eighteenth green. And there, gathered outside on the grass are . . . the Cuban fellas. They're sweating, glistening in the moonlight, as if they've been hard at work . . . and at this time of night . . .

They hold shovels and rakes. And they're smiling at me. And they give me a little thumbs-up good-goin' sign.

Mr. Finn doesn't show up that night. Nor does he show up the next day or on Monday or any day at all, ever again.

These days Riddle Key is a lot less lethal a place. People die, that's part of the deal, but not at such an accelerated rate.

And out on the eighteenth green—where the Cuban boys buried Mr. Finn—the sand trap rides a little higher and a little lumpier.

Now I sit in Mr. Finn's old office, showing new tenants the grounds, the housing, the amenities. And they always notice the books on my shelf. All of them hardback first editions of the works of Jay G. Garland, all personally inscribed to me.

"To Minka Lupino. If anybody ever murdered me, I'd want it to be you."

END OF PLAY

NINE POINT EIGHT METERS PER SECOND PER SECOND

Pete Barry

Nine Point Eight Meters per Second per Second premiered at Circle Players Theater in Piscataway, New Jersey, as part of an evening titled *Accidents Happen*, July 18–26, 2008. It was directed by the playwright. The cast was as follows:

BALTHAZAR   John P. Dowgin

It was later produced and selected as a finalist at the 34th Annual Samuel French Off Off Broadway Short Play Festival, in July of 2009. It was directed by J. Michael DeAngelis. The cast was as follows:

BALTHAZAR   Pete Barry

*A single comfortable chair in the void; slight movement and a sound of
wind make it clear that the chair is plummeting through the atmosphere.*
BALTHAZAR KENT, *a wiry-haired English gentleman, dozes.*
    *He jolts awake, looks around, and digs his BlackBerry out of his
pocket.*
    He dials.

BALTHAZAR: Hullo?
           Yes. I'd like to speak to a manager.
           Well you see I was hopping your flight
               five-four-nine from Heathrow to Los Angeles,
               and now I appear to be falling out of the sky.
           Yes, I'll hold.

(Pushes a button on the BlackBerry.)

           Michael. I'll be late to the four-o'clock in
           California. Stall the meeting. Call me back.
           Quickly.

(Pushes another button.)

           Hullo? Yes, sir, I'm falling. Still in my seat, though.
           It seems to have come with me. Where am I?
           Somewhere between London and Los Angeles. I
           know we had reached North America. I'm sorry
           if I can't be more specific.

I'd like to resolve this problem within the next two
    minutes, if possible.
I'm assuming that's the maximum amount of time
    I have before I hit the ground.
Yes, sir, I did the differential calculus, taking into
    account my drag, vector velocity, and the earth's
    gravitational pull at nine point eight meters per
    second per second.
How do I know the earth's gravity? The wonders
    of a liberal education.
Yes, I'm sure you are unfamiliar with liberal
    education, sir. Otherwise you would not be
    answering the telephone in an airport terminal.
Hold please.

(*Pushes a button.*)

Michael.
Get that bloke from accounting, the corpulent
    fellow, Hinkley. Ask him if it's true that if one's
    parachute should fail to open during free fall
    one should pump one's legs as if running as
    ground approaches. I've heard that somewhere.
    And call my wife and tell her to up my life
    insurance policy, if she knows what's good for
    her. Call me back. No buts, Michael.

(*Pushes a button.*)

Yes, sir, where were we?
It would help if you could tell me how to unfasten
    this belt buckle.
The chair is a flotation device? I hardly believe
    that helps if I hit the ground at several hundred
    miles per hour.
I highly doubt that it will bounce.

Where is the plane? Sir, it's your company's plane.
   It wasn't my responsibility to keep abreast of it.
It may have been destroyed in a terrorist attack, or
   perhaps my seat was inadvertently sucked out of
   a fire exit.
Frankly, sir, if the engineers who constructed that
   aeroplane are of your caliber of intelligence,
   it is quite possible that the entire machine
   spontaneously burst into its component sheet
   metal.
I just don't see how this is my problem.
Please hold.

(*Pushes a button.*)

Simone, darling how are you? Quickly, darling, up
   my accidental death policy.
No I don't believe it's going to matter, I'm going
   to pump my legs as I hit the ground, once I get
   out of this chair. Still, it's best to be prepared.
Well, I'm not sure if there's anything wrong
   with the plane. I'm not on the plane. Why is
   everyone so concerned about the damn plane?
Yes, I'm plummeting to earth, darling.
How is this my fault?
You tell me not to go to the office every day of
   the week! Your horoscope has been wrong
   several hundred thousand times to date!
Am I wearing my good suit?
HEAVEN FORBID I SHOULD FALL OUT
   OF AN AIRPLANE AND IT NOT BE
   TO YOUR EXACT SPECIFICATIONS,
   MADAM!
Look, got to resolve this thing, I'll call you back.

(*Pushes a button.*)

Yes, have you figured out this seat belt yet?

Michael?

Have you got Hinkley?

Have you stalled the meeting?

Then what are you calling me for?

I called you? Don't be stupid, Michael, do what
    I'm asking you to.

(Pushes a button.)

Hello, who is this, now?

Yes, the seat buckle is stuck.

Lovely.

Cut it? Sir, your company would have relieved me
    of my undergarments if they believed I could
    have used them as a sharp weapon.

Look, perhaps you have some sort of owner's
    manual.

I can't see how I can start running while sitting
    down.

All right, I'll try it.

(He fiddles with the buckle, and it pops open.)

Oh, look at that, something you suggested actually
    worked.

Fine, I'm abandoning the chair.

(He slides out of the chair, looks down, and scuttles back into it.)

SHIT.

Shit. All right. It's not land. It's water. The ocean.
    Shit. I wasn't prepared for this. I suppose we
    hadn't reached the continent. All right. I'm back
    in the chair. Wait. Is hitting water like hitting
    the ground? Maybe I could still pump my legs.

Or will I sink right through? Should I buckle
in? Or not buckle in? All right. Is this chair
solid? Is that good or bad? Should I hold my
breath? Will the impact harm me if I do? Are
you there? Is this chair safe? Oh my God is that
a shark? Is it true that—

(*Black, and SPLASH, and the deep, quiet sound of immersion in water.
Then the gentle white noise of ocean waves.*

Lights up.

BALTHAZAR *lies motionless in the chair, mouth wide open.*

His BlackBerry beeps.

Beeps.

Beeps.

He sits up and answers it.)

Hullo, yes? (*Long pauvse.*) Is Portia here?
Well let me check.
No, sorry, I don't believe Portia is here right now,
    you see I'm in the middle of the FUCKING
    OCEAN.
Yes I believe you have a wrong number. Now—
NO NO WAIT DON'T HANG UP.
Are you an American?
A Canadian? Even better.
You must alert the authorities. The, Mounties, or
    whatever you have.
My name is Balthazar Kent, and I am an extremely
    important—
What?

Yes, Balthazar, yes that really is my name.

Well, ha ha ha, and what's your name?

Well, hello, Marta, you sound like a very stupid girl.

Oh, you're top of your class at university? And employee of the week?

Well let me ask you this, Marta, did you clear over one point six million pounds for your company last quarter?

Oh, you didn't?

Well, you see, I did, Marta. So I'm rather an important fellow. And I'm currently late for a meeting in California. So if you've any brains in your head at all, you'll call the authorities right now, so they can get me to my meeting.

NO DON'T HANG UP.

Please ask a manager or someone else to make the call for you.

Thank you.

What is this, anyway? A telemarketing firm?

Why on earth are you calling a British mobile number?

Your manager has the authorities? Can you patch me through or whatever?

Hullo? Is this the Mounties?

Oh, you're just the regular police, then.

I can barely hear you, sir.

Well I am in the middle of the ocean.

The Atlantic, I presume.

I was on an intercontinental flight to Los Angeles, and—

Oh, on the news, eh?

Do you know what happened? (*Long pause.*) You have got to be kidding me. (*Pause.*)

I am never, ever, ever, ever, flying with this company again.

No, I suggest you don't, either.

What do you mean?

Just come pick me up.

I don't know, don't you people have helicopters?

I'm on a bloody BlackBerry! Can't it be tracked with some kind of satellite triangulation?

Well, why don't you ask Marta? She's top of her class at university!

NO DON'T—

Yes, hello, Marta, I was just wondering if you were studying satellite transmissions or global positioning systems at university.

You're studying theater. How nice.

Yes, you're right we did have two. Shakespeare and Milton. We didn't produce a single other author or poet.

Well of course I'm glad to be talking to you, Marta, I was getting worried I wouldn't hear the dulcet tones of your voice again.

No I won't explain what "dulcet" means. You should have studied that at university.

Look, I'm just getting a little tired of people not doing what I'm asking them to.

What time is it in California? I can't keep these clients waiting forever.

Yes, Marta, I really am in the middle of the ocean.

Will I die? What kind of bloody morbid question is that? How could I possibly calculate that kind of probability?

Am I prepared to die? What on earth do you...?

HAHAHAHAHAHAHAHAHA!

I'm sorry, Marta, the signal is very bad. I must not have heard you properly. I swear I thought you asked me... (*Pause.*) ... if Jesus Christ was my Lord and Savior.

You did just ask me that, didn't you?

Is he?

Erm. (*Pause.*) Yes. Yes he is, Marta.

It is good news, isn't it?

We wouldn't want to have to have a christening at a time like this.

I suppose there is plenty of water around for it and all, but still.

Listen, Marta, getting back to this I'm-stuck-in-the-middle-of-the-Atlantic bit.

You see, I must get to this meeting. Are you connected to the Internet?

Fantastic. Would you navigate to a Web address for me?

Certainly.

W-w-w-dot-l-e-m-p-s-h-i-r-e-dot-co. Oh, dot-u-k.

No, no, not "o-u-k." Just, Lempshire, dot-co, dot-u-k.

Yes, "uck."

Well, that's the Web address.

What is "uck"?

That would be "yoo-kay."

For "United Kingdom."

What is the United Kingdom?

It's bloody England, you stupid bird!

What is it United with? Scotland and Wales, I suppose. A bit of Ireland.

You yourself, in fact, used to be united with the British Empire.

Well, not you specifically. Your country.

Unless—you're not in Quebec, are you?

Then yes, you were a part of the Empire. In fact, Quebec, too, now that I think about it.

We got that from the French, tall lot of good Quebec ever did us.

What do you mean, you don't believe me? You

don't know this? You're in university, for God's
  sakes!
Yes, Marta, I apologize for taking the Lord's name
  in vain.
Have you got the site yet?
Fantastic.
Click on "Management."
Look for "Balthazar Kent."
Oh, God, don't they even teach spelling in
  Canada? Kent starts with a "K."
I'm starting to wish I had gotten some bloody
  American.
Good, scroll down.
Executive-level vice presidents.
There I am! Fantastic. What does it say? (*Long
  pause.*) You're joking.
They must have pronounced me dead before the
  authorities did.
What?
Replaced?
Carolyn Williams?
That fat bitch!
I'm not in the cold ground three hours, and she's
  already got my bloody job!
Oh my God the meeting.
She's probably there.
Go to log-in!
Log-in, woman, for the life of you!
Username k-e-n-t-b password x-t-three-capital-k-
  four-eight!
Enter!
Click "Meeting Schedule"!
Does it say rescheduled?
No?
Meeting lead Carolyn Williams?
NO!

Take dictation, Marta!
In the post reply box!
This is VP Kent! Am not dead! Am in fact
    alive! Meeting to NOT proceed. Request
    postponement until further notice! Enter!
What?
What do you mean closed?
Wait!
Look at the bottom right!
Does it say CLOSED?
NOOOOOOOOOOOOOOOOOOO!

(*Silence.* BALTHAZAR *leans back.*)

Yes, Marta, I'm still here. Shut it down.
Yes it's bad.
It means that the meeting was held without me.
It means that I will not meet the client, and
    Carolyn already has.
Which in turn means that I'm likely already out of
    a job.
It's over.

(*Silence.*)

My life no longer has any purpose. I am floating
    in the middle of the ocean. I no longer need to
    meet my appointment. My entire schedule is
    meaningless. I am as if one dead.
You may as well leave me out here. I have nowhere
    to be.
What possible bright side, Marta?
No, I don't have any family.
Well, my wife.
And son.
They hate me.

Why? I suppose because I hate them.

Well you don't notice how sad it is, actually, when you have a sufficient number of meetings.

Meetings are what hold modern society together, from playdates to funeral arrangements.

Human beings are simply aggregates of quantum particles colliding at random. Meetings provide structure to the human experience. Without meetings, we are in chaos.

I feel so empty.

I could just float here. In the ocean. Watch the sharks and the jellyfish.

I could live here, possibly. Like a hermit. Fashion a harpoon from my seat belt. Eat raw fish. Harvest rain and dew for drinking water. Day becomes night. The sting of the cold air will become familiar. This will be all I know.

But for now, Marta, I'll just talk to you, if you don't mind, until my battery dies. You will be the last human being I ever speak to.

And then I will be alone. In the middle of the ocean. A monk adrift in the endless surf.

(*Silence.*)

What do you mean, I'm not in the middle of the ocean?

Lake Superior?

How the hell do you know that?

They've triangulated my position?

So I'm saved?

I'm saved!

How big is Lake Superior? (*Pause.*) Well, that's not much better, now, is it?

Yes, I understand why it's called "Superior."

What is the matter with you, Marta?

> I'd just come to terms with my situation, and you
> raise my spirits only to dash them again on the
> broken steps of Fate!
> Well, what would Jesus do, Marta?
> You know what I think he'd do? He'd—

(*HOOOOOONK. An earsplitting horn.*)

> It's a ship. It's a ship, Marta! It's coming right
> for me! Hey! HEY! Ah. Turn! Turn port, or
> starboard, or whatever the hell way you turn, just
> turn! You're coming right at me! Hey! HEY—

(*Black.*

BALTHAZAR's *screams are drowned in a deafening rush of water.*

The sound of clanking chains.

Lights up.

The chair is askew, perhaps upside down. BALTHAZAR *sits on top, still on his BlackBerry.*)

> Yes, Michael, I'm aware that—

(*The chair rocks.*)

> Excuse me.

(*He looks up.*)

> Could you wonderful gentlemen be a bit more
> careful?
> You're very right. I don't know how a crane works.
> Never mind! I'll try to relax!

(*He returns to his phone conversation.*)

> Sorry, Michael, where was I?
> Thank you.
> So everyone can hear me right now? The
>   connection isn't spotty?
> That's fine. I just want them to know that what I
>   have to say is very important.
> Perhaps the most important thing I've ever said.
> Tell me when. (*Pause.*) Hello, ladies and gentlemen.
>   Please excuse the connection, I am in fact
> •   thirteen miles offshore.
> Thank you. Yes, thank you, Carolyn.
> And I'm glad that you were ready to step in,
>   Carolyn. When I hit the water I thought I was
>   dead. In a way I was. Powerless, cold, cut off,
>   alone. At the mercy of God's universe. And
>   when I found out I'd been given up for dead,
>   well. That was a hard hit. I began to realize that
>   the only real difference between my life in the
>   ocean and my life at home was the speed and
>   number of events. In neither place did I feel
>   anything but indignant rage. In neither place
>   did I have any control over the course of my
>   life. In neither place did I have any meaningful
>   human relationship, with you, my coworkers,
>   or with my wife and son. Might I not be better
>   off floating in the ocean than visiting pain upon
>   my friends and family, for all my absence, my
>   austerity, my blind drive to serve only myself?
>   (*He coughs.*) Excuse me. I believe I may be
>   having some hypothermia, I'll try to be more
>   brief. I'm not entirely sure if my right leg can
>   be saved.
> So I asked you here today, ladies and gentlemen,
>   not to ask for reinstatement, but to confer on

you the truth of my spiritual journey. Carolyn,
     I know you have family. Have you seen them
     lately? Daniel, you have brothers. Call them
     and tell them you love them. Do not float in
     your own icy ocean waters. Life is not about
     meetings. Life is about the people in the
     meetings.
Thank you.
Yes Carolyn?
Oh, I don't know, what with everything that's
     happened—
Well I'll think about it. If I'm needed, then
     certainly I'll step back into the role. I'll call the
     client tomorrow and explain.
Yes, thank you, Carolyn. Please don't cry, my dear.
I know. Why don't you sign off and call them right
     now?
Certainly, dear. (*Pause.*) Is she gone?
Thank God.
SHE TOOK MY FUCKING JOB?
And none of you questioned that?
Yes, I'd say you'd better not if you don't want a
     lawsuit in the future. "Dead man wants job
     back"—that'll be in all the tabloids.
Hopefully she's writing her resignation in tears
     right now.
Well then. What lesson have we learned here?
That's right, Michael! Don't rush into things.
Good.
What time is it in London, now?
Nine o'clock Saturday morning. Fine. Let's meet
     this afternoon, two o'clock, conference call.
You've what, Ronald?
Oh, you'll have to cancel cricket practice? How
     terrible I've got a GANGRENOUS LEG. Tell
     your cricket pals to shove it.

See you all at two o'clock, sharp.
Michael!
Repopulate my schedule, please. It must have been
    erased somehow.
Let me check.

(*He toggles through the BlackBerry's menus. He smiles.*)

Ahhh.
Thank you, Michael.
Enjoy your weekend. Keep your phone on! I'll see
    you Monday. Bright and early.

(*He hangs up and pockets the BlackBerry. Clang from the chain.*)

Watch it, you hives of sexually transmitted disease!
    Slowly!

(*Black.*)

END OF PLAY

NORM-ANON

Warren Leight

CHARACTERS

JUDY RODGERS
BOB ALLEN, JR.
ANNIE ROSS

Onstage, three happy, well-adjusted people.

JUDY: Hi, my name is Judy Rodgers.

BOB: Hi, I'm Bob Allen, Junior.

ANNIE: And I'm Annie Ross. And though we may look different...

BOB: All three of us have something in common: a secret about our past.

JUDY: A secret that, as we grew older, kept us isolated from others. You see, all three of us are:

ALL: Adult Children of Normal Parents.

JUDY: For years I denied it. When my friends talked about their dysfunctional homes, and codependent parents, I tried to mix in. I pretended that my childhood had also been one of constant instability and emotional trauma. The truth was, I was living a lie. The truth is, my parents were normal. And so was I.

ANNIE: In college, my roommate—Sylvia, was having a hard time of it. She stayed inside our dorm room, on the floor, for two weeks, listening to Aimee Mann CDs. One day I asked her to come out for a walk with me.
    "I can't," she said. "I'm depressed."

"Depressed," I asked. "What's that?"

You see, I had never heard the word, and I had no idea what she was talking about. I felt so embarrassed.

BOB: I can relate to what Annie . . . Ross, is saying. At work I used to wonder, am I the only one here not subject to mood swings, or obsessive-compulsive behavior. I didn't feel guilty about it, or superior—I mean, guilt or shame or grandiosity never really solve anything. And we all have to do the best we can with what we've been given, but sometimes I did wonder, just for a little while . . . AM I the only one? I enjoyed life, and still do. But sometimes not so often, not for any length of time, I felt a little . . . alone.

Until I found NORM-ANON.

JUDY: Yes, all three of us are grateful members of Norm-Anon. Norm-Anon: a support group for happy people. Healthy people, who grew up in clean, well-lit homes.

There aren't many of us.

ANNIE: And sometimes it helps to get together.

BOB: To talk about . . . what it was like, coming from those homes. How great the holidays were.

JUDY: How much we miss Mom 'n' Dad.

ANNIE: And Gran'pa.

BOB: And the girl, or fella, next door.

JUDY: Once a week or so, we get together, to talk about feelings. Of course, we know feelings aren't facts. And feelings, good or bad, pass. And we all know, without question, really, that everything always works out for the best. Still, on those days when everything isn't coming up roses, it's good to get together with people who understand.

BOB: Right now, you may be asking, how do I know if I'm an adult child of normal parents?

ANNIE: Well, if you have to ask, you're probably not. But, we do have a short handy checklist, that can help you decide: Ask yourself the following questions:

JUDY: Do you find yourself genuinely happy for the success of family or friends?

BOB: Do anniversaries and holidays fill you with a sense of joy?

ANNIE: Do you have twenty/twenty vision? A perfect dental history? And good skin?

JUDY: Do you often find yourself telling the truth, when a lie would do just as well?

BOB: If you answered yes to any or one of these questions, it's a good bet—not that any of us likes to bet—that you're one of us. An adult child of normal parents—
     If you're tired of being with people who act out, or feel sorry for themselves, or need to learn things you knew when you were four, maybe it's time you tried Norm-Anon.

JUDY: Call us.

ANNIE: We're all in the book.

BOB: Thanks.

JUDY: C'mon guys, let's go get some sodas.

ALL: Bye for now.

END OF PLAY

NOTHING

Philip Dawkins

Nothing received its premiere at the Cell Theatre in Albuquerque, New Mexico, with the Fusion Theatre Company's short play festival, *The Seven: That One Thing*, June 18–June 21, 2009. It was directed by Bruce Holmes, and was performed by Morse Bicknell and Kelsey Montoya.

CHARACTERS

ADULTS
DAD
MR. TELLER
PA SYSTEM (MRS. MALBY)

KIDS (12–14)
SON
DAN TOLLISON
AMBER CARLSON
JENN GROUT

ALIENS
ALIEN FACE ON TV
ALIEN WARRIORS

DAD *and* SON *at the dinner table. A big bowl of spaghetti on the table, a covered meat dish, a television set next to the table.* SON *poking at his food, disinterested.* DAD, *trying, nervous. Some time and then.*

DAD: How was your day today?

SON: Fine.

DAD: Just fine?

SON: Yeah, fine, whatever.

DAD: What did you do?

SON: Nothing.

DAD: Nothing?

SON: Yeah.

DAD: All day at school, and you did nothing?

SON: Yeah.

DAD: (*Beat.*) Well I had a pretty good day. I made that sale that Carl and I had been working on. You remember I told you about that really big account? (*Beat.*) So, that was pretty exciting. (*Pause.*) Look, we both know you'd rather be at Mom's right now, I get that, but—could you at least pretend like you're not completely miserable?

SON: I didn't say anything.

DAD: No, you're right, you didn't say anything.

SON: What do you want me to say? You asked me how my day was, I said fine.

DAD: You said, "Fine, whatever."

SON: It was fine, whatever.

DAD: Could you help me out a little, here? I'm making an effort. I'm trying.

SON: So am I!

DAD: Okay, I'm sorry, yes, you are trying, I'm sure, but—

SON: My day was totally boring, okay? What do you want? You want me to make something up?!

DAD: *Yes! Make something up!* (*Ooo, that came out a little harsher than intended. Damn. Beat.*) I'm . . . never mind.

(*Beat.*)

SON: There was this one thing. In homeroom today. You know those televisions that hang from the ceiling in the corners of the classrooms? Well, right in the middle of attendance, the TV just turns on. All by itself. (*At this point, the television beside the kitchen table turns on loudly. Static. Both* SON *and* DAD *look at the TV. What's that about? They don't know. Continuing hesitantly.*) And...all of a sudden, this face appears on the screen, a face of something alien almost. Something unhuman.

DAD: Something *in*human.

SON: Whatever. (*An alien face materializes on the TV screen.*) Oh my God.

DAD: Then what?

SON: Then, um, I don't know...um...it starts talking? I guess. It says—

FACE ON TV (ALIEN): Greetings, classlings. Do not attempt to leave your desks. Your school has been taken over by the perilous members of the Cobalt 4 Battle Fleet.

DAD: No way.

SON: It's totally true. And suddenly, Dan Tollison, who always sits in the back of class and sleeps through first period anyway, wakes up! (*He pulls the silver dome off of the tray, and* DAN TOLLISON*'s head is there, waking up startled.*) And Dan's like—

DAN: What the heck is going on?

SON: And the alien on TV is like—

ALIEN: Silence, sleepy one!

SON: And these fire-hot lasers shoot out of the alien face's eyes! (*The face on the television explodes, and the TV goes static.* DAN *screams.*) And we all scream and duck under our desks.

(*He puts the cover back over* DAN's *head.*) And everyone's like "Ahhhhh!!!"

DAD: Ahhhhhhhhh!!! (*Lifts up the meat dish cover and* DAN *is screaming AHHHHHHHHHH, covers him back up again.*)

SON: And Mr. Teller's like—

(MR. TELLER *runs on from stage left to right.*)

MR. TELLER: It's an alien invasion!!! Run for your lives!

SON: But just as he gets to the classroom door, five aliens kick it down and slither into the room, pointing big bubble-shaped blasters at us. (*Five aliens run onstage pointing blasters at* DAD *and* SON.) And I don't know where I get the courage, but I stand up and I say, "Don't shoot. We are a peaceful homeroom!"

DAD: And then what?

SON: Then, Amber Carlson, who's totally annoying and used to pick her nose and put the boogers behind her ears when we were in fifth grade—

DAD: Oh, I know Amber. Her parents belong to that weird religion, right?

SON: Right. So, Amber Carlson's like—

AMBER: (*Popping up from behind the table.*) I *knew* it, they've finally come for us!

SON: Then she screams and faints. (AMBER *screams, faints.*) But, she's holding her pink cell phone.

DAD: I thought you weren't supposed to have your cell phones in class.

SON: Dad, we're not supposed to have space *aliens* in class either.

DAD: Right. Continue.

SON: So, Amber Carlson drops her cell phone and it slides onto the floor, and lands right between the feet of the biggest baddest alien warrior. (SON *takes the cell phone from his* DAD*'s belt, and slides it between the feet of one of the aliens.*) And he looks down at Amber Carlson's cell phone and says—

ALIEN WARRIOR: Eeezzzoo Boober spotch grob grob, norb!?

SON: Which was a special alien language, so we had to call in our librarian, Mrs. Malby, to translate.

(*Sound of a school PA system.*)

PA SYSTEM (MRS. MALBY): Mrs. Malby to Mr. Teller's classroom. Mrs. Malby to Mr. Teller's class. Thank you.

MRS. MALBY: (*Running on, looking very scared, and very librariany. She is holding a large book entitled* Cracking the Alien Dialect.) The alien says, "What is this? Some kind of earthling bomb?"

SON: So I say, "Tell him it *IS* a bomb, and if they don't do what we ask, we'll blow them back to whatever galaxy they came from."

MRS. MALBY: Minnie Moozer Klobberstoch, Icky pursablooey grob grob—oh, what's the word for galaxy!?!

SON: But the alien says—

ALIEN WARRIOR: BEELARG!!

SON: Which means—

MRS. MALBY: Silence!!

(*The* ALIEN WARRIOR *picks up the cell phone, sniffs it, shakes it, starts to laugh.*)

ALIEN WARRIOR: Ar Ar Ar! Eeezle noffle prob. (*All the aliens laugh. Ar Ar Ar.*)

SON: Then, I get an idea. I turn and yell to the class and to Mrs. Malby, "Quick, does anyone know Amber Carlson's cell phone number?!" And the biggest Alien Warrior stops laughing and yells—

ALIEN WARRIOR: Beelarg, Norfleflunger! Beelarg.

SON: (*To the* ALIEN.) "No, I will not beelarg!" (*To the classroom.*) "Who knows Amber's number?!?" And I start to get scared because Amber Carlson's not very popular and I think maybe no one knows her number, but then, in the back of the classroom, one student stands up from underneath her desk.

(*An attractive girl appears from behind the table.* JENN GROUT.)

JENN GROUT: I do. I know Amber's number. She's my neighbor, and sometimes we carpool.

SON: It was Jenn Grout.

DAD: *The* Jenn Grout? The one you have the major crush on?

SON: How do you know I have a major crush on Jenn Grout?

DAD: You told me.

SON: I did?

DAD: I do listen, you know?

ALIEN WARRIOR ONE: BEELARG, Norfleflungers!!!

SON: "Quick," I yell to Jenn Grout, "dial Amber's number."

(JENN *pulls out her cell phone and dials* AMBER's *phone.*)

SON: *Hurry!*

JENN GROUT: It's ringing.

SON: All's silent, and then . . .

(*The cell phone in* ALIEN WARRIOR's *hand rings . . . something poppy, something tweeny.* ALIEN WARRIOR *looks at his hand, puzzled.*)

ALIEN WARRIOR: Blupp duh—?

SON: And then . . .

DAD: Yeah?

SON: . . . his face explodes!

(DAD *grabs a handful of spaghetti from the bowl on the table, and throws it at* ALIEN's *face.* ALIEN *writhes in pain and acts as if the spaghetti is his face melting.* DAD *continues doing this to the remaining four* ALIENS, *who all act as if their heads are exploding.*)

And one by one all the aliens' heads start popping like zits, and they sink to the ground in a slithering pile of their own head guts.

(*He lifts up the meat dish cover.*)

DAN: What's happening?

SON: I don't know!

(*Replaces the meat dish cover.*)

MRS. MALBY: The vibrations from the cell phone must be a frequency intolerable to alien eardrums.

JENN GROUT: You're saving the day!!!

SON: Then, suddenly, there's this rumbling, and it sounds like the cracking of ten thousand knuckles and the entire roof rips off of the school!

(SON *and* DAD *grab the four corners of the tablecloth and fling it and all its contents off the table.*)

And above us is the sound of ten million ceiling fans, and there hovering above our heads is a giant, rotating flying saucer.

(*The table begins to lift off the ground—maybe* SON *and* DAD *lift it on their own. Under the table are a ton of lights and gadgets that look like the bottom of a spaceship. It continues to float up and up and up until everyone is huddled underneath it looking up in astonishment. The noise should be that of a huge aircraft taking off. Their hair blows; they have trouble staying on their feet.*)

We look up in amazement, and Jenn Grout hugs me tight, and I can totally feel her boobs without even trying. And then all of a sudden, the spaceship disappears into the first-period sky with a loud BAMMM!!!

(*A light flash! Loud boom/crack. When lights return, all have disappeared except for* DAD *and* SON, *who sit on the floor surrounded by remnants of alien invasion.*)

And when we open our eyes, the roof is back on the school, and the TV is all in one piece and it's like nothing ever happened? Except that Amber Carlson's cell phone is mysteriously missing.

DAD: Wow.

SON: Yeah.

DAD: Well... I can't wait to hear what happens tomorrow.

(*They share a smile.*)

END OF PLAY

PARTICLE BOARD

Elizabeth Meriwether

Particle Board was originally produced by Ars Nova, producers Kim Rosenstock and Jason Eagan. Shira Milikowsky directed the following cast:

HAROLD CRETTS	Daniel Berson
SLY JONES	Audrey Lynn-Weston
TRISHA FOME	Kristin Slaysman
DAMARA	Rebecca Henderson
DOCTOR	Ben Correale
JAY	Stephen Haskell

NOTE
We originally produced this play with two microphones set up on either side of the stage. SLY JONES spoke into one, and the other characters used the other and left the stage after they were done speaking. HAROLD was on a platform off to the side, away from the action. Everyone performed directly to the audience. Think one of those documentaries on PBS or the History Channel. Oh, yeah, every time HAROLD tells a joke he hits himself with a piece of wood and yells out, "Ow!" We used foam board so no one got hurt.

A man walks up to a microphone. Taps it a couple times.

HAROLD: This thing on?

(*He laughs. And then hits himself on the head with a piece of wood.*)

Ow. My wife came up to me the other day and she said, "Honey, is that a piece of wood in your hands?" And I said, "*Wood* you like to hold it?"

(*He laughs. And then hits himself on the head with a piece of wood.*)

Ow.

(SLY JONES, *carrying notecards, enters on the other side of the stage.* HAROLD *freezes.*)

SLY JONES: Harold Cretts was this country's first and foremost Particle Board comedian. Some consider him the founding father of the Particle Board shtick. "Shtick" is a Jewish word meaning something that Jews think is funny. And Christians pretend to think is funny. Particle Board is of course the cheap wood invented during World War Two when supplies were hard to come by, it's manufactured out of wood chips of all different kinds of trees and stuck together with resin. Which comes from the Latin, To Rez. Or to hold from behind while crying.

HAROLD: If you ask me what war I fought in, I'd say it was "*Wood War Two.*"

(HAROLD *hits himself with the wood and yells out "Ow!"*)

SLY JONES: Much like Particle Board, Harold Cretts was himself made up of wood chips. If wood chips were a metaphor for being born in Brooklyn in 1935 and being Jewish. When asked how Particle Board comedy was born, Harold Cretts replied, "I had a piece of wood in my hand and then I hit myself with it." Always quick with words, Harold never ceased to charm anyone he came across—children, women, and a tiny Gay named Fantastic Jack. Jack ignored his fourth official warning and one restraining order to run up and give Harold a hug at the 1957 World Series. Harold smacked the boy in the face with his Particle Board and sent him to the hospital with a surface wound, where it was revealed that his name was not Fantastic Jack but rather Robert Duvall. Robert would of course grow up to be Robert Duvall, star of *Tender Mercies* and *Secondhand Lions.* When asked, Duvall claimed to have no recollection of his days as Fantastic Jack, the tiny Gay. This is just one in a series of strange and wonderful anecdotes that happened to Harold as he traveled around the world with his wood, talking to people of all colors and shapes. Sometimes those shapes were even fat people.

HAROLD: So my wife asks me if she looks fat in those pants, and I say, "No honey, *but my wood looks fat in your pants!*"

(HAROLD *hits himself in the head with the wood, and yells out "Ow!"*)

SLY JONES: One funny story is that Harold spent an uncomfortable elevator ride with Walter Cronkite where neither of them said a word. The incident is chronicled in his well-loved memoir, *Oh, My Wood!*

HAROLD: I got on the elevator and I turned around and there was Walter Cronkite. At the end of the elevator ride, I got out of the elevator and walked to my car.

SLY JONES: Candor. Integrity. American. Cantankerous. Hilarious. Average. Complicated. Sexy. Wet. Exorcist. Not mean. Clinically insane. All these words have been used to describe Harold Cretts. Whatever he was, the women went nuts, citing most often that it was his use of the Particle Board that first caught their eye.

(TRISHA FOME *enters and speaks out.*)

TRISHA: Oh, I remember the sound of it hitting his head. If I had to write it down, I'd probably spell it S-L-P-A-T, Slpat. Joke. Slpat. It looked really painful. And I remember there was a little bruise forming at his hairline, and you know by the end of the night I'm pretty sure there was a lot of blood coming down his face. It was hilarious. I remember that night I wasn't wearing socks and, ooo, I felt just like Myrna Loy. I went up to Harold after the show and asked him if I could touch his wood—and then oh gosh, I was so young, I just started blushing—it was probably the pink wine and the late hour but Harold took me in his arms and French-kissed me. He gave me oral herpes that I've had my whole life. When it flares up, my husband always laughs and says, "Looks like Harold's back." It's funny he calls my herpes a name. My husband is almost as funny as Harold Cretts. But he's not.

SLY JONES: What was it about the wood?

TRISHA: I don't know. It's just funny when people hit themselves. Especially handsome men like Harold. That's really funny.

(TRISHA FOME *exits.*)

SLY JONES: The women came and went but few stayed. Once a few did stay, literally. Harold is often credited with inventing the "foursome," which to weaker men would just seem like a bad idea. For many women, what first drew them in was often what eventually made them leave—you guessed it.

(DAMARA FATELLI *enters.*)

DAMARA: I said, "Harold, let's go to bed and make a baby." And he starts crying. And I'm like: "What's wrong?" And he's like: "Nothing." And then maybe I'd put on some stiletto heels and walk on his face. And it was like that for five years.

SLY JONES: Why did you stay, Damara?

DAMARA: There was something about him. Kinda made you feel like a warm buttered roll. After all the other schmucks who made me feel like chop suey. And I don't say that lightly. I dated a lot of Chinese. Great in bed. They don't call it soy sauce for nothing. They really nailed me like I was a railroad track. Are you going to have to bleep that out because it was racist?

SLY JONES: How was Harold in bed?

DAMARA: Well there was a lot of crying, like I said, but there was also a lot of joy. Joy mostly in the form of crying. But I knew he loved me. He liked it when I stayed really still, you know really quiet and still and stiff.

SLY JONES: Like a piece of wood?

(DAMARA *takes a moment to think, reflect, then:*)

DAMARA: (*Softly.*) Oh God.

(*Another beat.*)

Thank you.

SLY JONES: What some might call inspiration, others called an obsession, an addiction. Wood addiction or "waddiction" can be crippling, even fatal. Harold hit rock bottom on *American Bandstand* with Dick Clark.

(HAROLD *is a broken man.*)

HAROLD: So Dick, Dick, you won't believe what my wife...my wife...she said, "Harold, (*incoherent mumbling*)..." And I said...I said...(*incoherent mumbling*)...I said...(*incoherent mumbling*)..."You're a bitch..."

(HAROLD *hits himself over and over with the wood, then holds it to himself.*)

(*Softly, crazy.*) "Bandstand, Bandstand..."

(HAROLD *beats an imagined Dick Clark away with his wood.*)

Get away Dick, no, no, get away, I'm dancing, I'm dancing with my wood—I'M DANCING, DICK, I'M DANCING...

(DOCTOR *enters.*)

DOCTOR: Harold came to my facility the first time he tried to live without his wood. It only lasted a couple days. I suggested inpatient care, and that he needed to spend a good thirty days. At that point his hands were barely recognizable with so many splinters and his head was badly bruised and scarred. I guess he hit a rough patch in his career, and he thought if he hit his head harder and harder it would make his jokes funnier. It didn't. But he meant a lot to a lot of people. He was like a rock-and-roll star for my daughter, she just jumped around the whole time he was on with Johnny Carson. I didn't care much one way or another but I guess I liked the part where he hit himself. I didn't have the heart to tell my daughter that he'd come in for rehab years later. It was a sorry sight. It's not how I would have wanted to spend my life, you know, hitting myself with wood, but then you know, I don't think comedy is funny. And as I said, he was out of there after about three days. We tried to talk him out of leaving, but he just sat there quietly. I could see it in his eyes. He couldn't live without it and you know what, I don't think he wanted to. I think he left the rehab center and went right to a hardware store. It had to be Particle Board, the cheap stuff. He was down to nickels and dimes at that point. Must have told them he was building a tree house. No one knew he was digging his grave.

SLY JONES: "A Side Splitter." That was the headline in the *New York Post*. It is still unknown how Harold bought the saw, some people think the FBI gave it to him because they just wanted him to die so they could stop following him. It remains unclear if he was aiming to saw the wood in half or himself, regardless, it didn't end up being the wood. And the man who had worked so hard at keeping the world from seeing his insides finally showed us everything. Conspiracy theories abound. Some claim that vital organs were missing and that Real Harold Cretts took some of Fake Dead Harold Cretts and went to Vancouver and worked as a librarian. But that just doesn't make any fucking sense. Some say that Harold Cretts was a Jewish leprechaun—in Yiddish lore, a *tekl-mentch*. They say he is now living inside a tree in California and he will come back out in fifty-five years when someone bakes a magic Jewish cookie, called the *cookie-le*. One Michigan teenager claims that he is the reborn Harold Cretts.

(JAY FEDDO *enters*.)

And this teenager is obviously a jerk.

JAY: I just think he's really funny.

SLY JONES: I hate you.

(JAY *opens a Diet Coke and drinks it.*)

Harold Cretts meant many things to many people. Some of those people were fat. Some of those fat people were nice. Some were once tiny Gay boys. Like me.

(*A beat.*)

I am Robert Duvall.

(*He holds up a picture of Robert Duvall.* JAY *drinks his Diet Coke.*)

JAY: Whatever.

SLY JONES: This is Harold's last piece of wood.

(*He holds up a blood-splattered piece of wood.*)

If you look closely, you see a pattern. It could be a Ford motorcar or it could be the constellation Fantastico, the Greek God of Tragic Love and in some translations, a Bowl Used For Cooking Baby Deer. Harold knew Fantastico is my favorite constellation, because I wrote about it in a letter to him when I was five years old. Now when I want to see Harold Cretts, the funniest man alive, the Human Nail, I just close my eyes and look to the stars.

(*He closes his eyes.*)

(*Softly.*) Fantastico. Fantastico.

JAY: That's so gay.

SLY JONES: (*Ignoring him, continuing softly.*) Fantastico. Fantastico.

JAY: (*Earnestly.*) Can you really see him?

(JAY *doesn't close his eyes, but he looks up.*

SLY *holds out his hand;* JAY *takes it. They both look up at the sky.*)

SLY *and* JAY: (*Softly.*) Fantastico, Fantastico.

(HAROLD, *still on the other side of the stage, chuckles.*)

HAROLD: Just say the *wood*—

(HAROLD *holds the wood up to hit his head. Lights out.*)

END OF PLAY

PEOPLESPEAK

John Augustine

PeopleSpeak was originally presented in *Summer Shorts 2* (J. J. Kandel and John McCormack, producers) at 59E59 Theatres from August 6 through August 28, 2008.

The set and lighting design was by Maruti Evans; costume design by Michael Bevins and Megan Sanders; sound design by Chris Cotone; casting by Billy Hopkins and Jessica Kelly; press by David Gersten & Associates; production stage manager was Micahel Alifanz. Robert Saxner directed the following cast:

SIOBHAN	Sherry Anderson
CASSIE	Patricia Randell
BRIAN	Nick Westrate

CHARACTERS

SIOBHAN: A woman of substance. A permanent temp. Somewhere in her thirties to middle fifties. Any race.

CASSIE: An extremely verbal garment center executive. Between 25 and 40. Any race. But cast younger than actor playing Siobhan.

"A witty and acerbic play."
—*The New York Times*

"I loved it. John Augustine is crazy."
—Dr. Ruth Westheimer

BRIAN: A happy, playful waiter in his twenties to forties. This actor also plays the construction worker, the cabdriver, and the man in the doughnut kiosk. And the other minor characters. Any race.

TIME
Now.

PLACE
Café Sha Sha, and various brief NYC locations.

NOTE
The set is minimal. And changes in "scene" are done simply: i.e., the taxicab is represented by using chairs with wheels on them. Changes for the actor playing the waiter should be done very simply and easily. They should flow with no time "waiting" for actor to change. Find simple, clean ways to do this.

The affirmations Siobhan sings are original melodies written by John Augustine and are included.

In the dark we hear a "self-help tape" A few sentences such as:
"You are loved. So much you are loved. But was there ever a time in your life when you wanted to die? When you thought to yourself, 'No one will ever love me.' Have you ever thought this? Have you? You are not alone."
Lights upon SIOBHAN *standing in her apartment. She is holding a gun. She is perhaps crying softly. She looks at the gun. Puts it to her head. Takes a breath. Yes. No. Yes. Gun down. Gun up. Ready to pull the trigger when suddenly:*
. . . Her cell phone rings. It is in her hand already. It is one of the silly annoying familiar rings.
She answers but does not lower the gun.

SIOBHAN: Hello? Oh, hello, Mother. No, I'm at home—I haven't gone back to work yet. Well, it is called a "leave of absence" because I am on a "leave of absence."

What am I doing *right* now? (*She eyes the gun.*)

Oh nothing. Just wondering what to do next.

Nothing is wrong. I'm fine!

Well, maybe I do. But I think if anyone has a right to sound angry, it's me.

Oh. *Lots of people* have it worse? Like who…?! (*Perhaps she lowers the gun here.*)

Well, she was *born* that way.

Yes, I am grateful not to be a human torso. But I don't think it is fair to compare my problems with that woman.

I DO have sympathy for her.

She what??

Oh stop it, Mother. She *likes* being in the circus. At least *she* has a job she *likes*. I would give my right *arm* to be in the circus. That didn't come out right.

I was absolutely NOT making a joke. Believe me, Mother. *Nothing* is funny to me. Nothing!… (*Puts gun back up to head.*)…Yes, Bob Hope movies are funny. And Jack Lemmon. Yes, Jim Carrey is funny.

Whoopi Goldberg? Not so much. But I think she's a good actress. I liked her in *Ghost*.

NO. I am in PAIN! It does not help me to think about Jim Carrey when I am in PAIN! Can we change the subject please?

No. Going shopping is like the *last* thing I want to do. I get all my clothes wholesale anyway. You know that. It's one of the perks of working in the garment center.

I KNOW I am still just a secretary! You think I don't KNOW that? And they don't say "secretary" anymore. *(Holds up gun.)* No. I don't want lunch.

(Scratches her head with gun.) Because, I have this thing I need to do. *(Holds up gun.)* And now I think I need to get it done today.

I am smiling. *(She isn't.)* Oh you can *hear* that I'm not smiling? OK. Hold on. I have to build up to it. *(She smiles a crazy big happy smile.)*

(Trying to actually sound happy.) There. How is this? Can you hear the smile in my voice now? Is that better for you?

You're welcome. Yes, they came in the mail yesterday.

I don't want to sing them for you now. It makes me feel stupid. Yes, it's very nice that you write musical affirmations for me. You're right. Not everyone's mother does this.

...Oh, OK! But then I'm hanging up. *(She picks up a piece of paper.)*

(Singing.)

> I'm wealthy...Money comes to me.
> Money COMES to me.
> Thank you very much.

I'm happy...Love is everywhere.
Love is EVERYwhere.
And I let it in.

I'm safe now. All my doors are locked.
All my windows down. (*Quick beat wondering if she is
reading the next line correctly.*)
Killers lurk outside.

(*Speaks.*) Very good, Mother. You should put it on YouTube.
But I think the third verse needs work.

Yes, I do feel better. I can't hear you anymore—There's a
dead zone in my apartment. Pun intended.

(*Lights begin to shift to: Café. The* WAITER *enters and sets up a sign
that reads,* PLEASE WAIT TO BE SEATED. *He also sets up whatever he
needs to for the café set. His cell rings, overlapping with* SIOBHAN*'s last
lines.*)

SIOBHAN: I'm losing you. I didn't pay my phone bill. If you can
hear me I'm hanging up.

WAITER: (*Answering his cell.*) Hey there, friend. What up? Uh-huh.
Uh-huh. Wait. Hold on. (*To someone in the audience.*) You can
pay on your way out. (*In phone.*) OK! So let me tell you.
Well, it was really crowded. But I noticed him right away.
And I was like staring at him and staring at him. And I was
sending him psychic messages. You know how I do. I told
you I am very psychic. Anyway. I was looking at him and I
was screaming in my head, "Look at me. Look at me!!"

And then you'll *never* guess what he did next.

That's right. He looked at me. Are you a Pisces too?

(SIOBHAN *enters café. She notices the* PLEASE WAIT TO BE SEATED *sign and waits to be noticed.*)

But isn't that creepy fabulous? And he was like staring right at me for a really long time.

No, he was NOT undressing me with his eyes. He's not that way. Besides, it was a clothing-optional beach. He didn't need to.

SIOBHAN: (*She sings.*) "I'm angry. No one sees I'm here. No one SEES I'm here. Waiters never come."

(*She drops a book to get his attention. He notices only slightly. She bends down to pick it up as . . .*)

WAITER: Uh-huh uh-huh uh-huh uh-huh.

(*The* WAITER *takes the* PLEASE WAIT TO BE SEATED *sign and turns it around. On the other side it reads:* PLEASE SEAT YOURSELF. *And the* WAITER *moves off.*)

SIOBHAN: Whatever.

(*She moves to an available table.*)

WAITER: Yes. He is married. Yes, I am kind of seeing him. Does that make me a bad person? It does? No I don't think it does. Why does that make me a bad person? I'm not married.

SIOBHAN: (*Reading from index cards.*) "People notice me. I am a relevant person. I deserve to be loved. I deserve to have coffee when I sit in a café. Maybe I deserve to have wine."

WAITER: But creepy how we were both at Sandy Hook, right? Isn't that a coincidence? It is too a coincidence. Don't ruin my serendipity. Serendipity. It means . . .

(SIOBHAN *picks up table tent and strains to read the phone number. She makes a call on her cell.*)

I'm not sure what it means. But it's something good. Like being nude at a beach at the same time is serendipity. I think.

(*The café landline phone rings.*)

Hold on. The café phone is ringing. It might be my boss. Café Sha Sha. This is Brian.

SIOBHAN: Do you have take-out service?

WAITER: Yes, we have take-out service.

SIOBHAN: And do you also have table service?

WAITER: Yes, we have table service.

SIOBHAN: Then could I get some table service? Over here. At this table. (*He looks around. She waves a kind of hostile wave.*)

WAITER: Ohmygod. That is so cute. You are adorable. (*Into cell.*) I'll call you back. I have a live one here. (*To* SIOBHAN.) YOU are a problem solver. You saw a problem, and you solved it.

I know most waiters would give you attitude now. They'd be all up in your face with "oh, no she didn't." But I'm not that kind of waiter. I like people with spunk.

What can I getcha, honey? I've always wanted to say that to someone. Like I'm Eve Arden or some sassy waitress in an old movie. People my age don't even know who Eve Arden is.

SIOBHAN: Maybe I should get something to go.

WAITER: No, stay here. I like you. You're … well … you're tall.
And I like that in a customer. I'm kidding. That's my humor.
You're sitting down. You could be short for all I know.

SIOBHAN: Coffee please, black.

WAITER: Oh my God. Same here. We are so much alike already. I
can tell we're going to be great friends. Ask me how I take
my coffee.

SIOBHAN: I'm gonna regret this …

WAITER: Go on. Ask me.

SIOBHAN: OK. How do you take your coffee?

WAITER: Black. Like my presidents.

SIOBHAN: Uh-huh.

WAITER: Sorry. And I promised the boss I wouldn't make political jokes. Don't tell him. He's a Log Cabin Republican and
we agreed to disagree.
    Coffee (*whispers*) black. Coming up.

(WAITER *exits. She dials her phone.*)

Noise from the street Car alarm, beat box, etc. WAITER *turns into* CON-
STRUCTION WORKER *in hat and orange vest. Sunglasses. And stands at
a corner.* CASSIE *appears as if on a street somewhere. Each time* CASSIE
walks by—CONSTRUCTION WORKER *changes his sign from 61 STREET to
60 STREET, 59 STREET, and so on.* CASSIE'*s phone rings.* CONSTRUCTION
WORKER *is also on the phone.*)

CONSTRUCTION WORKER: You have a NICE ASS, honey.

CASSIE: (*Caught off guard but not offended.*) Thank you. You have a nice ass too.

CONSTRUCTION WORKER: I am talking to my wife!

CASSIE: Oh. (*Now she is offended.*)

(CONSTRUCTION WORKER *walks off while holding phone and becomes the* MAN IN DOUGHNUT BOOTH.)

CASSIE: (*Looking at cell.*) Who is this calling... Siobhan!

Hey there! I have been a MESS without you. I've missed ALL my appointments. EVERYthing in the office is in shambles. I can't do anything for myself. And that is a tribute to YOU! You keep me organized.

So, how are you? Are you done grieving? Or recovering? Or whatever you were doing? I don't mean to sound— however I sound. I'm just anxious to have you back. Are you ready to come back to work?

SIOBHAN: Hi. Yes. Well. I don't know. Hello?

CASSIE: How are you feeling? I really want to know.

SIOBHAN: I think I'm doing pretty well for someone who just doesn't give a fuck anymore.

CASSIE: Oh, well that's good.

SIOBHAN: I'm having a hard time.

CASSIE: Oh, I know you are, angel. Anyone would. I am so sorry. But remember. You are an ox. You are a great big strong ox. And I mean that in the nicest way. You don't look like an ox. You're just very strong like an ox. Do oxen still exist? Or are they extinct. Google that for me, honey. I always like to learn new things. But back to you. You're doing well?

(CASSIE *walks toward* MAN IN DOUGHNUT BOOTH.)

SIOBHAN: No, I'm not. I am having a really hard time with this whole thing.

CASSIE: Siobhan, honey. I am there for you. Or here for you. (*To* DOUGHNUT MAN.) Could you give me a bagel with a schmear? (*In phone.*) I am here *and* there for you.

(*To man.*) A schmear. Cream cheese, honey. Where are you from? Afghanistan? Oh, sorry. Just the coffee. No cream cheese. Forget the bagel. Forget the coffee. (*Into phone.*)

Didn't you read the book I sent over? *When Bad Things Happen to Good People?*

SIOBHAN: No. I'm reading my *Louise Hay* book again and my *Love Is Letting Go of Fear* book and I have my mother's musical affirmations. Oh. And a book called *Toxic Parents.* I like that title. And some other book someone gave me— About how not to be angry at the god*damn motherfuckers who are ruining my life* book.

CASSIE: No. You know what? None of those books work. You have to read *When Bad Things Happen to Good People.* You! are a good person.

SIOBHAN: Uh-huh.

CASSIE: Siobhan? Repeat. You are a good person.

SIOBHAN: You are a good person.

CASSIE: No, say *I* am a good person.

SIOBHAN: YOU are a good person?

CASSIE: Forget it, honey. We're both good people.

(SIOBHAN *cries.*)

Siobhan? Forget work for today. Let's meet at Bergdorf. We'll steal designs and I'll knock them off. We can shop till we drop.

MAN PASSING ON STREET: I hate that expression. Shop till you drop. It's stupid.

CASSIE: Who asked you? Shut the fuck up!

SIOBHAN: What?

CASSIE: Not you, honey.

MAN ON STREET: (*Into cell.*) Some old lady just told me to shut the fuck up. What is wrong with people?

CASSIE: I am not an old lady! I haven't even had Botox yet, ya big lug. I'm sorry. You little lug. Meet me at Bergdorf.

MAN PASSING ON STREET: OK. After I finish my call.

CASSIE: Not you, putz. My friend.

SIOBHAN: (*Through her tears.*) Bergdorf? Where is that again? (*She hyperventilates.*) I don't know where that is. I don't know how to find it. I don't have a GPS on my phone.

CASSIE: Oh, honey. Forget it. I'll grab a cab and come to you. Now, no more tears. Do you hear me? No more tears.

Pretend you're a shampoo. Stop crying. No more tears. I'll be right there. Where are you?

SIOBHAN: Downtown.

CASSIE: Oh God. You're not at that Paris Commune, are you?

SIOBHAN: Café Sha Sha.

CASSIE: Good. 'Cause I don't do Paris Commune ever since Ari and Tony left. It's still lovely—but I want to keep my memories.

SIOBHAN: What?

CASSIE: Nothing, honey. A little joke to myself. Taxi!

(*She gets into a "cab" represented by chairs with wheels. The cabdriver is on his cell and driving. He is speaking in another language.*)

FOREIGN TAXI DRIVER: Lazoomish. Lazoomish. Kapechaka? AH HAA! Lazoominsh. Nein! NEIN! Ashkanazi.

CASSIE: Could you not talk on the phone while you drive? It's rude. And anyway—Isn't there a law in New York?

TAXI: Zoom zoom zoom. Jibberish BITCH Americans Jibberish jibberish. Just kidding. I LOVE America! Zoom zoom zoom. Lady. I no talk on phone.

CASSIE: Well, thank you.

(*The driver starts to text instead.*)

NO! Please DO NOT TEXT while driving. That is worse than talking! Are you INSANE? Not you, honey, the cabdriver. You hear me? It is RUDE to text on the phone when you are driving. Can't people go one second when they're not on the phone?

SIOBHAN: No, I guess they can't.

CASSIE: I'm going to report you to someone.

DRIVER: (*Not understanding what she said.*) Yes. Yes. Thankyouvery-much. Lazzominsh Lazoomish Kapeechka. Chaka. Chaka. Chaka-kahn.

(*Taxi drops her off at the table.*)

CASSIE: (*Still on cell.*) I am so tired of taxis in the city. I am walking everywhere from now on.

SIOBHAN: We can hang up now. We're both here.

CASSIE: That's right. Where is the waiter? (*She hangs up. Studies* SIOBHAN *for a second.*) How are you? Before you tell me, and I do want to know—oh, someone is texting me. 'Scuse me for one sec. Oh shhhh-nanigans. I need to make a quick call. Read your book for a second.

SIOBHAN: I deserve to be loved.

CASSIE: Yes, you do. Hold that thought, honey. I need to call into the office. Because *you're* not there to help me. Otherwise I wouldn't be so rude.

(*On cell.*) Hi. It's me. Listen. I'm taking the afternoon off. "You know who" has had a major tragedy in her life. And she needs me to listen.

What's the problem? How many pieces do they want for the Chicago store? Can we make delivery on that?

Well, call China—the number is on my 'puter. 'PUTER. Computer. I don't have time to say the whole word. I don't have a secretary! (*To* SIOBHAN.) No offense.

Just do it! I have a friend in CRISIS for crying out loud. Try and keep up with me. Ask that new designer person if you need help. He should have the number for China. No. Do NOT have him call me. He has been *creeping on my book* for a whole year. *Creeping on my book.* Facebook. Never mind. Go ask a young person.

SIOBHAN: Friends listen to me when I speak. My needs are as important as other people's needs.

CASSIE: Could you do your affirmations a little quieter, honey? I'll be off in a second, angel.

SIOBHAN: I deserve to take up space.

CASSIE: And you do. That's right. You go, girl. (*Into cell.*) Honey. I need to hang up. "You know who" is very needy right now because of that *thing* that happened to her. I can't tell you now. She's sitting right here. I'll text you later. Call CHINA!

(*The* WAITER *comes back. He is on cell, listening. He puts two coffees down.*)

I didn't ask for coffee, but thank you.

WAITER: (*To* CASSIE.) I'm an intuitive. I know things.

CASSIE: Oh. Well, thank you.

WAITER: No worries.

CASSIE: Do I look worried?

WAITER: (*Into cell.*) And what did he say? And what did she say?

CASSIE: Where can I smoke?

WAITER: Out the front door and around the back. Behind the building.

(*He points. She goes.*)

CASSIE: He knew I needed coffee? But he couldn't *intuit* I need to smoke?

WAITER: (*To a customer in the audience.*) Yes, I will be with you in a minute! Put your hand down or I will call you out like you're a number in a bingo game. (*Cell.*) And what did she say? She SAID that?

(*He looks at someone else in the audience.*) I'm sorry. I don't know where your waiter is. (*Cell.*) And what did HE say? Uh-huh uh-huh. Wait a second I'm getting a text.

(*He texts and speaks while texting.*) Not free 4 din 2 night. Sorry. Send.

Hi. I'm back. Yes. It was him. The married guy I'm kinda dating. Am I a bad person? I am? I don't think that I am. Tch. Is that your call waiting? UH! Yeah. Go ahead. I'll hold.

(*He waits and looks around. To same audience "customer."*)

Sorry I was rude. What did you need? (*In cell.*) Oh hi, hold on. (*To customer.*) Hold on a second. (*To cell.*) I'm at work. Somebody wants something. (*To customer.*) What? (*Cell.*) No. Just hold a second. Hold on. (*To customer.*) What do you need, a check? Oh. Well why didn't you say so? Pay on your way out. (*Cell.*) Hold on. I'm getting another text from the married guy. (*Reading and texting.*)

(*Lights down on café. Lights up on* CASSIE *"outside" the café holding an unlit cigarette.*)

CASSIE: (*On cell.*) I'm out with my assistant. She's talking my ear off so I came out for a cigarette. God. (*Looking at audience.*) You should see all the smokers out here. I'm trying to quit. I'm down to three unlit cigarettes a day. No, I just hold them. It's something to put in my mouth. Ha ha. I was at the Kenneth Cole sample sale. Clean simple lines never go out of fashion. No. Then I went to Dulcifino. And there was a really pretty pink blouse. And one was coral, and one was turquoise. I know, sweetie. Sweetie. I know the colors aren't right for here. They are for my trip to Florida. You can't wear black in Florida. Well, you just can't.

Yes, they *are* pastel, but they are pretty. Why are you being so hostile to pastels? I choose colors for a living. Hellllooo... I have a magnificent sense of color.

We're leaving next week. It's Shavuot. So we have to go. It's the birthday of the Jewish religion. That's all I know. I'm not a very good Jew. But apparently it's very important. Bradley jokes that I'm only Jewish by injection. We have to see his family. Well they can't live forever. And where there's a will, there's a way. LOL.

(*Lights black out and come right back on. The* WAITER *is now sitting.* SIOBHAN *is pouring him coffee.*)

WAITER: Well. I hate the word "marriage" as a concept. Why not call it a civil union? It's not like marriage worked out for all those people anyway. The guy texting me is married for crying out loud. Hold on that's him calling now. Hey, Bradley. (*Laughs.*) A shirt and pants and an apron. Yes. It's hot. It's very hawt. Boxers. Or briefs. I don't remember. You can find out later. No, I'm not free to talk like this now. I am working. (*To* SIOBHAN.) Men! Can live with 'em, can't kill 'em. (*To cell.*) ANYwho. I have to hang up. Call me later. Maybe I can get free. I have to go. (*Listens.*)

Stop it. I'm sitting next to some sad woman with a tragedy or something. I don't know. When I find out, I'll tell you. But I think it's something really really bad. She was crying and everything. I know. Who are all these people who can have coffee during the day? Doesn't anybody work? (*To her.*) Not you, I'm glad you're here. (*In phone.*) Bradley! I'm hanging up. Bye. Call me. (*He hangs up.*)

(CASSIE *comes back to table.* WAITER *gets up.*)

CASSIE: OK. I'm all yours now. What are you doing in my chair. Get up. (*Her cell rings.*) It's my husband. I have to take it. It's the last one. I promise.

(*The waiter sits on the other side of* SIOBHAN *so she is now between the* WAITER *and* CASSIE.)

Yes, dear. No. I left the office. I am out with Siobhan. My friend Siobhan. (*Lowering her voice.*) My assistant. She's the permanent temp in my office. Yes. The one in AA and DA and SA. She's in *all* the anonymous groups. I don't want to tell you. She is sitting right next to me. It's supposed to be anonymous. (*To* SIOBHAN.) Right, honey? (*In cell.*) Bradley. Bradley! You've met her a gazillion times. She delivers your dry cleaning.

Right. Siobhan. It's an Irish name. She's my little shiksa friend. I was shopping the stores for product when she called. Siobhan! S-I-O. No S like Sam...S-i-o-b-h-a-n.

Well, I don't know. The first syllable is pronounced *shhh* like SHUT UP. And Vaughn. Like, von. The *bh* must make a *v* sound. I don't know! They're Irish. They were probably drunk.

Oh give me a break. I'm tired of all this politically correct nonsense. The Irish drink, Jews shop and actors are waiters and that's the end of that. Stereotypes are stereotypes for a reason. Uh-huh. Well, she needed to talk, so I took the day off. That's the kind of person I am. Bradley!

I told you what happened to her. Yes, I did. I told you. Well, I'm out in public—I can't tell you again. Try and replay the conversation in your memory. I thought you were busy tonight. I just made plans to go to yoga—I thought you had a client dinner. Oh. Well, order in. Who's calling you? OK. Well, call me back. (*To* SIOBHAN.) Gotta tinkle, honey. Be right back.

(*She goes to the restroom.* WAITER *calls Bradley.*)

WAITER: Hey, Brad. I'm suddenly free tonight if you want to come over. The thing I was doing got canceled. What? You are bad. Yeah. I can take a picture of it on my cell—but I would need to go to the bathroom.

(WAITER *leaves.*)

SIOBHAN: Wow. Wow, and wow. Wherever you go—there you are. Someone said that.

Sometimes I feel like my brain is going to explode. I don't

know how to be alive in this world anymore. Sometimes
I feel completely invisible. And then sometimes I feel like I
am the elephant in the living room.

I had this stupid idea that when I got sober and stopped
doing drugs and stopped being a sex addict—that my life
would be better. But then there are all these PEOPLE
that come along—and you didn't notice them before
because you were self-medicating—so not only "wherever you go there *you* are," but "wherever you go—there
THEY are."

And then for the five minutes a day I'm NOT thinking
about myself... I turn on TV and I hear the same three top-
ics hashed and rehashed to death! The same ten sentences
are repeated on the *Today* show and the This show and the
THAT show... The same shit. Over and over.

I am worn out by consumers... and consumption and all
the me me me.

(*A customer enters with a violin case under his arm and stands by the*
WAIT TO BE SEATED *sign. She turns her attention to him.*)

What do you think of me. Me and my life. Me and my little
motherfucking life. And I am sorry to use the word fuck. I
tried to think of another word to express how I feel... and
you know what? There isn't one. "If you were more intelligent you could express yourself without resorting to the
use of profanity."

Oh really? Well FUCK YOU! I am NOT more intelligent.
'Cause you have FUCKING used that up in me. I have lost
that chance. I have missed that boat. That ship has sailed.

Do you like my nautical references more than saying fuck?

I am not a seafarer. I was NOT raised on a lovely mother-fucking lake. With "water rights." I did not even SEE an ocean until one week ago. And that was an accident. I must have taken a wrong turn at Albuquerque.

That's a Bugs Bunny reference. You kids today don't know about Bugs Bunny. He was the first person I saw dressed up in drag. He used to put on lipstick and kiss Elmer Fudd. And that's when I realized—why do I have to wear lipstick? And yet, I do. I still have luscious lips. Don't you think?

Are you all staring at my luscious lips?

Oh God. I think my medication is starting to wear off.

(*To violin man.*) You'd better go. I don't think you're going to get service today. The waiter is off taking pictures of his penis.

(*The man looks horrified or confused and leaves.*)

Well, that shut him up.

They should list the side effects for going *off* your medication.

Side effects include… "having an actual feeling." Actually *hearing* the people around you. Realizing your life is a mess. Your relationships shallow.

Bugs Bunny probably wouldn't be allowed to be taught in school today. He'd be on Prozac. Ricochet Rabbit would be on lithium. I'm bing bing bing! Ricochet Rabbit! Oh my God. I don't think I should have stopped cold turkey…

(CASSIE *returns.*)

CASSIE: I'm back. And I am all ears.

SIOBHAN: People don't really care. Don't you find that people mostly just want to talk about themselves?

CASSIE: No, I don't find that at all.

SIOBHAN: You don't?

CASSIE: No. For instance. The other day I was at a convention. I was the guest speaker...

SIOBHAN: You're doing it now.

CASSIE: What?

SIOBHAN: You're talking about yourself.

CASSIE: I am not. I'm explaining to you how I don't talk about myself. By way of example.

SIOBHAN: Go on.

CASSIE: And I was giving a speech. A pep talk to the poor women there. Mostly homeless abused women. Horrible, unattractive homeless abused women.

Some of them still fat—which I never understand. How do you stay fat when you are homeless?

The government should study that. Fat homeless people. How? We could solve world hunger problems if we crack that nut. These women probably really DO have a thyroid problem. Sad...

SIOBHAN: I've lost the thread.

CASSIE: I'm telling about how if homeless women would just dress better they could get a job. That's really their biggest problem.

SIOBHAN: Uh-huh.

CASSIE: And it's great! Because at the end of my lecture—we give them all donated clothing and free cell phones. And we show them how to make phone calls and put on makeup.

Well, some of them were prostitutes—so we show THEM how to put on LESS makeup. It's really one of the best things I've done in my adult life. I really feel good about myself.

SIOBHAN: Side effects of going off your medication include: You will absolutely hear the narcissism of the people around you.

CASSIE: You know, you never really did tell me what happened to you.

SIOBHAN: You will question every decision you have ever made in your life.

CASSIE: People are asking me what your problem is—and I am embarrassed to tell them, I don't know. And I should know. I am your boss and best friend. And it is not my prurient interest that wants to know. I care. I care deeply. Do I need to explain prurient? Tell me what happened.

SIOBHAN: I have told you all about it several times. In gruesome detail.

CASSIE: You did? Well, tell it to me again. I probably wasn't listening because I was so upset for you.

SIOBHAN: Do not go off your medication without your doctor's approval—as this may make you too aware of the people around you.

CASSIE: 'Cause I am in pain too. I am a feeling person.

SIOBHAN: Can we be quiet together for a minute?

CASSIE: Sure, honey. I love being quiet. I am a very quiet person. Silence is very profound to me.

(SIOBHAN *makes a "sshhhh." Raising her finger gently to her mouth.*)

CASSIE: OK. We'll be quiet now. Just enjoy each other's company. Until you're ready to talk and you can tell me what happened to you. OK. Let's stop talking.

(*She sits quietly. Quiet. Quiet. Then.*)

Was it about all your credit card debt? Infidelity? Cancer? AIDS?

SIOBHAN: Yes. It was all of that. Now please. Shhhhh.

CASSIE: OK. It's nice to be quiet. People should learn to not speak. There is too much people speak. And I am the first to admit it. I'm going to India next year for six-week silence. I will love that. You know . . . if you ever wanted to slip into one of my homeless women talks . . . you could take home an outfit or two. Oh shi-nannigans. There's my beep. Do you mind if I text? I'll do it quietly.

(*She moves to another part of the café.* WAITER *takes this opportunity to move over to* SIOBHAN.)

WAITER: I had a revelation yesterday...I had a midafternoon appointment and I don't like to come home early unless it's winter...If I'm interacting with people—even here—I am alive I am fresh. It was midafternoon and I was home...And I knew there had to be a reason I would go home early.

And there was a movie star standing outside my apartment. Filming. It was a sign. And there are people in this business that function at a million kilowatts. And I can't believe I'm not producing something. And here is this powerhouse. And I knew something big was going to happen to me that day.

SIOBHAN: Did it?

WAITER: No. But it doesn't always. The seed may have been planted. The seed. Who knows? Maybe I will see that actor again. Maybe she will come in here and recognize me from the street.

SIOBHAN: And do what? Give you a job?

WAITER: It could happen. There's a reason I'm not further along. Here's my excuse. For not being further along.

I stopped doing anything after September 11. And that's not an excuse. But it is. And it's true. My little brother was born on that day and he can speak three languages now. He's won awards for little-kid things already. He's practically applied to medical school already—and I still work here.

A whole generation is growing up and I still work here, stuck. Stuck in the Sha Sha. I feel so disconnected sometimes. And when I meet someone—like the movie star (*Smiles at* SIOBHAN.) or even you...I feel better. Like there is hope.

SIOBHAN: Really?

WAITER: Being here with you. Right now. This is a very pure moment for me.

CASSIE: Ohmygod. My husband. First he's free. Then he's not free. Then he's free? Then he's not free.

WAITER: Siobhan and I are having a quiet moment.

CASSIE: Fabulous. I love quiet moments. What a perfect way to meditate. Silence. Yum. Silence.

WAITER: Yes, silence. (*Silence.*) I'm going to channel an entity now. There is someone who wants to come through. Someone who wants to speak to you.

SIOBHAN: OK...

(*The* WAITER *speaks in different voices. The italics are "the entity."*)

WAITER: *First I want to thank this waiter for allowing me to speak to you today.* Oh, that's OK. Go ahead. *Thank you.* You're welcome. I love channeling. *Well we thank you. But you need to breathe and allow me to come through.* OK. *You should probably breathe too.* You breathe too. (*She does.*) *You are not to kill yourself today. You have more to do.*

SIOBHAN: How did you know?

WAITER: You're going to kill yourself? Ohmygod. *Please don't interrupt me.* Sorry.

SIOBHAN: Sometimes I just want to die.

WAITER: *You people are so funny. You do not ever die. But do not leave this planet now.* I agree. Bad karma. *I am here for you. Waiting. And helping. This too—shall pass.* That's true it will. *And killing your earth body is not how you are meant to exit this world. It's* just not smooth. It is not the way out. *There are many of us here waiting to greet you. (Laughs.) But we are not in any hurry to see you here. Stay there. Have fun.* He's right. You should listen to him or her or them.

SIOBHAN: It just gets so hard sometimes.

WAITER: So, take a pill, gurl. Get a therapist. Read a book. Learn a life lesson. *I'm not through.* Oh, sorry. I thought you were. *I have more to say.* Well, go ahead. I am all ears. *Stop seeing married men.* What? Who, me? *Yes, you. It's not the agreement you should be making in this life.* He started it. *You men confuse the need for sex with the need for nurturing. You must learn how to nurture each other. This goes for your straight friends too.* OK. Are you done now? My shift is almost over. *I think so.*

CASSIE: Are there any words for me?

WAITER: He's gone now. *No, I'm not. I'm still here.* Oh, sorry.

CASSIE: What should I do?

WAITER: Stop shopping. There is too much stuff in the world.

CASSIE: I can't believe the spirit told me to stop shopping.

WAITER: He didn't that was me. *But I agree.* Yeah. How many little black dresses do you need?

CASSIE: Seven.

SIOBHAN: I don't feel better. When will I feel better?

WAITER: *You may never feel better. And as soon as you know that—* you will feel better.

CASSIE: Does that make you feel better?

SIOBHAN: Not so much.

WAITER: *You must get back in touch with your inner child.*

SIOBHAN: My inner child is dead.

WAITER: She's a rough customer. *I will help you. Picture this . . . A little bunny frolics by a stream. A cute little happy bunny. A butterfly lands on his nose. The bunny giggles.*

SIOBHAN: Goooo ga . . . Gooooo . . . little bunnies. (SIOBHAN *makes happy baby faces.*)

WAITER: *Very good.* Give me one. I want to get in touch with MY inner child too. *No, no, no. You must get in touch with your inner adult. Your inner child is way too present.* How rude.

CASSIE: What about me? What should I do?

WAITER: *You are fine. You add color to the world.*

CASSIE: That's true I do add color.

WAITER: Would you like anything else before I go? My shift is almost over. *Young man! Isn't there something you need to cancel?* Oh, right.

CASSIE: That reminds me. (*She calls.*)

WAITER: (*He texts.*) Bradley. I can't see you. I only date available people. End of story.

CASSIE: Bradley. If you get free . . . come down to Café Sha Sha and have coffee with me. The waiter here channels. It's great fun.

WAITER: Now. Let's all act happy. It's a choice. Smile. It gives your face value.

SIOBHAN: You sound like my mother.

WAITER: Hey! Mothers keep the earth alive...Except the ones that kill it. Like mine. But that's a different story for another day. Just smile and psych yourself out. Denial is a good thing sometimes. (*He smiles.*)

CASSIE: I love it. He is right. Like right now? (*She smiles.*) I'm very depressed. But would you ever know it? No. Because I buck up. I move on. And I will continue to shop. I won't apologize for it. I am helping the economy. I'll stop shopping when I cross over.

SIOBHAN: I will smile too. No matter how angry I am.

WAITER: *Revenge is not the answer. If you are going to seek revenge— you better dig two graves.* I got that in a fortune cookie once.

CASSIE: Don't think about it. Whatever it is.

WAITER: Don't.

SIOBHAN: Don't think about it.

CASSIE: Nam myoho renge kyo.

WAITER: Smile. You smile too. *I always smile.*

CASSIE: Yes.

SIOBHAN: Yes...

(*They all smile.* SIOBHAN *takes out her gun.*)

SIOBHAN: (*Singing.*) I'm safe now. All my doors are locked. All my guns are cocked. Killers lurk outside.

WAITER: That's a little dark.

CASSIE: It is, but that's what makes you interesting. (*She begins song.*) We're safe now...

WAITER AND CASSIE: (WAITER *joining* CASSIE.) All our doors are locked. All our windows down.

SIOBHAN: (*Sung.*) But killers lurk outside.

WAITER: (*Sung.*) But maybe they'll go away.

CASSIE: (*Sung.*) They all got captured now.

WAITER: (*Sung.*) The bunnies lurk outside. (*Entity.*) *And they frolic by a stream.*

CASSIE: That's right.

SIOBHAN: Bunnies frolicking. Happy. Little. Bunnies.

(CASSIE *and* WAITER *continue to smile.* SIOBHAN *tries—but it is hard. She alternately smiles and looks worried—and holds her gun or perhaps gets up to look outside...waiting...watching...as...lights start to fade to black. Slower fade on* SIOBHAN *and gun. Blackout.*)

END OF PLAY

AFFIRMATIONS FOR SIOBHAN BY HER MOM

THE RENTAL

Mark Harvey Levine

The Rental was first produced in August 1998 at the MET Theatre in Los Angeles, California. It was directed by Chuck Rose, with the following cast:

> SONYA Carolyn Lawrence
> HAROLD Gary Paul Clark

The Rental received its Equity premiere in May 2005 at the Phoenix Theatre in Indianapolis, Indiana. It was produced and directed by Bryan D. Fonseca, with the following cast:

> SONYA Sara Riemen
> HAROLD Michael Shelton

SONYA's *apartment, early morning. There is a knock at the door. Sonya staggers out, half awake, tying on a robe. At her door is* HAROLD, *a thirtyish, normal-looking man in a nice coat. He carries a bouquet of flowers, a clipboard, and a picnic basket.*

HAROLD: (*Through door.*) Hello, Sonya? It's Harold!

SONYA: . . . Who?

HAROLD: (*Through door.*) Harold! Valerie sent me. Valerie Persky?

SONYA: Valerie . . . ?

(*She opens her door a little. She gapes at all the stuff he has.*)

Oh my God!!! What did she do?

HAROLD: (*Handing her the flowers.*) Happy Birthday from Valerie Persky. I'm Harold, your boyfriend.

(*He kisses her in a familiar manner, and enters.*)

SONYA: I . . . I . . . What?!

HAROLD: (*Quickly.*) Let me get this stuff in the fridge . . . Honey, did I wake you? I did. I'm so sorry. Sit down, relax, I'll be right back. Is this the kitchen? Great.

(*He exits to kitchen.* SONYA *grabs a baseball bat she has by the door.*)

SONYA: Excuse me! Excuse me! Hello? Who are you?

HAROLD: (*Offstage.*) I'm Harold! Harold, your boyfriend.

SONYA: My boyfriend?!

HAROLD: (*Offstage.*) Yeah...You know, for your birth—?

(*He reenters and sees her with the bat. He ducks behind the couch.*)

Aaaah! Don't shoot!

SONYA:...It's a baseball bat.

HAROLD: All right, don't hit.

SONYA: I'm pretty sure I'd remember having a boyfriend.

HAROLD: From Valerie! I'm from your friend Valerie! Wait, wait...I come with a card.

(*He holds out a standard "enclosure card," which she grabs and opens.*)

SONYA: Well, this IS her handwriting. (*Reading.*) "Sonya...what do you get for the girl who deserves everything? Well, you deserve a really great boyfriend, so I got you one, for today at least. Don't wear him out, ha ha. Happy thirtieth! Love, Valerie." (*Pause.*) You gotta be kidding.

HAROLD: You had no idea I was coming. Okay, okay...this happens occasionally. Once they sent me to the wrong house; I thought I was gonna have to date an eighty-year-old guy named Lou...

SONYA: (*Waving bat.*) They?! Who's they? What is this?

HAROLD: Wait! I'm your birthday present! From Rent-a-Boyfriend, Ltd.!...Apparently, I'm a SURPRISE birthday present.

SONYA: Rent-a-Boyfriend, Ltd.?!

HAROLD: I can explain, if you promise not to shatter my skull.

(*Still suspicious, she lowers the bat.*)

Thank you. (*The company speech.*) "Rent-a-Boyfriend, Ltd., has been providing the finest in temporary romantic relationships to the discriminating woman since 1985." I've been rented to you for our sixteen-hour "*affaire de coeur*" package. I'm sure you'll enjoy it, it's one of our most popular ones.

SONYA: I'm going to kill Valerie for this.

HAROLD: Listen, this is a generous gift. And I can promise you a relationship that, though brief, will create a burning, romantic memory that will shine in your heart to the end of your days. (*Pause, she snickers.*) They make me say that.

SONYA: So you're a...a gigolo?

HAROLD: No, no, no. A professional boyfriend. It's a specialized craft. There's six months of training, three months of supervised infatuation...

SONYA: Valerie rented me a boyfriend.

HAROLD: It's a very thoughtful present. She told me that...um, that you've had a lot of...disappointments in this area. Well,

Sonya, you're about to have the most fantastically romantic day of your life.

SONYA: This is crazy...

HAROLD: (*Really selling it.*) Is it? Sonya, today you have someone who cherishes you the way you should be cherished. Who adores the way you curl your fingers in your hair, the way you move across a room. The way you hold a baseball bat. Someone who lives and breathes and dies upon the merest glance of your cobalt blue eyes...

(*Sonya's starting to crack.*)

...and all you have to say is yes, I deserve this. Yes, at long last. Yes.

SONYA: ... Yes.

HAROLD: (*Whipping out a contract.*) Sign here.

SONYA: (*Signing.*) I don't believe I'm doing this. But you know what, I DO deserve it.

HAROLD: Of course you do. And initial here, and here.

SONYA: (*Initialing.*) After all the creeps, the bad dates, the blind dates, the personal ads, the—(HAROLD *kisses her full on the lips the moment she finishes signing.*)—mmmph!

HAROLD: Thank God we got that over with. Finally, I can hold you in my arms. Hello, sweetheart. Happy birthday.

SONYA: Wh— Okay. We've started, right?

HAROLD: Right. Your boyfriend has come to whisk you away

on a fun-filled birthday celebration! I've got a picnic here
I think you'll like. Salami and egg sandwiches! Chinese
noodles in sesame oil! Chocolate raspberry mousse cake!

SONYA: How do you know what my favorite foods are?!

HAROLD: Valerie told me. But remember, I'm your boyfriend. I
know all about you. You like Louis Prima records and old
Dick Van Dyke reruns. Your books are in strict alphabetical
order. You never wear beige. You live in constant fear you've
left your purse somewhere.

SONYA: My God.

HAROLD: But Valerie never told me you wake up first thing in
the morning looking breathtakingly gorgeous. I thought
that only happened in the movies.

SONYA: Wh–what? Oh God. I must look like hell.

HAROLD: You're stunning. Look at you. Your eyes are—

SONYA: Wait, wait...this is a little much for me right now,
okay? I don't like to be cherished before my first cup of
coffee.

(*He takes out a "travel cup" of coffee and hands it to her.*)

HAROLD: Ah! I brought you some. Dark-roast Kenyan. Your
fav—

SONYA: (*Overlapping.*) —My favorite...of course. I don't believe
this.

HAROLD: Sonya, my dear, this is just the beginning...

(*She sits stunned on the sofa, sipping coffee.* HAROLD *starts to massage her feet.* SONYA *protests, then, with an "I give up" wave, lets him.*)

First, I make you breakfast. Then it's off to Lavender Springs Spa, where you get a mud bath and a massage while I see how many sonnets I can compose about you. Then our picnic lunch in a secluded grove,—

SONYA: (*Stunned, softly overlapping.*) Uh-huh...

HAROLD:—a drive along the coast, sailing in the bay—

SONYA: (*Falling under his spell.*) Yeah sure...

HAROLD:—Our reservations at La Coupole are for seven-thirty, and afterwards a horse-drawn carriage takes us to—

(*He produces two tickets from his pocket.*)

SONYA: The Eric Clapton concert?!!! Oh my GOD!!! I love you!!!

(*She throws her arms around him. Then realizes what she's doing.*)

I'm sorry! I mean... Wow. You ARE good. Are you sure you're just here for one day?

HAROLD: It'll be a day to remember.

SONYA: (*Makes a little noise of disbelief.*) I... gotta get dressed. Would you... excuse me for a minute? Don't go anywhere.

HAROLD: Of course.

SONYA: I'll be right back. (*As she leaves.*) Oh my God... Oh my God!

(*She exits. He produces a Dustbuster-type sweeper and begins to casually clean.*)

(*Offstage.*) So...um...Harold. Do you do this often? I mean...how many...uh, girlfriends do you—

HAROLD: Sonya...right now there are no other women for me. I've never met anyone like you.

SONYA: (*Offstage.*) Oh...my...GOD.

(*She hops in, half dressed, putting on shoes.*)

Well, I've certainly never met anyone like—What the HELL are you doing?

HAROLD: Dusting.

SONYA: Don't! Don't...do that. Just...sit. Sit! Stay! You win. You are officially the best boyfriend I have ever had. Or ever will have.

(*She exits. He appears a little concerned over this last remark.*)

HAROLD: Really?

SONYA: (*Offstage.*) Are you kidding? Gold medal, Boyfriend Olympics, one-day sprint.

HAROLD: I was a little worried. We got off to a kinda weird start there, what with you swinging a baseball bat at me.

(SONYA *reenters, fully dressed.*)

SONYA: (*Peeved.*) You've been my boyfriend ten minutes, already we're reminiscing? Anyway, I didn't SWING it, I brandished it.

HAROLD: . . . in a threatening manner.

SONYA: How do you "brandish" in a nonthreatening manner?

HAROLD: All I'm saying, is, is we started off on the wrong—

SONYA: What the hell did you expect, a strange man comes bursting through my door, kisses me . . . you kissed me! You're lucky I didn't bash your brains in!

HAROLD: (*Beaming.*) We're having our first fight! Oh honey!

(*He hugs her.*)

SONYA: I'm not sure I'm ready for this kind of relationship.

HAROLD: I'm sorry, sweetheart. Let's forget about it.

SONYA: Yeah . . . yeah . . . we let it go too long . . .

(*He laughs. She leans back and relaxes into his arms.*)

I have to admit, this is nice. Y'know, this is all I wanted. Just to be in someone's embrace. Is this too much to ask?

HAROLD: Absolutely not.

SONYA: You know what? I want to walk down the street swinging our arms like we're fifteen.

HAROLD: Okay.

SONYA: I want to sit at a restaurant and stare into each other's eyes and completely annoy everyone else.

HAROLD: You got it!

SONYA: I can't wait to show up at yoga tomorrow. You'll drop me off with a quick kiss, and then watch as I—you're not gonna be here tomorrow.

HAROLD: Forget about tomorrow.

SONYA: It's just... kinda hard. Here I am, in your arms. And then you just leave? It's not fair. This is all I get? One really romantic day? For the rest of my life?

(*She starts to cry a little.*)

HAROLD: The nice thing about this kind of relationship is you KNOW when—Sonya? Are you—? No—don't cry! Oh God.

SONYA: I'm okay.

HAROLD: No, crying's bad. There's not supposed to be any crying.

SONYA: Oh, I cry all the time.

(*He grabs a tissue and starts to dry her tears himself.*)

I'm okay...

(*He hands her tissues—and then more tissues, until she has way too many. He places them on her, floats them at her, etc. She laughs.*)

HAROLD: Much better. You know, I just discovered something. I can't stand to see you cry.

SONYA: Oh, Harold. You're very sweet, y'know.

HAROLD: Sonya... there's something else... I love you.

SONYA: What?!

HAROLD: I love you! Can't you see it in my eyes?

SONYA: (*Since she is wiping her eyes.*) Not at the moment, no...

(*She continues to wipe her eyes.*)

> (*Jokingly glances at him for a split second.*) Yeah, now I can. Got it. (*Finishes wiping her eyes, then looks at him again.*) You can't be serious.

HAROLD: You don't believe in love at first sight?

SONYA: Do you mean it, or is this part of the package?

HAROLD: I'm your boyfriend. I really love you.

SONYA: How can you love me?

HAROLD: How could I not? You're warm, funny, smart—

SONYA: Stop stop. Look, I don't know if you're crazy, or I am, but—

HAROLD: Don't you deserve to be loved?

SONYA: Of COURSE I do. EVERYONE does. But this—you just—I mean, you don't REALLY really love me. You're doing this because Valerie paid you.

HAROLD: We have today, because someone paid for it, sure. But I do "REALLY really" love you. I love you, Sonya.

(*She stares at him. They move in closer... they almost kiss, but—*)

SONYA: Wait a minute. As presents go, this beats a basket of bath gels. But don't come in here telling me you love me.

HAROLD: But I do.

SONYA: Well, that's just swell! Where were you when I needed you? Like when my car was stolen. Or when my grandmother died? I could have used a boyfriend! You weren't there! I had to deal with that alone!

HAROLD: Sonya, I—

SONYA: And are you gonna be there tomorrow or the next day when something really good happens and I want to tell you about it? You gonna be there?

HAROLD: No, I'm not gonna be there.

SONYA: You love me. Ha! You're just like all the other men.

HAROLD: No, I'm not! I'm a trained professional!

SONYA: I mean, yes, I like romance. Yes, picnics are fun. But I want someone who . . . wants to do laundry with me. Or do absolutely nothing—with me.

HAROLD: We could do that too! I'm here to give you what you want!

SONYA: What I WANT is someone who not only knows my favorite coffee but also my soul. Love me? You haven't even MET me!

HAROLD: Listen, I thought I'd—

SONYA: You thought you'd give the girl a small thrill for once in her life?! I make my own thrills, darling. Hey, we're having our second fight!

HAROLD: I'm offering you love—

SONYA: No, thanks! Already got some! I've got my whole family! They drive me crazy, but they love me! And my friends—I have great friends! THEY love me! My God, look what Valerie did for my birthday. I have plenty of love, pal.

HAROLD: Do you.

SONYA: Yes I do. And I sure as hell don't need a Don Juan wannabe. Guess what, Harold, we're breaking up! I'll remember the ten minutes we had with great fondness. But y'know what? This isn't half a couple standing over here. Okay? I'm a whole couple all by myself. With a great family, incredible friends—I even kind of like my job! Y'know? So if I end up meeting someone, fine! If I don't, ALSO fine! Got it? I don't need you!

HAROLD: No, you don't.

SONYA: You better believe I don't! (*Still yelling.*) Did you just agree with me?!

HAROLD: Yeah, I did. Because you're right. You don't need me. But if you ever find someone...who deserves to love you...I will envy him. Good-bye, Sonya.

(*He exits. Pause. He returns, slightly embarrassed.*)

(*Company speech.*) "This has been a date from Rent-a-Boyfriend, Ltd. If you've enjoyed our service, please...tell a friend."

(*With a curt bow, he exits.* SONYA *stands stunned for a moment.*)

SONYA: (*Shouting after him.*) Hey! I enjoyed your service! Now get back here and MAKE ME BREAKFAST!

(*Blackout.*)

END OF PLAY

REUNIONS

Billy Aronson

Reunions was originally presented by the Ensemble Studio Theatre (Curt Dempster, artistic director) as a part of Marathon 2002. Jamie Richards directed the following cast:

TABBY	Hope Chernov
SARAH/CONNIE	Katherine Leask
ALAN/BRANDON	Thomas Lyons
RICK	Grant Shaud
NANCY	Maria Gabriele

CHARACTERS

TABBY ECKERSLY: Is an independent publisher.
SARAH BURK NELSON: Is a mother.
ALAN ROADS: Doesn't know what he is.
RICK ARZOOMANIAN: Is a pirate.
NANCY MCCANN: Is a giraffe.
CONNIE CUMMINGS: Is Santa Claus.
BRANDON TAVELLE: Is a warlock.

TABBY, SARAH, *and* ALAN *stand there talking.*

TABBY: Because in publishing the manuscript is everything, if you don't like the manuscript I mean that's all you've got, it's your life.

SARAH: Sure.

TABBY: And I was getting manuscripts that, well some of them were fine but I couldn't get behind them, not with every bone in my body.

SARAH: Uh-huh.

TABBY: And then one day I just woke up and it was clear as day that I had to just go ahead on my own.

SARAH: You're your own boss, that's so great.

TABBY: I have complete control, every single manuscript I believe in with every bone in my body, every fiber.

ALAN: I taught high school for eleven years! Then I quit and sold computers! Now I'm back in graduate school!

SARAH: I can't believe it's been nine years since I had a job.

TABBY: But you're a mom. That's so great.

SARAH: It's amazing, watching them figure stuff out, you learn so much.

TABBY: That's what everybody says.

SARAH: They're born with these real personalities, then they grow into these people that you really like, they're your pals, this whole team just came out of your body.

TABBY: It must be amazing.

SARAH: They can get you so angry, you never knew you could be so angry, or so in love, in whole new ways.

TABBY: I've really got to do that when I meet the right person.

SARAH: It's worth waiting for the right person.

ALAN: I keep meeting the right person but I can never convince her that I'm the right person!

TABBY: Now that I'm in control of my work it'll be easier.

ALAN: Let's head to the tent! There's going to be dancing!

SARAH: If I leave Bob with the kids one more minute he'll kill me.

TABBY: Has anybody seen Donna Cunningham? We said we'd share a table.

SARAH: Did you hear Connie Cummings is going to be here?

TABBY: Connie Cummings, really? I can't believe it.

SARAH: My kids are dying to meet her.

TABBY: When I tell people I went to school with Connie Cummings they think I'm making it up.—Hey is that Rick Arzoomanian? (*To off.*) Rick. Rick.

(RICK *enters. He's a pirate.*)

Tabby Eckersly. Remember?

RICK: Hey, Tabby.

TABBY: Did you know Sarah Burk?

SARAH: Sarah Burk Nelson.

RICK: Sarah, sure.

ALAN: I'm Alan Roads! I was friends with Gary Fine!

RICK: Hey, Alan.

TABBY: I read that you were a pirate in the paper, that's so great.

SARAH: Really.

RICK: I was getting nowhere on land. Just knocking on doors, year after year. So I put together a crew and headed out to sea.

TABBY: You just did it.

SARAH: That's so great.

RICK: It was tough out there for a while. There was nothing happening and the sun was killing us.

TABBY: Sure.

RICK: But then I saw this ship and I felt that it was ready for new ownership.

TABBY: You just had a feeling.

RICK: I felt the time was right and this was my chance. So I set my sights and I went for it with everything I had.

TABBY: Wow.

SARAH: I read about this.

RICK: It was a real battle, it was tougher than I thought. It cost me this eye, but we kept on fighting and we did it.

TABBY: That's something.

RICK: We pulled a real coup, and when I opened the treasure there were rubies and sapphires and diamonds packed together so tight. And just like that we went from struggling to stay afloat to being a major player on the sea.

TABBY: I'd been reading manuscripts that meant nothing to me, well some were okay but I couldn't get behind them so one morning I just woke up and decided to go independent and now it's great.

SARAH: I've missed working but you can't believe the way kids are born with these real personalities, you've got this whole team of people you love.

ALAN: I got sick of teaching so I went into sales and now I'm back in school!

RICK: Has anyone seen Chris Dumars?

SARAH: Are you in touch with Chris?

RICK: I haven't seen Dumars in years.

TABBY: Did you hear Connie Cummings is going to be here?

RICK: I heard she might.

ALAN: Let's head to the tent for the dancing!

TABBY: I was going to wait for Donna Cunningham and get a table.

SARAH: I've really got to get back to Bob and the kids or he'll kill me.

(SARAH *goes.*)

TABBY: But to have all that treasure, right at your feet, all of a sudden.

RICK: I felt shocked, and I felt proud.

TABBY: Now that I'm finally working on manuscripts I really believe in it's so liberating.

RICK: There were emeralds and sapphires and rubies—

ALAN: Guess I'll head to the tent!

(ALAN *goes.*)

TABBY: And didn't it totally make up for all the years, you know all the knocking on doors?

RICK: I had this feeling for the first time that I really was a pirate. I wasn't just pretending or going through the motions.

TABBY: At first I'd look down at these manuscripts and I couldn't believe I'm really attached to such brave and honest material that I can totally pour myself into.

RICK: We're a major player and heat isn't a problem, and we don't have to worry about the wind.

TABBY: My brain isn't chained to this garbage that I can't really get behind. I kept telling myself it would happen but it really has happened.

RICK: And I feel like this is just where I should be right now. And I'm headed exactly where I should be headed.

TABBY: Donna Cunningham's supposed to be here, we're going to get a table, you should join us.

RICK: That would be good.

TABBY: (*To off.*) Donna, is that you? Donna.

(NANCY *enters. She's a giraffe.*)

Nancy McCann. I'm sorry. I thought that you were Donna Cunningham.

RICK: Nancy. Hi.

TABBY: So you're a giraffe.

NANCY: (*Softly.*) Yes.

(RICK *and* TABBY *look at* NANCY. NANCY *looks at them.*)

RICK: That's Donna Cunningham over there.

TABBY: (*To off.*) Donna, it's me Tabby. Do you have an extra seat for Rick Arznoomanian? (*To* RICK.) She has an extra seat, you should join us.

RICK: That would be good. Except... is that Rich Kravitz at her table?

TABBY: Rich Kravitz and Donna used to go out.

RICK: I don't feel like sitting yet.

TABBY: But wouldn't you have a lot to say to Rich since he's a pirate too?

RICK: I think I'll stay here.

TABBY: He's a really successful pirate, you know that right, from the papers?

RICK: I don't read the papers.

TABBY: He was on magazines too, and TV for months.

RICK: I'll stay here and see who's around.

TABBY: You're sure?

RICK: I'll stay here I think.

TABBY: I really have to say hi to Donna.

RICK: Okay. I'll be here.

TABBY: Okay.

(TABBY *goes*. RICK *talks to* NANCY.)

RICK: It was a real battle all right, it cost me this eye. But we hung in there and we did it, and when I got to the treasure there were rubies and there were sapphires packed in there so tight. And there were diamonds, and now we're a major force on the sea. We're smaller than some. We're a small major force. So we're not so widely recognized. But we're expanding. (*To off.*) Connie Cummings. Connie.

(CONNIE *enters. She's Santa Claus.*)

CONNIE: (*To* RICK.) Stuart Beamish? Oh hi.

RICK: Rick Arzoomanian. Remember?

CONNIE: Rick, so you're a pirate, and Nancy you're a giraffe, what great things to be.

RICK: I'm a pirate all right, Connie.

CONNIE: It's a terrific time to be a pirate. And to be a giraffe.

RICK: And you're Santa Claus.

CONNIE: It's strange sometimes, to actually be the real Santa.

RICK: Sure.

CONNIE: To really be based in the North Pole. To actually fly the whole globe in one night.

RICK: It must be something.

CONNIE: Everybody makes a big deal about how I'm the first woman Santa and that's great, what it says to girls and what it means.

RICK: Sure.

CONNIE: But on a day-to-day basis it's much more about dealing with the media. Protecting the image, making it fresh for a new millennium.

RICK: Sure.

CONNIE: The elves handle construction pretty much on their own but you have to keep an eye on that, and deal with reindeer unions.

RICK: Uh-huh.

CONNIE: But when winter rolls around it's still about the joy, bringing joy to the world.

RICK: I'd been getting nowhere on land, year after year.

CONNIE: Uh-huh.

RICK: So I got a crew together and headed to sea and I saw this ship, and I had a feeling that it was ready for new ownership and so we took it on and—

CONNIE: Uh-huh.

RICK: —and when I opened the treasure I saw, there was—

(BRANDON *enters. He's a warlock.*)

BRANDON: Connie Cummings. Brandon Tavelle. Remember?

CONNIE: So you're a witch.

BRANDON: (*Wounded.*) I'm not a witch, I'm a warlock.

CONNIE: What a great thing to be, Brandon.

BRANDON: Always knew I had something. Through all the crap I endured. The winking and whispering at those cliquey drinking parties. Anthony Oaks and Sally Bottini. Or Little Miss Muppet and her brainless cronies in the back of the lecture hall saving four seats with an apple so they could point at me and giggle. Or the marching-band-lacrosse-gang with their esoteric handshakes and midnight singsongs which they always topped off with the obligatory run down the hallway to howl their lewd nicknames and puke in my shoes. I wanted to jump off the tower, but I buried myself in the library, found this book about spells and my God that was me. I could pull toads out of people's ears. I could turn those toads into snakes, and make the snakes disappear in a burst of flame. I knew I could do it, and now: I do. And it has this effect. A power. Not just on my parents. Total strangers come up to me, with this look, you can see it. They open their mouths, not a damn sound comes out, because they're speechless.

CONNIE: It's a terrific time to be in witchcraft.

BRANDON: (*Destroyed.*) I'm not a witch. I'm a warlock.

(BRANDON *storms off.*)

RICK: And when I opened the treasure there were rubies. And sapphires. And diamonds. And they were all packed in there so tight.

CONNIE: Huh.

RICK: Emeralds and rubies, and silver, there was silver in there. And I felt shocked and I felt proud, and so lucky, that it was all right there, all at once. Everything I needed was right at my feet, we'd gone from struggling to stay afloat to being a major force. And now the heat doesn't bother us, and the wind is no problem. We're going in just the right direction as a major force on the sea.

CONNIE: When I go flying on Christmas Eve I go down the chimney of everybody, every person on earth, rich and poor, every nation, from home to home to home it's such a rush as you get going, you get into this rhythm and it's intoxicating.

RICK: It must be.

CONNIE: To make their lives so full and so special with these things they've been dying for all year, things they want and they need that are thrilling and wholesome, pure joy that's really good for them, electric and lasting and real.

RICK: That's something.

CONNIE: To drop off their dreams and head back to the sky and hear billions of people gasping and screaming your name, can you imagine? Giving intensely personal perfect pleasure to every human being on earth and having that be your job? It's not even a job it's a privilege, I'm tremendously fortunate to be able to make life on earth worth living and bring the entire planet to this state of indescribable ecstasy again and again there's nothing like it.

RICK: Huh.

CONNIE: And the next day and the next to see entire families still caught in the glow of this golden moment and know you've lifted their hearts and brought a sense of hope and dignity and given them the strength to grow and really reach for their dreams and to feel in your gut that every chimney you went down was completely worthwhile.

RICK: Mm.

CONNIE: The stockings hung with glee for godsake, and the cookies and milk by the fireplace, and the songs all over the radio and TV specials on every network with every major pop star they can drag out singing your praise and the drawings, entire kindergarten classes doing drawings and collages and plays and your picture's on their lunch boxes I mean couldn't you die?

RICK: (*Nods.*)

CONNIE: There's nothing else I could stand for three seconds after this, any other work would be torture because absolutely nothing else gives such undisputed pleasure with total universal recognition and I'm so ridiculously lucky to be doing exactly what I'm doing I could laugh every second of my blest and spectacular life. (*To off.*) Hey, Stuart Beamish. It's me. Connie Cummings. I'm fucking Santa Claus.

(CONNIE *goes.* RICK *gasps for breath, staggers, fists clenched, suffocating.*)

RICK: She's lucky all right. Her uncle was Santa Claus. Like that didn't help. If my uncle was Santa Claus I'd be handing out presents. But my uncle wasn't Santa Claus. I was on my own. Knocking on doors. Dying in the heat. Till I saw that ship. And there was rubies. And silver. And diamonds. Where's Chris Dumars?

(RICK *staggers away, falls, crawls off.* NANCY *stands there.* TABBY *runs on, laughing and sobbing hysterically.*)

TABBY: Oh Nancy hi, did you know Donna Cunningham is pregnant, it's so great, they'd been trying for so long, and she's got this great guy, he gets along great with her friends, and Rich Kravitz has these adorable girls and the sweetest wife, and Sarah Burk's about to have her fourth, and Bob is such a great dad, and I'm finally working on manuscripts that really mean something to me, they're new and beautiful and fresh and so strong I can go out and push with every muscle in my body, every cell, all my blood and my skin and my guts and soul.

(TABBY *runs off.* NANCY *stands there.* ALAN *enters stepping carefully, struggling for balance.*)

ALAN: Nancy McCann! I'm Alan Roads! I was in your freshman comp! You wrote such great papers! I used to follow you across the green! Gary Fine and Gary Bowman said I should stop stalking you and ask you out! Meanwhile I didn't know Gary and Gary were going out with each other! I sure wish they were here now but they're dead! All my friends are gone and I have nothing to say and no idea what I'm doing! Hey the music's starting, let's dance Nancy McCann! You had great ideas and now your head's way up in the trees and I'm still down here, but I'd feel way up there if you'd dance with me! So let's dance, Nancy McCann! Can we dance?

NANCY: (*Softly.*) Yes.

(*A pop tune from years ago plays, such as "We Are Family."* ALAN *holds on to* NANCY. ALAN *and* NANCY *begin to dance.* RICK *and* TABBY *enter dancing together.*)

(*At first the dancing is self-conscious.* ALAN *and* NANCY *are timid and reserved.* RICK *and* TABBY *dance cautiously, carefully showing off to one another. But as they continue to dance, both couples let go, become more expressive, joyous, and free.* CONNIE *joins the dancing, as do* BRANDON *and* SARAH.)

END OF PLAY

RIPPER GIRL

Elizabeth Wong

Ripper Girl is an excerpt from *Dating & Mating in Modern Times*, a collection of twelve cocktail monologues for women by Elizabeth Wong. It was originally commissioned by the Playwriting Center of Theatre Emory for the Brave New Works Festival and produced by Theatre Emory, producing director Vincent Murphy.

The play premiered on September 20, 2003, at the Mary Gray Monroe Theatre in Atlanta, Georgia. Managing director was Pat Miller; set and lighting design was by H. Bart McGeehon; sound design was by Judy Zanotti; costume design was by Michael Reynolds; the vocal coach was Sheri Mann Stewart; the videographer was Ned Zimmerman; the stage manager was Gretchen E. Butler; Elizabeth Wong directed. The role of Cassie was played by Alex Newell.

It was first presented as a staged reading at Emory University. Dramaturgy was by Kate Snodgrass; stage manager was Emily F. McMullen; Elizabeth Wong directed. The role of Cassie was played by Laurel Ilvonen.

CAST
CASSIE: A teenage girl, *très* smart, vulnerable, yet always hiding behind self-deprecation and nonchalance; rebellious, insecure, classic underachiever; her escape is skateboarding but she's not competitive or planning on making it a career; in fact, she's not sure of much.

PLACE
Her messy bedroom.

TIME
Now.

PLAYWRIGHT'S NOTE
Special thanks to Vincent Murphy for his enduring support of me
and women's writing; and to my nephew Alex for lending me his
skateboard and introducing me to the world of Tony Hawk.

CASSIE, *late teens, has a well-used, banged-up skateboard with lots of
stickers affixed.*

CASSIE: We don't date. Kids my age, we hang out. We just kick
it. So basically, if you want a boyfriend, it's not like he asks
you out. Guys just corner you at some party, and if you suck
face, that's it. No one gets all that formal. I tried having a
boyfriend once, but I got sick of waitin' by the phone for
him to call, so I just grabbed my board, and headed out to
a place I heard about, down by the culvert. It's a dried-out
drainage pipe, a really cool find. I heard some of the biggest
rip dogs come down here, but no one was around. Had the
pipe all to myself. Which was fine with me. I'm alone a lot.
Which is fine. I'm not what you call popular, and like, well,
I'm pretty dumb. Stupid actually, that's what my father says
when he sees my report cards.

(*Deftly, she flips up her board with her foot, and catches it with
confidence.*)

I was gettin' into my style. Flowing and slashing like
Jackie Chan. I was in a groove, and feelin' no pain. Just this
rush of speed, the rumble below my feet, the sound of my
wheels on concrete. This pipe was so sweet. So I got kinda

bold. I tried for a goofy foot tail grab and totally missed big-time.

(*She jumps, hits the ground hard, and rolls and rolls and rolls to a stop.*)

Heard this sick pop. Like the bone here is sticking out, and I'm freakin'. I've never been hurt bad before, and this was bad. Then this guy, like from nowhere, like out of thin air, like some crazy-ass angel, comes running up to me. I'm holding my leg like this. Dude goes, "You were rad. For a girl, you have this awesome rubber-band style." I go, "Shut up." He goes, "You're gonna be okay, don't talk okay?" I go, "Just shut up." He goes, "I was up there watchin', you were awesome." I go, "You thought so?" He goes, "Absolutely. And oh, by the way, I called 911." I go, "I'm gonna pass out." He goes, "You should tighten your nuts. Your trucks are loose."

On the way to the hospital, he tightens my bushings. Which was prime, coolest thing anyone has ever done for me. Pathetic, but true. I woke up in the ambulance, dude was sitting next to me. He goes, "What's your name, girl?" I go, "Cassie, I think." "Well Cassie, I'm Curtis. And you are gonna be okay to rip another day, so lay back and let these good folks do their thing, okay?" So I lay back. And listen to Curtis. He and his friends Phil and Reuben ride the culvert religiously, and he was surprised to see me there, but awestruck by my smooth style. He told me how he'd been down at Wiggy's, and at Consolidated, and lots of other places. And how his friend Reuben paid gravity tax on the same trick as me, cracked his skull on mister concrete, wrecked up his collarbone and broke a finger, finger, finger. So I got off easy. Considering.

(*She sits up a bit, leaning on an elbow. Dreamily.*)

His voice was real nice. I just listened. Going in and out of consciousness like I was. Every time our eyes met, he just really looked at me. Like no one ever looked before. I didn't just disappear into nothing. I could even see my reflection. Like in a flash, I just knew. Here was this totally cool guy, a totally cool guy who happened to be totally impressed by ME! Sheesh. I don't think I've impressed anyone before, not my father, not my stepmom, none of my teachers. A real novelty moment for the memory books fersure. (*Beat.*) I'm not much of a talker. I don't got a lot to say. And uh, well, I'm not really good at basic conversation. I'm an idiot and a slacker, that's what my father says, especially when he tries to help me with my homework.

(*She gets up.*)

Whatever. I'm not after any sympathy for my screwed-up existence. But in the hospital, I told Curtis stuff I normally just keep to myself. Like how I'm not very good at baking cookies, or doing geometry, or makin' friends. Like how my mom died, and I miss her so much. And like how my father married this person who looks like my mom but who isn't. How like the only time I feel things go right for me is when I'm riding my skateboard. When I'm rippin', I feel like I'm a genius. And you know what? Curtis? He was a good listener too.

　　And after I was done with my litany of self-loathing, dude said, "Cassie, I'm gonna come back tomorrow, and tomorrow, and when you get out of here, I'm gonna visit you at your house. If that's all right with you. And oh, here's some flowers. I got 'em from the gift store downstairs in between times when you were passed out cold."

(*Flips up board with her foot, catches it.*)

Flowers.

(*She hugs her board, wraps her arms around it tightly.*)

I didn't know what to say. Which was typical. But Curtis didn't seem to care. This totally cool cute guy, a complete stranger, gave me flowers. (*Smiles shyly.*) Daisies.

(*Lights slowly out.*)

END OF PLAY

THE RUMOR

Dan Kois

The Rumor was originally produced by the 24 Hour Company at the Atlantic Theater in New York City on June 3, 2002. It was directed by Stu Zicherman with the following cast:

PR FLACK	Danita Winfield
REPORTER 1	Tor Ekeland
REPORTER 2	Brice Gaillard
CHUCK BONNER	Garrett Savage
CHRIS TINGLEY	Sean Williams
LARRY WAKEFIELD	Bradford Olson

CHARACTERS

PR FLACK
TWO REPORTERS (playing multiple roles)
CHUCK BONNER
CHRIS TINGLEY
LARRY WAKEFIELD

PRODUCTION NOTES

A note on the type: A slash / in a line marks the point of interruption for the next line. For instance, in the following exchange:

R2: The guy got the game-winning RBI, he can't spare ten minutes / for us?

FLACK: He's with ESPN.
  The cue for the Flack's line "He's with ESPN" is Reporter 2 saying the word "minutes."

Occasionally, lines will continue through an interruption. For instance, in the following exchange:

R1: Your former teammate, Eric Davis / made headlines

TINGLEY: Ah, Eric.

R1: a few seasons ago by saying that he wouldn't share a glove...
The cue for Tingley's line "Ah, Eric" is Reporter 1 saying the word "Davis." Reporter 1 continues through her next line *without pause.*

Lights up on a table with three microphones. Reporters are arrayed before the table, waiting for the press conference to begin. A PR FLACK *is briefing them.*

FLACK: We'll have Larry Wakefield, Chris Tingley, and Chuck Bonner out to talk about the game in a moment. FYI, Boston lost tonight so the Yanks are a half game out.

R1: What about Castillo?

FLACK: He's with ESPN.

R1: Fuckin' ESPN.

R2: The guy got the game-winning RBI, he can't spare ten minutes / for us?

FLACK: He's with ESPN.

R1: Fuckin' ESPN.

R2: Will Bonner be addressing Tony's column in the *Post*?

FLACK: I can't speak to that, Linda.

R2: So, yeah?

(WAKEFIELD, TINGLEY, *and* BONNER *enter and sit at the table. They have all recently showered and still have wet hair.* WAKEFIELD *wears a Yankees hat and a warm-up jacket.* TINGLEY *wears a muscle shirt with cut-off sleeves and is chewing gum.* BONNER *has a towel hung around his neck.*)

R1: Nice throwin' today, Chuck!

BONNER: Thanks.

R1: Love that sinker to / Mendoza.

R2: Chris, were you looking fastball on the homer?

TINGLEY: Yeah.

FLACK: Chuck has a prepared statement to read.

(*Clamor.*)

Chuck has a prepared statement and then they'll all take questions.

BONNER: Thank you.

(*Reads from a prepared statement:*)

"We live in a society where baseball players are looked up to as heroes. Right or wrong, I know that as a player for the greatest team in the world, my life is a public one. But I try to keep my private life as private as possible. However, recent rumors, including an irresponsible column in yester-day's *New York Post*, force me to respond.

"I know that I live in America, the greatest country in the world, and that part of that greatness is freedom of the press. But I resent these rumors and I resent the fact that I have been forced to dignify them with a response. So I will just say it, right here, right now, so that there can be no confusion: I am not ambidextrous."

(*Clamor.*)

FLACK: Prepared statement, guys, then questions.

BONNER: "I am a right-handed pitcher. I pitch with my right hand. I cannot, nor do I want to, throw with my left hand. I only pitch with my right hand. Thank you."

FLACK: Questions? (*Clamor.*) Gary.

RI: Chuck, Tony Franklin's *Post* column didn't mention any names at all.

BONNER: Right.

RI: It just said, I'll quote here: "There's a persistent rumor around town that one Yankees star who spends a lot of time throwing the ball with his right hand is actually ambidextrous and has started to think about declaring his manual orientation." Why do you think the column's about you?

BONNER: I don't know who the column's about. You'll have to ask Tony Franklin that.

RI: Sorry, I'll rephrase. Do Yankees fans think the column is about you?

BONNER: I can't control what people think. That's obvious. And I can't convince people what to think. I can only say what I know and what the truth is and that's I'm right-handed and I throw with my right hand. That's it. End of story.

(*Clamor.*)

FLACK: Yes, Anne.

R2: Coach, is there an ambidextrous player on the Yankees?

WAKEFIELD: I don't know. Not that it's anyone's business, but I don't know. I never walked in on anyone throwing with both hands, if that's what you mean.

(*Clamor.*)

FLACK: Barry?

R1: Coach, can you explain the comments you made to *Esquire* magazine last month?

WAKEFIELD: Whaddya mean, explain?

R1: Well, / I mean—

WAKEFIELD: What's to explain?

R1: Coach—

WAKEFIELD: Next question.

(*Clamor.*)

FLACK: Okay—

WAKEFIELD: "Explain." Are the majors are ready for an openly ambidextrous player? I said sure. What's to explain?

R1: Do you still feel that way, after all the attention / this issue has gotten?

WAKEFIELD: Yeah, sure I do. We're all big boys here.

FLACK: Latonya?

R2: Chris, how do *you* feel? Are the majors ready for a player who openly has the ability to throw with both hands?

TINGLEY: In this day and age it would be irrelevant. If the guy is doing his job on the field, you know, I don't think there would be any problem at all.

BONNER: I agree.

TINGLEY: There's practical considerations, though.

BONNER: Yeah.

TINGLEY: Like, what hand does he wear his glove on?

BONNER: Sure, yeah.

(*Clamor.*)

FLACK: Bobby?

R1: Nice game today, Chris.

TINGLEY: Thanks, Bobby.

R1: Your former teammate, Eric Davis / made headlines

TINGLEY: Ah, Eric.

RI: a few seasons ago by saying that he wouldn't share a glove with an ambidextrous teammate.

TINGLEY: I remember.

RI: He said, I'm paraphrasing here, but he said, "I have no problem with switch-hitters, but I don't want someone on my team going around throwing with both hands."

TINGLEY: Right.

RI: "That's just plain weird," he said.

TINGLEY: Right.

RI: Do you think his feelings are shared by many big leaguers?

TINGLEY: No.

BONNER: No.

TINGLEY: Nuh-uh, it's just, ballplayers are never / gonna...

BONNER: We're not the most open-minded / people on earth...

TINGLEY: Right, but we're still / fairly...

BONNER: We're not going to, y'know, walk into an ambidextrous bar and start, like—

TINGLEY: —playing darts.

BONNER: With both hands.

TINGLEY: No.

WAKEFIELD: But on the whole, I think major leaguers are pretty accepting.

TINGLEY: Eric, I love Eric, but he's sort of from the old school, you know.

BONNER: (*Nodding.*) Old / school.

WAKEFIELD: Old school.

(*Clamor.*)

FLACK: Yeah, Alia.

R2: Coach, what kind of player should be that trailblazer? The Jackie Robinson of ambidexterity?

TINGLEY: Good question. / Good question.

BONNER: Good question.

WAKEFIELD: Well—it shouldn't matter—but it'd be best if he's a real superstar, like Jackie was.

TINGLEY: That's why there's rumors about Chuck, you know. When you're getting near three hundred wins, that's a big deal, and if he was ambidextrous, which he's not, but if he were, he'd be a real ambassador.

BONNER: Sure.

WAKEFIELD: Beyond that, I don't know. Whoever he is— like Jackie—whoever he is, he shouldn't be such a, a, in-your-face ambidextrous guy. He should be proud, but he should have that—dignity.

BONNER: It's best if he's not flamboyantly ambidextrous.

TINGLEY: Using both hands all the time in public, right.

(*Clamor.*)

FLACK: Lance?

RI: Fellas, even the most conservative estimates from scientists suggest that two to four percent of Americans are ambidextrous. So it would seem like at least fifteen / to thirty leaguers...

BONNER: That's high. That's just math.

WAKEFIELD: Lance, this isn't the general population, you know? This is baseball. Single-handedness is very important, it's a really prominent part of the culture of baseball, you know, the locker room and all. /

RI: But still, there must be at least one or two / who are in the closet.

BONNER: Sure. / Sure.

TINGLEY: Sure. We've played with guys, with guys who, you know, who weren't *out* out but who it was a known secret: on the team, you know?

RI: And no one had any—

BONNER: No. No problem.

(*Tiny pause.*)

RI: Was this on the Dodgers?

BONNER: I'm not, no, I'm not / identi—

R1: Was it—

WAKEFIELD: That's fruitless, Lance. Next question. That young lady over there has been waving her hands for a while.

FLACK: Yes, Miss . . .

R2: Lucinda Martin, *Both Hands Magazine.*

BONNER: Oh, Christ.

R2: Mr. Bonner, do you have a problem with ambidextrous people?

BONNER: No, I do not.

R2: Does this so-called rumor threaten your handhood? Do you see something wrong / with ambidexterity?

BONNER: No.

WAKEFIELD: Can someone—

R2: Do you feel—

FLACK: Miss, please let Mr. Bonner answer your questions.

R2: Sure, fine.

BONNER: I have no problem whatsoever with ambidextrous people. Okay? I, I'm not one, but I, like I said before, I have played with them before, and I have friends, and I'm just saying—it's not me. I'll tell Yankees fans right now, the greatest fans in the world, ambidextrous people are people just like you and me.

R2: Mr. Bonner, I'm ambidextrous.

BONNER: That's great.

R2: Like many ambidextrous people, my favorite baseball player is Chuck Bonner. You actually have quite a fan base among the ambi community. Would you like to speculate on why this is?

BONNER: (*Pained.*) No, that's great. I'm always grateful for my fans, no matter who they are or how many of their hands they can use with equal ability.

R2: What would you say if I told you we had pictures—

FLACK: Okay, / that's enough.

R2: Pictures of you throwing with your left hand in high school?

TINGLEY: Someone shut her the fuck up!

R2: What would you say?

BONNER: I'd say you were a liar. You can do anything with photos these days.

R2: But these pictures—

R1: Shut up! Let the rest of us go!

TINGLEY: Those pictures are bullshit, just for the record.

R2: You can't lie to yourself forever, Bonner!

FLACK: (*Very firm.*) That is absolutely enough, Miss Martin. If

you cannot speak civilly to these players I will have you
removed. Next question, right here in the front.

RI: Chuck, can you prove you're not ambidextrous?

WAKEFIELD: Oh, for Chrissakes—

RI: Our readers want to know if a major New York figure is
hiding a newsworthy fact about himself!

TINGLEY: This is not / *newsworthy*.

BONNER: Carter, ask anyone who knows me. Ask anyone
who—

RI: Can you prove it?

BONNER: Fine. Fuck. Fine.

(BONNER *tromps out into the reporter pool.*)

Gimme your—gimme your notebook.

TINGLEY: Chuck—

BONNER: Gimme your fucking notebook. And your pen. Here.
I'm writing with my left hand. Look at this!

(*He holds the notebook up. In extremely childish, sloppy lettering:*
FUCK YOU.)

Is that proof enough? Is that proof enough? How about this?

(*He throws the notebook at* REPORTER 2 *with his left hand, missing by*
a mile. His throwing motion is exaggeratedly awkward, almost girlish.
He is furious, near tears.)

TINGLEY: Chuck!

BONNER: How about that? Did you get your pictures? Did you
   get all that? Why does everyone think I'm hiding something, that I'm—why? No, tell me. Why? Do you ask Greg
   Maddux if he's ambidextrous? Do you ask Randy Johnson?
   Well, do you?

TINGLEY: (*Softly.*) No.

BONNER: No! What if I *was* an ambidextrous man? What if I *was*?
   How would this fucking witch hunt make me feel? What
   kind of message does that send to the world?

TINGLEY: Chuck, honey...

(TINGLEY *takes* BONNER'S *hand and strokes it.* BONNER *is crying,* TIN-
GLEY *gently kisses* BONNER'S *forehead.*)

BONNER: I'm so tired, Chris.

TINGLEY: I know.

BONNER: What if I was? What if I was tired of keeping secrets?

(*Pause.*)

TINGLEY: Then you'd have to stop keeping them.

R1: What are you saying, Chuck?

TINGLEY: (*To the reporter.*) Shut up.

BONNER: (*Ignoring the reporter.*) What if I was tired?

(*Pause.*)

R2: Chris? Is this something you and your husband have discussed?

(*Pause.* WAKEFIELD *makes a cutoff gesture to the* FLACK.)

FLACK: Okay, this press conference is over—

BONNER: No.

TINGLEY: Chuck?

BONNER: *No.*

(BONNER *looks over at* WAKEFIELD, *who nods solemnly.* BONNER *faces the crowd.*)

I have something I would like to say.

(*Blackout.*)

END OF PLAY

SANDCHAIR CANTATA

Nicole Quinn

Sandchair Cantata was originally produced as a staged reading by Actors & Writers, Olivebridge, New York, on October 19, 2002. It was directed by Nicole Quinn with the following cast:

WORRIER	Sarah Chodoff
PRAGMATIST	Sigrid Heath

CHARACTERS
WORRIER
PRAGMATIST

Lights up on: A beach.

Two forty-something women in sand chairs at surf's edge. They wear bathing suits and baseball caps, each with a book in her lap, watching their respective kids in the water. The conversation ebbs and flows, the rhythm of waves.

WORRIER: (*A lament.*) I'm old.

PRAGMATIST: We're well preserved.

WORRIER: Pickled.

PRAGMATIST: Pears.

WORRIER: Pairs?

PRAGMATIST: Luscious fruit.

WORRIER: (*Indicates the ocean.*) You think they're okay?

PRAGMATIST: Yep.

WORRIER: Really?

PRAGMATIST: Yep.

WORRIER: Smells like summer.

PRAGMATIST: Seaweed.

WORRIER: Sunscreen, SPF thirty.

PRAGMATIST: (*Thrilled.*) Vacation.

WORRIER: (*Thrill shared.*) Vacation.

(*They take it in, the beach.*)

PRAGMATIST: Good book?

WORRIER: It's okay. Yours?

PRAGMATIST: Better in bed.

WORRIER: Who?

PRAGMATIST: The book.

WORRIER: Oh.

PRAGMATIST: (*Nods her head toward the water.*) Or him.

WORRIER: (*Wrinkling her nose.*) No.

PRAGMATIST: (*A minor wound.*) Why not?

WORRIER: Boring.

PRAGMATIST: Looks or personality?

WORRIER: Both.

PRAGMATIST: (*Reassessing.*) Grumpy maybe.

WORRIER: Or mean.

PRAGMATIST: Nice smile.

WORRIER: (*Revelation.*) Oh, yeah. Laughing eyes.

PRAGMATIST: Great butt!

WORRIER: (*Doubtful.*) Really?

PRAGMATIST: (*Indicating someone else.*) No, hers.

WORRIER: Buns of steel.

PRAGMATIST: Youth.

WORRIER: (*Devastated.*) I'm middle-aged.

PRAGMATIST: Yes we are.

WORRIER: When did it happen?

PRAGMATIST: Every day.

WORRIER: Every day.

(*Each retreats, reverie, water as lodestone.*)

PRAGMATIST: (*Confession.*) I hate my book group.

WORRIER: (*Surprised relief.*) I hate mine too!

PRAGMATIST: The dynamic's...

WORRIER: ...All wrong.

PRAGMATIST: Too social.

WORRIER: Mine too. (*A beat.*) Do the waves seem rough?

PRAGMATIST: No.

WORRIER: You're sure?

PRAGMATIST: Yep.

WORRIER: (*Whimsical.*) Your kids are *so* happy.

PRAGMATIST: (*Pleased.*) Yeah.

WORRIER: (*Poor me.*) Mine are so whiny.

PRAGMATIST: Don't say yes so much.

WORRIER: (*Startled, miracle cure.*) Really?

PRAGMATIST: You're a paper tiger.

WORRIER: (*Defensive.*) Am not.

PRAGMATIST: Are too.

WORRIER: (*Anger rising.*) Am no...

PRAGMATIST: (*Loud, in her face.*) Are too, are too, are too!

(WORRIER *backs down, fairly cringing.*

A breath.)

    See?

(*They sit in silence, watching the waves of children.*)

WORRIER: (*Licking her wounds.*) Want a frozen lemonade?

PRAGMATIST: And french fries. (*She indicates the kids.*) They'll fly if we buy.

WORRIER: Alone?

PRAGMATIST: It's not far. We can watch them from here.

WORRIER: I don't know.

PRAGMATIST: Don't know what?

WORRIER: If it's a good idea.

PRAGMATIST: Give them a budget and let them work it out. We get chair service.

WORRIER: But...

PRAGMATIST: Or *you* could go.

WORRIER: (*A large life question.*) What am I doing!?

PRAGMATIST: Getting lemonade? French fries?

WORRIER: Children. Raising children, that's what I'm doing.

PRAGMATIST: My treat.

WORRIER: I'm always the bad guy. "You can't do this," "Don't do that." I make them go to bed. I take them for shots.

PRAGMATIST: You take them for ice cream.

WORRIER: (*Hopeful.*) Ice cream.

PRAGMATIST: The great equalizer.

WORRIER: (*Squinting out front.*) What's that boy doing?

PRAGMATIST: (*Yelled out front.*) Hey, you! Orange trunks! Blue Warhead mouth, get off my kid!

WORRIER: Jerk!

PRAGMATIST: He's a kid.

WORRIER: But he...

PRAGMATIST: He wanted someone to tell him to get off. I did. He did.

WORRIER: (*Okay, smarty pants.*) Like the one you threatened to bite?

PRAGMATIST: Like that.

WORRIER: Did you ever bite her?

PRAGMATIST: Nope.

WORRIER: (*Smug.*) Who's the paper tiger?

PRAGMATIST: I didn't have to. But I would have.

WORRIER: Sure.

PRAGMATIST: *She* believed me.

WORRIER: She was three.

PRAGMATIST: They can be very cunning at three.

(*The* WORRIER *glances around, then panics, dancing in all directions from her chair.*)

WORRIER: Where are they!!!

PRAGMATIST: (*Calm.*) Down there. The tide carried them.

WORRIER: (*Screeching, hand gestures, basic mania.*) Olivia! Over here! Move, back, back! Get your brother! Now!

PRAGMATIST: (*Sure she's come unhinged.*) You okay?

WORRIER: (*A breath, a confession.*) Every day in the papers, there's another kid taken. And teenagers.

PRAGMATIST: (*Sympathetic.*) It's too much.

WORRIER: Is everybody a pervert or a victim?

PRAGMATIST: We just hear about it more. The media.

WORRIER: It's not right. Not fair. Priests. Teachers. Relatives. Strangers.

PRAGMATIST: We do the best we can.

WORRIER: Living in fear is the best we can do?

PRAGMATIST: This isn't the projects, or Auschwitz, we're at the beach. Lighten up.

WORRIER: It could happen here.

PRAGMATIST: Sure it could.

WORRIER: (*Self-righteous.*) Kids are snatched from their homes.

PRAGMATIST: (*Proverbial.*) Lives lived in fear...

WORRIER: Oh, please.

PRAGMATIST: ... Lives half lived.

WORRIER: (*Blurts it out.*) I bought a gun.

PRAGMATIST: (*Many answers come to mind, to mouth, but she says:*) Be sure you can use it.

WORRIER: (*Launches into it, living it again.*) This crazy guy, or maybe it was drugs, he pushed his way past the pizza delivery man under our stoop. The kids and I were terrified. "Who are you?!!" I screamed it at him till the pizza man dragged him out by the collar yelling at me to "Lock de gate, lock de gate!" We were prisoners in our own house, watching the crazy guy try to pull the ironwork out of the concrete, while the pizza man pedaled away as fast as he could.

PRAGMATIST: (*Wow.*) The pizza guy was great.

WORRIER: And our neighbor across the street, he came out to help too.

PRAGMATIST: (*Wow again.*) He did?

WORRIER: He brought a baseball bat, but his back was out so he had to use the bat as a cane to hobble across the street.

PRAGMATIST: One crazy guy versus you, the kids, the pizza man, and the bat-cane avenger. Not too shabby.

WORRIER: (*Revelation.*) Yeah.

(*They retreat into themselves, the ocean as a dodge.*)

PRAGMATIST: My sister's dying.

WORRIER: Oh.

PRAGMATIST: Could be years.

WORRIER: Okay...

PRAGMATIST: Years of cutting and radiating and cutting...you know.

WORRIER: Oh.

PRAGMATIST: I'm trying to figure out how not to be paranoid when I'm old, like my mother was. My sister's just trying to figure out how to get old.

WORRIER: (*Reassuring herself.*) Middle age is looking pretty good.

PRAGMATIST: (*To herself.*) I'm glad it's not me.

WORRIER: (*To herself.*) Me too.

PRAGMATIST: (*Comfort food.*) French fries.

WORRIER: (*Yells to the kids.*) Hey, guys, you fly, I'll buy!

(*A breath.*)

(*Curtain.*)

END OF PLAY

THE SCARY QUESTION

Wayne Rawley

The Scary Question premiered on February 6, 2004, at Annex Theatre in Seattle, Washington, as part of their monthly cabaret series *Spin the Bottle*. The cast was as follows:

LINDA	Shannon Kipp
BRIAN	Wayne Rawley

CHARACTERS
BRIAN: Linda's boyfriend.
LINDA: Brian's girlfriend.

SETTING
Linda's living room couch.

NOTE
A double asterisk (**) in a line means the person with the next line should begin speaking.

AT RISE: LINDA *and* BRIAN *are sitting on the couch,* LINDA *at one end and* BRIAN *at the other.* LINDA *is reading some document for work.* BRIAN *is flipping through his own book or magazine.* BRIAN *is having trouble concentrating and looks nervously up at* LINDA *a couple times before speaking.*

BRIAN: Question.

LINDA: Hm?

BRIAN: Question.

LINDA: What question.

BRIAN: For you.

LINDA: Question for me?

BRIAN: Yes.

LINDA: Are you okay?

BRIAN: (*Defensive.*) Yes!

LINDA: Okay.

BRIAN: I need to ask you a question.

LINDA: Okay.

BRIAN: How long have we been together?

LINDA: Eight months.

BRIAN: That's right!

LINDA: I know!

BRIAN: You like 'em?

LINDA: Huh?

BRIAN: You like 'em, the eight months?

LINDA: Of course.

BRIAN: Me too.

LINDA: Good.

BRIAN: Hell, yes it's good!

LINDA: Okay.

BRIAN: Okay.

(*They go back to reading.*)

That's not the question.

LINDA: I'm supposed to read this for work.

BRIAN: I'm distracting you?

LINDA: No—

BRIAN: Because I don't want to distract you—

LINDA: No. That's okay. There is something on your mind. I want to know what it is.

BRIAN: I love you.

LINDA: I love you too.

BRIAN: When did we first say I love you?

LINDA: Um, four months ago.

BRIAN: Right!

LINDA: I know—

BRIAN: You knew!

LINDA: That's right.

BRIAN: Four months!

LINDA: You cried.

BRIAN: I was happy!

LINDA: So was I!

BRIAN: Okay!

LINDA: Okay.

BRIAN: Eight months, four months.

LINDA: I've never been happier.

BRIAN: Me either!

LINDA: Good.

BRIAN: Good does not begin to describe it.

LINDA: Okay.

BRIAN: Okay.

LINDA: Okay.

BRIAN: So—

LINDA: Honey, please just ask your question!

BRIAN: I'm sorry!

LINDA: What?

BRIAN: I just—

LINDA: What.

BRIAN: This isn't exactly easy—

LINDA: What isn't?

BRIAN: It's important, and I'm just not sure...

LINDA: Oh, my God. Brian. Stop it. Is it bad? You're scaring me.

BRIAN: It's scary. I'm scared to ask it—

LINDA: Brian, ask it!

BRIAN: Okay! So I'll just ask it. Then. Okay.

(*He gets down on one knee next to* LINDA.)

LINDA: Brian?

BRIAN: Linda, I wanted to ask you this for so long... What would you do if the Zombies attacked?

LINDA: What?

BRIAN: What would you do if Zombies attacked.

(*Pause.*)

LINDA: I'm sorry, ★★I don't know what you mean.

BRIAN: The Zombies. If they attacked. What would you do?

LINDA: What Zombies are you talking about?

BRIAN: Any Zombies—any and all Zombies. A horde of Zombies★★ from the cemetery, whatever—

LINDA: Horde of Zombies?

BRIAN: What I'm asking★★ is this—

LINDA: This is what★★ you wanted to ask me?

BRIAN: Should the proper set of circumstances align, be they atmospheric, environmental, chemical, industrial, viral, biological or supernatural that caused—

LINDA: That's weird, Brian, that is—

BRIAN: THAT caused the crazed, unholy and recently deceased to rise from the grave in search of succulent human flesh—

LINDA: Gross!

BRIAN: Yes. You're right. It is gross. Nevertheless—what would you do?

LINDA: Why are you asking me this?

BRIAN: Because it's important—

LINDA: No it isn't.

BRIAN: YES! It is!

LINDA: Why is it important?

BRIAN: Because I love you and you know what? I really do love you—and I want...I hope...that is to say, I'm ready for our relationship to...move. To the next level—

LINDA: You want to get married?

BRIAN: Whoa, wait a minute; you're asking me to marry you?

LINDA: I thought you were asking me to marry you!

BRIAN: I was asking about Zombies!

LINDA: Brian! What do you mean next level!

BRIAN: The next level! The level—above the current level!

LINDA: Moving in together?

BRIAN: Ah-hah— Well, okay, you know, I'm not sure. I'm afraid—

LINDA: Of Zombies?

BRIAN: Well, you didn't come to Zombie night.

LINDA: You're mad about Zombie night.

BRIAN: I'm not mad—

LINDA: You said it was okay that I didn't come to Zombie night!

BRIAN: It was—

LINDA: You said you didn't mind if I skipped Zombie night!

BRIAN: (*Finally, as if it has been bothering him for days.*) Well, why would you want to skip Zombie night? It was awesome! We watched *Night of the Living Dead*, *Dawn of the Dead*, *Return of the Living Dead* and *Return of the Living Dead II*, which sucked I admit that, but *Return of the Living Dead* was awesome and why didn't you want to come?

LINDA: I don't like Zombie movies.

(*Pause.*)

BRIAN: Wha? **What do you—

LINDA: I don't like Zombie movies.

BRIAN: That doesn't register with me, that—

LINDA: I don't like **them.

BRIAN: That doesn't compute. **Don't like them?

LINDA: No, You're getting it right. I. Don't. Like. Zombie. Movies.

(*Pause.*)

BRIAN: What?

LINDA: Brian, this is ridiculous!

BRIAN: No, it is not! No it is not ridiculous!

LINDA: They are gratuitous.

BRIAN: It happens to be a very viable genre.

LINDA: They are disgusting.

BRIAN: They ARE quite often a very pointed and highly savvy commentary on the mindless consumerism of late seventies, early eighties Middle America.

LINDA: No they aren't!

BRIAN: Zombie movies are my life!

LINDA: No they aren't!

BRIAN: No! That's not totally true, they aren't totally my life, but I love them! I love them, Linda! I love them!

LINDA: Okay! Great! I'm glad you love them! Love them! I love modern dance!

BRIAN: That's not really dance. They're just hopping around, anyone can do that.

LINDA: See! See! I don't like Zombie movies, you don't like modern dance!

BRIAN: No! No! That's you— That's a diversion! That's you trying to create a diversion!

LINDA: You have lost your mind!

BRIAN: It's true I have! I have lost my mind. When I wake up in the morning, the first thing I ask myself is "I wonder if she is going to smile today," and when I think that, I smile. And if I do something, in the day, that makes you smile? And you smile? And I see you smile? I die. Every time. Because, and I am being honest, I do not think there is anything more beautiful that has ever existed in the world than you smiling. All I want out of my life is to maybe see that most beautiful thing in the world just once a day. But, and I am also being honest—I have great fear about making it work with a woman that has no Zombie plan.

LINDA: A Zombie plan.

BRIAN: A small amount of thought given to a possible plan of escape should the dead rise from the grave and begin to walk the earth.

LINDA: Brian, I don't have a Zombie plan.

BRIAN: I know. I'm sorry. I've ruined everything. It's too soon— It's too—I'm sorry. I'll go.

LINDA: You're leaving?

BRIAN: I'm pushing you. I promised myself I wouldn't do that.

LINDA: Flamethrowers.

BRIAN: What?

LINDA: Do we get flamethrowers?

BRIAN: (*Sad. She just doesn't get it.*) No. A flamethrower won't do us any good. They're Zombies. They're not gonna stop just because they're on fire. By the time they are burned enough to become incapacitated, they will already have eaten your brain.

LINDA: What about grenades?

BRIAN: Hand grenades?

LINDA: Yes.

BRIAN: No. The collateral damage would **be too massive.

LINDA: What does that mean? **Like blowing up the house?

BRIAN: Like blowing up yourself, these Zombies **are like right outside—

LINDA: Okay. So what if I've got a flamethrower—

BRIAN: Linda, you can't—

LINDA: Listen, I've got a flamethrower, you grab the aluminum baseball bat out of the hall closet. You stand at the door— they're around the house right?

BRIAN: Completely surrounding the house and probably break-

ing through the barricades we've set up in front of the
windows at this point.

LINDA: You stand at the door, I open the door for you and you
run out swinging that bat at everything that moves. You
clear a path to the car, because they're rotting, their heads
come right off with one crack of the bat, so you clear a path
to the car; we make it to the car. I jump in the backseat,
you drive.

BRIAN: Keep talking.

LINDA: You start the car and speed off, screeching the tires with
smoke coming off them and everything, I pop up through
the sunroof with the flamethrower—they are all chasing us
at this point right?

BRIAN: (*Impressed*.) Yeah. Yeah, they're chasing us all right.

LINDA: I pop up through the sunroof with the flamethrower and
torch the bastards right back into the grave that spawned
them. They'll never catch us 'cause we're in the car. And
they aren't like superhuman or anything—

BRIAN: No, they aren't any stronger or faster than normal
humans—

LINDA: Right, so they can't catch us, 'cause we're in the car and
they are all on fire, running around bumping into each
other setting each other on fire, burning up to incapacita-
tion, and we escape. This time.

BRIAN: That could work.

LINDA: Then you and I find the resistance movement and join
up.

BRIAN: Seriously?

LINDA: Yep.

BRIAN: You would join the resistance movement?

LINDA: The world is crawling with the living dead, Brian. We have to find the last bastion of humanity and align ourselves with them. Besides, if our species is going to survive, we are going to have to learn to work together.

BRIAN: Oh, my God. That is so true. I love you.

LINDA: I love you too.

(*They kiss.*)

BRIAN: Do you really want to live together?

LINDA: Of course. I can't wait. But we should. Wait. For months. I think.

BRIAN: Agreed. It's a big step. You are so right.

END OF PLAY

SNAP

Daryl Watson

Snap premiered on behalf of Real Theatre Works at the Battle of the Bards, New York, on February 25, 2005. The competition was hosted at Crobar by Partial Comfort Productions. The play was directed by Jenny Koons, and the cast was as follows:

COACH LATRELL	Malcolm Barrett
CLARENCE	Robert Barrett
MARCUS	Brian Hastert
SUSAN	Mayteana Morales
WAYNE "THE MOUTH TRAIN" EVANS	Nyambi Nyambi

CAST OF CHARACTERS

COACH LATRELL
CLARENCE
MARCUS
SUSAN
WAYNE

This play is dedicated to
Malcolm, Shamis, Jackie,
Chad, Karla, and Leah

SCENE ONE

The entire stage is dark.

COACH LATRELL: ATTENTION!

(*Lights up on a gymnasium.* CLARENCE, MARCUS, *and* SUSAN *are standing in a row, facing forward.* COACH LATRELL *paces back and forth.*)

You know what I see in front of me today?

(*A beat.*)

I ain't talking to myself, muthafuckas! I said, do you know what I see in front of me today!?

ALL: No, sir!

COACH LATRELL: I see bacteria! I see maggot freshmen! I see cutlets of dog shit in the early stages of decomposition! That's what I see. Do you agree?

ALL: Yes, sir!

(LATRELL *stops in front of* CLARENCE, *who is an extremely tall boy.*)

COACH LATRELL: What's your name?

CLARENCE. Clarence?

COACH LATRELL: You a tall muthafucka, ain't you? If you did a backflip, you'd kick God in the mouth!

(*Everyone laughs.*)

The hell y'all laughing at? You think this is funny? You think y'all don't have weaknesses? The first rule in playing the dozens is everybody's got a weakness! (*To* MARCUS.) What's your name?

(MARCUS *opens his mouth wide to reveal crooked teeth.*)

MARCUS: Marcus.

COACH LATRELL: GODDAMN! Need you an orthodontist! Can't tell if you're smiling at me or flashing gang signs! Close your mouth before you get somebody shot. I can just see you now, walking down the street: "Yo, what's up, fellas—POP! POP! POP! POP!" (*To* SUSAN.) What's your name, princess?

SUSAN: S-S-S-Susan.

COACH LATRELL: The hell's wrong with you? You challenged or something?

SUSAN: I-I-I have a st-stu-stutt—

COACH LATRELL: A what!?

SUSAN: A stu-stu-stu-stutter. I have a stu-stutter.

COACH LATRELL: You ain't lyin', jack!

SUSAN: I have a stutter, and...

COACH LATRELL: And WHAT?

SUSAN: . . . I'd a-a-a-ap-appreciate it if you di-di-di-didn't use that as an excuse to ab-b-b-b-b-buse me.

COACH LATRELL: Oh. Okay. Well, if you'd like, we can all take out our notebooks and do some journaling instead. You know? Like, really get down on paper everything you're feeling. Would you like that?

SUSAN: Y-y-yes.

COACH LATRELL: Yeah? You'd like to do you some intense journaling?

SUSAN: Yes. V-v-very much—

COACH LATRELL: TOO DAMN BAD, STUTTERING SALLY . . .

SUSAN: S-S-Susan.

COACH LATRELL: On your belly, maggots! All of you! Push-ups now! And count every one off with, "Yo' daddy so dumb." Don't just stand there! Do it.

(*Everyone drops down and starts doing push-ups, saying, "Yo' daddy's so dumb."*)

That's right! Welcome to the Clarence Thomas High School Dozens Team! You think this is abuse? You ain't seen nothing yet! Why you stopping, Marcus?

MARCUS: (*Breathing heavily.*) It's my asthma, sir!

COACH LATRELL: Asthma?

MARCUS: I can't breathe so good.

COACH LATRELL: Okay...so help me out here. Where's the part of this conversation that has shit to do with me and what I'm doing?

MARCUS: I can't bre—

COACH LATRELL: Because asthma don't sound like a Coach Antoine Latrell problem. It sounds like a Marcus problem. Something wrong with your DNA. Take it up with yo' mama, 'cause that don't got shit to do with me!

SUSAN: Coach, come on, he c-c-can't b-b-brea...

COACH LATRELL: Is there a CD player skipping around here?

SUSAN: N-n-n...

COACH LATRELL: Or are you actually trying to communicate with me?

SUSAN: F-f-f-f-f-f-f-f-f-fuck you!

(*A beat.*)

COACH LATRELL: Say that again.

SUSAN: F-f-f-fuck you! Skinny-ass m-m-m-m-m-m-muthafucka!

COACH LATRELL: All right, everybody. Practice is over for today.

(*Everyone gets up to leave.*)

Not you, Susan!

(CLARENCE *and* MARCUS *exit. A beat.*)

Well done.

SUSAN: Wh–wh–wh–wh—

COACH LATRELL: DON'T! Don't! Just stop! Damn! I'll explain. You learned the second rule of playing the dozens. No matter what, when somebody throws a snap at you, you throw one right back. You got potential. Now . . . there's a freshman exhibition tournament next week. And you're going to be in it.

SCENE TWO

SUSAN *is jumping rope.* COACH LATRELL *is watching over her.*

COACH LATRELL: (*Singing.*) I don't know what I've been told!

SUSAN: (*Singing.*) I don't know what I've been told!

COACH LATRELL: Yo' underwear is ten years old!

SUSAN: Yo' underwear is ten years old!

COACH LATRELL: Yo' breath is bad, yo' booty stank!

SUSAN: Yo' breath is bad, yo' booty stank!

COACH LATRELL: That ass is like a septic tank!

SUSAN: That ass is like a septic tank!

COACH LATRELL: Sound off!

SUSAN: Fuck you!

COACH LATRELL: Sound off!

SUSAN: Three, four!

COACH LATRELL: Sound off! Fuck you!

SUSAN: And yo' fucking family too!

COACH LATRELL: Drop the jump rope!

(SUSAN *drops it.*)

Now give me a snap!

SUSAN: You're skinny and st-st-stupid! And you got lint in your hair!

COACH LATRELL: No, no, no, no! We've been at this for days! This is not about just insulting me! When you play the dozens, you gotta make that person ashamed for being alive, for having the family that he has, for the car he drives, for the fucking toothpaste he uses! You gotta find where he's weakest, focus on that and keep hitting him there and don't let up until he falls to pieces! You gotta be quick! Gotta be on the ball! Don't forget the motto: "We don't fight with our fists; we fight with our *wits*."

SUSAN: I hear you. I hear you.

COACH LATRELL: You heard me, but you not listening to me. Girl, your sister so skinny, people in Somalia send *her* food!

SNAP! That's the dozens! Now come on! The exhibition's tomorrow!

SUSAN: I—

COACH LATRELL: Your sister so bucktoothed, she could kiss a man and comb his mustache at the same time.

SUSAN: I-I-I—

COACH LATRELL: Your brother so poor, he got married just for the rice!

SUSAN: I can't!

COACH LATRELL: Why not?

SUSAN: Are you d-d-d-deaf? I g-g-got this st-st-stutter! I'm gonna g-g-get eaten alive out th-th-there!

COACH LATRELL: You didn't stutter when you were singing with the jump rope!

SUSAN: Singing's the only thing I'm g-g-good at! I don't even want to b-b-be here! My d-d-dad used to play on the d-d-dozens team b-b-back when he was in high school, and he just wants me to f-f-f-follow in his f-f-f-footsteps and my mama—

COACH LATRELL: Yeah, yeah, yeah, but, um, back to what I was talking about, you gotta find your rhythm, Susan. I can't help you do that. Only you can do it. And you gotta do it by tomorrow. Or you're going to lose.

SCENE THREE

The exhibition. Two microphones lie in the center of the floor. SUSAN *and* COACH LATRELL *are in one corner. Her opponent,* WAYNE "THE MOUTH TRAIN" EVANS, *is trying to rally the audience.*

COACH LATRELL: Now just remember everything I told you.

SUSAN: You told me I was going to lose.

COACH LATRELL: Well, remember the part where I said I believed in you?

SUSAN: No.

COACH LATRELL: Well, I believe in you and—

WAYNE: (*To the crowd.*) Wazzup, muthafuckas! Wayne "the Mouth Train" Evans is in the house! Y'all ready to get this party started? Yo, I'm gonna tear this scrub apart!

(*He grabs a microphone.*)

Come on over and get your medicine, baby! I promise you won't feel a thing.

COACH LATRELL: Grab your mike and show him who's boss. You can do it.

(SUSAN *picks up her mike. A bell rings. They start circling each other.*)

WAYNE: (*To* SUSAN.) Yeah. Yeah. Where you at? Huh? Where you at? You ain't nothing. Yo, check this out: Your house is so small, I put a key in the lock and broke a window! OHHH!

(SUSAN *speechless.*)

> What's the matter? Where you at? Look at that poofy-ass hair! Hair so damn nappy, you gotta take Tylenol every time you comb it! OOOOOOH!

SUSAN: Y-y-your d-d-d-daddy...

WAYNE: Oh, what the fuck is this shit? You got me battling a girl who stutters? Yo, your mouth is so big, you could eat a banana sideways.

(*A bell rings; end of Round* 1. SUSAN *walks over to* COACH LATRELL.)

COACH LATRELL: What the fuck are you doing out there? He's taking your ass to the floor like 409!

SUSAN: Ooh, th-that's a g-g-g-good one. Can I u-u-use that?

COACH LATRELL: No, you cannot use that! Why are you just standing there? Why don't you say something?

SUSAN: I don't got anything to say.

COACH LATRELL: Everybody got something to say! Look at that goofy-ass muthafucka! He's a clown! You could tear him apart.

SUSAN: He's b-b-b-etter than m-m-me.

COACH LATRELL: He's quicker than you. You just gotta slow him down. Remember: place your strengths against his weaknesses. What are your strengths?

SUSAN: I d-d-don't know! I can sing. That's it.

COACH LATRELL: I didn't know you sang.

SUSAN: I t-t-told you y-y-yesterday!

COACH LATRELL: Girl, you stutter half the damn time as it is. *God* don't even know what you're saying!

(*The bell rings.* WAYNE *runs into the center of the ring and grabs his mike.*)

WAYNE: Let's get this over with.

(SUSAN *enters and picks up her mike. They circle each other.*)

Yo, your sister's so flat, she had to tattoo "front" on her chest!

SUSAN: You-you-you—

WAYNE: What's up, girl? I can't tell if you're trying to talk to me or beat box! OOOH!!!

(SUSAN *tries to speak but is too overwhelmed.*)

Yo, your sister's so ugly, she was a stunt double for *Predator!* Ooooh! And as for yo' mama? Yo' mama—

SUSAN: (*Singing.*)
     No!
     Don't you say nothing 'bout my mama!

(*Everyone goes dead quiet.*)

     (*Singing.*)
     No!

Don't you say nothing 'bout my mama!
No, no, no, no!
Don't you say nothing 'bout my mama!
'Cause then I'm going to have to start talking 'bout yours.

(COACH LATRELL *starts snapping.*)

(*Singing.*)
'Cause your mama's so fat
and that's no lie!
It takes two trains and a bus
just to get on her good side.
A big-booty butt
Mountain hips wide as hell
Her underwear is
double double double double XL
And to top it all off
She's as dumb as a stool
She thought Boyz II Men
was a day-care school!
She's dumb and she's fat, dumb and fat
Yo' mama's dumb and she's fat.

WAYNE: Your ma—

SUSAN: Your mama's so fat she eats wheat *thicks!*

WAYNE: You—

SUSAN: Your mama's so fat, she tried to get an all-over tan and the sun burned out!

WAYNE: Your mama's so stupid, she jumped out a window and went up!

SUSAN: Your mama's so stupid she thought Hamburger Helper

came with another person! Your mama's so stupid, she sold her car for gas money! Your mama's so stupid, I taught her the running man, and I haven't seen her since.

WAYNE: Okay...

SUSAN: Your mama's so stupid she got fired from the M&M factory for throwing out the Ws!

WAYNE: Okay...

SUSAN: Your mama's so dumb she failed a blood test.

WAYNE: All right! You win!

SUSAN: Your mama's so dumb...

(SUSAN *can't stop. One snap after another keeps flying out; it's as if a dam has been released.* COACH LATRELL *gets into the "arena" to pull her out.*)

COACH LATRELL: Susan!

SUSAN: (*Screaming.*) Your mama's got an Afro with a chin strap! Your mama's got more weave than a dog in traffic! Your mama's got so many teeth missing, it looks like her tongue's in jail!

COACH LATRELL: (*Pulling her away and hugging her.*) SUSAN! IT'S OVER! IT'S OVER, SUSAN. It's over, baby. You did it. You did it.

(*Fade to black.*)

END OF PLAY

SOURPUSS

Dan Berkowitz

The first public performance of *Sourpuss* was in *Monologues and Madness* at the Cornelia Street Café, New York City, in August 2008. The piece was performed by the author.

A MAN *walks into a spotlight center stage.*

MAN: I'll tell you why I don't do drugs anymore. Ten years ago, a friend's traveling in Germany, sends me a package. Inside, wrapped in tissue paper, is a lump of something, kinda brown. Naturally, I assume it's hashish, so I swallow it. An hour later, when I'm not high, I track my friend down at his hotel. Wake him up at three-thirty in the morning, Düsseldorf time—on his honeymoon—to complain about the lousy hash. It's only after he yells, "Why didn't you read the note in the fuckin' box?" that I realize what I had ingested was not hash, but was, in fact, a chunk of the Berlin Wall.

Three days later—when I *am* high on hash—I'm at a party, doing tequila shots. My friend Jack starts laughing and goes, "Man, remember that time you took the sledgehammer to Warren Beatty's Jaguar? Jesus, you really beat the crap out of that car!" And everybody's laughing and I'm laughing, and then I find myself saying, "When did I do that?" And Jack must not have heard me, cause he starts laughing even harder, and goes, "And then when Warren pulled the gun on you, the way you fell to your knees, and stretched your arms out like Christ on the cross, and sobbed, 'Don't shoot! Dukakis needs every vote!'" Which, of course, told me it must have been 1988.

And I suddenly realize there are vast swaths of my life of which I no longer have any recollection at all. And some

417

of them sound like they were fun. I mean, for example, I thought I'd never even *been* to the Tournament of Roses parade. And then I find out one year I not only rode *on* the Disney float, but had sex with Snow White. And two of the Dwarfs. *During* the parade. But the hash had wiped out a lot of brain cells. Well, and the pot too. And probably the coke. And the acid and the mescaline. And I suppose the mushrooms, though I only did them once or twice. I think.

(*Pause.*)

I am *so* glad vodka doesn't affect the brain.

(*Blackout.*)

END OF PLAY

THANK YOU SO MUCH
FOR STOPPING

Halley Feiffer

Lights up on ASHLEIGH, *standing on the side of the road. She is the picture of a perfectly put-together young lady, save for the palpable anxiety that we can see is bubbling inside her; even so, she has a smile plastered on her face. She waves frantically at an approaching car.*

ASHLEIGH: Hi excuse me?!? Hi!! (*Sound of the car slowing down and pulling up to her.*) Hi, um. (*She makes a gesture for "please roll down your window." Sound of the window being rolled down. With a big smile, like the gracious hostess.*) Hiiii. Thank you *so* much for stopping. I'm *so* sorry to bother you, I'm just having a *little* bit of a problem, I'd love your help, I'm *so* sorry, I *never* do this, it's just... *kind of* an emergency—oh no don't worry, it's not the end of the world or anything, I'm fine it's just—oh, this is so embarrassing— (*She chokes on her words; she is suddenly emotional.*) —Oh it's just so hard to ask for *help!* (*Beat. She collects herself quickly.*) I'm sorry. I don't know what got into me. Excuse me. So: thank you so much for stopping here's the thing: I just, as I was driving—I'm going over to my mother's house—(*Points to her car in the distance.*)—yup that's me, right over there, the Prius, uh-huh—so, as I was driving, I just...

Accidentally killed my husband. (*Grimaces.*) I know, it's *so* embarrassing, I just— (*Suddenly remembers something.*) Oh! My gosh, I can't believe it, I forgot to introduce myself, I'm so sorry, how rude. (*Sticking out her hand.*) I'm Ashleigh, what's your name? Susan? That's my *mother's* name! No I am not kidding, it really is! And what's your name? Jerry? That's my *brother's* name! No don't get too excited Jerry I was kidding that time. (*Laughs loudly at her own joke.*) So *anyway*: I just killed my husband, and I was wondering if you guys—

—Oh, well that's a good question, I'm sorry, I should've explained that right away: what happened was, we were driving over to my mother's house—I said that—and we were just sort of joking around, and he was, you know, joshing with me about how bad a driver I am, and I got kind of peeved, 'cause—well, I don't know why, I'm usually very even-tempered, but things have been sort of tough lately— (*Gets sort of emotional again, tries not to let it show.*) —and anyway I got sort of peeved, and I said: "Well if you hate the way I drive so much why don't you get out of the car?" and he said "Maybe I will" and I said, "Good, then do that," and I pulled over, and he got out, and then, as a joke, sort of, I sort of pretended to like you know, hit him with the car, but here's the thing I actually *am* a pretty bad driver, and here's the thing I *did* hit him, and I definitely didn't *mean* to, but then I thought, Well hey, people get hit by cars all the time, I didn't hit him that hard, I'm sure I didn't do any serious damage, but here's the thing: I did. (*Grimaces.*) Yeeeeeah. You know it's the sort of thing that could happen to anyone, but when it happens to you, you're like AAAAAAH WHAT DO I DO?!?!?!? You know? So what I'm *wondering* is: would you guys mind if I just kind of *loaded* him into your backseat, and we could just drive him over to the hospital real quick? It'll just be real quick—I have to be somewhere myself in half an hour—

I'm sorry?

Oh, well I can't very well put him in *my* backseat, I've got both the kids back there.

Yeeeah, I do, two little ones. Little Susan and Little Jerry! No just kidding those aren't their names. But that reminds me actually—and I hate to be needy—but do you guys have any babysitting experience? I'm so sorry I hate to be needy but as I said things *have* been sort of tough lately, and—

(*Sound of the car pulling away.*)

Oh no, wait what? Oh no no no wait, don't—what are you—*what*?!

(*Sound of the car retreating into the distance.* ASHLEIGH *looks after the car, forlorn. After a few moments, to herself.*)

I guess that's what I get for asking for help.

END OF PLAY

36 RUMSON ROAD

Barbara Wiechmann

---

36 Rumson Road premiered at Home for Contemporary Theatre and Art in New York City as part of their Midnight Madness Festival in 1991. It was directed by the author with the following cast:

JONI	Michael Houston
SONIA	Jeanne Dorsey

JONI GRILLO *and* SONIA DINUNZIO, *two middle-aged Realtors with great outfits, sit at a local bar drinking very sweet whiskey sours.*

SONIA: So be it fate...

JONI: You're not looking good.

SONIA: There's nothing I can do.

JONI: What is it?

SONIA: 36 Rumson Road.

JONI: What?

SONIA: The house won't sell.

JONI: I thought you sold it.

SONIA: I can't sell it.

JONI: It's written all over your face.

SONIA: It's a lovely house. A gorgeous house. I can't sell it. For love or money. I can't sell it. I don't know what it is. I tell you the leak coming from the garage is very minor. It's a terrible thing you know. I put my heart into the place.

JONI: You love the house.

SONIA: I do. It's a beautiful house.

JONI: But you can't sell it.

SONIA: I don't get it.

JONI: Sonia, you're so stuck on this house it's terrible.

SONIA: I love the house. I *love* the house.

JONI: The house is *great*. Why doesn't it sell?

SONIA: She tells me the kitchen. The kitchen needs redoing. What's wrong with the kitchen? The kitchen is great. The kitchen is gorgeous in the house. They don't like the brown tile. They don't like the brown tile all over the house.

JONI: The house has brown tile?

SONIA: There is a lot of brown tile in the house. There are a lot of brown *tones* in the house. As I said, a Tudor is a darker house. The whole thing is darker in a Tudor. It can take the brown.

JONI: Of course.

SONIA: Do you want your fruit?

JONI: Lemme keep the cherry. I thought the house was listed with Marlene?

SONIA: No. No way. I got the listing. I bled for that listing.

JONI: I know you, Sonia.

SONIA: And you know what I think of that place. A showplace. I want to tell you I've been to hell and back just to get the whoosies to make up their minds to put it on the market. Marlene—let's face it—is the kind of broker who wants a property to just land in her lap. You and I know it doesn't work that way. I mean where's the craft in that?

JONI: Sure.

SONIA: Listen—soon as I heard the Blaumsteins were relocating, I cornered the wife in the Grand Union. The frozen-food aisle. Maneuvered the skinny bitch over to the Sara Lee section and slammed her up against the frozen fudge layer cakes. She's helpless. I'm casual. I start up a conversation. Ease her into domestic talk. Turns out she doesn't know what to do. She's torn. She loves the house. She's in love with the house. She's heartbroken about selling—but hubby's relocating. Should she keep it on the off chance they'll be vacationing in Monmouth? *She doesn't know.* Hubby wants to sell. He's unyielding. They're fighting. She's in tears. What to do. I toss a few Sara Lee crumb cakes into her cart. We share a laugh. I wanna say, "What would you *like* to do with the house— what would you *like*?" I mean she's driving me crazy. I'd like to say, "Sell it, *sell it!*" but a term keeps running through my mind—a phrase—I can't put my finger on it.

JONI: Is there a phrase such as "Stuff it up your ass"?

SONIA: Exactly. So here's what I tell her. I take her aside. I look her square in the face. I say, "Keep the man not the house." I say, "Keep the man."

JONI: Beautiful.

SONIA: Keep the man.

JONI: That's craft.

SONIA: And boom—I get the listing.

JONI: And after all that it won't sell.

SONIA: You know why? I'll tell you why it doesn't sell. You know why? The house doesn't take a good picture. You know why? It's got the garage in front. That's the garage. (*She demonstrates with hands.*) And that's the house. I have pictures from every angle. I paid ninety-four dollars for those pictures. Shit. I paid for what? For shit. You're never gonna get a good shot. It's all blocked by trees.

JONI: You see the shots Jerry got of Mystic Manor? Gorgeous.

SONIA: You know why he gets ahead? He gets good pictures. Every time. The house could be a pile of sticks and the shots come up beautiful. You see the shots he got of Winkle Circuit? Beautiful. He got the blue with the cranberry shutters. Beautiful. (SONIA *is by this point overcome.*)

JONI: What is it? What is it?

SONIA: What is it? I'll tell you what it is. I can't get a good picture. That's it right there. I'm fucked. I'm fucked on the visuals. I'm screwed on the visuals.

JONI: Well it doesn't help the door is beaten in when you go to show the place.

SONIA: No, no it does not. Who's gonna buy a place with the door beaten in? They come to see a house, the door's beaten in, they think it's a bad neighborhood. They think vandals.

JONI: You wanna know what I think?

SONIA: What do you think?

JONI: I think Marlene.

SONIA: I think Marlene too. It's dog-eat-dog, Joni. I got to tell you that between her and me, it's dog-eat-dog.

JONI: Sure.

SONIA: You know what she did to the poodle?

JONI: What poodle?

SONIA: That open house we threw? She comes, spends the entire afternoon gobbling up our cheese and with fifteen minutes to close up, finds the garage and locks a poodle in it. She imprisons this poodle in the garage—without food, without water, knowing it could be *days* before the house is opened up again. A teacup poodle. This big. Arthritic. She knows it's not going to last.

JONI: Where'd she get it?

SONIA: It's hers! The woman has no values.

JONI: She killed her own dog?

SONIA: She suffocated her poodle. Just to get me. She locked it in the garage without food or water, so it would die and stink and rot and—

JONI: The house won't sell.

SONIA: *Exactly.*

JONI: It's good you have a sense of humor.

SONIA: You know, Joni, you're fun. You're a lot of laughs. You like to have a good time, you know.

JONI: Who doesn't?

SONIA: Frank was telling me—the other day he says to me, "Sonia, lighten up. Sonia, you're no fun anymore." He says, "Let's go to the track—blow some cash." So we go to Monmouth. Nothing. It's no fun. No fun. (*Pause.*) I wanna be somewhere. You know, Jone—I wanna be somewhere with my life. I should be on top. I got this house too much on my mind.

JONI: Frank thinks you're no fun?

SONIA: So listen. We go to the Red Oak for a Greek salad— something light in the summertime—we go to sit down in the booth, and I happen to notice that there's crap all over the seats. I say, "Frank, we can't sit here, there's dirt all over the seats." You know what he says? Listen to this. He says, "Sonia, we're fucking dirty people, we can sit on fucking dirty seats."

JONI: Did you tell him to stuff it up his asshole?

SONIA: Joni, I'm a fun girl.

JONI: You sat?

SONIA: Of course. There are still good times to be had.

JONI: Absolutely.

SONIA: Now Marlene. She would not sit on those seats. For love or money. You see what I'm saying—she's not a sport. She's not a good time.

JONI: What because she won't sit on dirt she's not a good time?

SONIA: No. No, not because she won't sit on dirt. Because she won't sit on it even as a *joke*—you see?

JONI: Oh sure—as a joke. As a joke I'd sit on anything.

SONIA: *Exactly.* That's because you, Joni, are fun. You're a fun person. I'm a fun person too.

JONI: You're a very fun person. You just have this house too much on your mind.

SONIA: You know what it is? I can't get a good picture. That's what it is. I'm fucked on the visuals. (*Pause.*) Joni, you think I put on a few?

JONI: No.

SONIA: Frank thinks I put on a few.

JONI: I don't see it.

SONIA: We bleed our guts for these houses.

JONI: We do.

SONIA: We bleed our guts for what? For what. For Marlene to come and beat the door in. For Marlene to come and leave her dead poodle in the garage to die and stink and shame me. For Marlene to come. (*Pause.*) It's a shame, though. I looked at you the very first time, I said, "There's a girl who likes to laugh, to have a good time."

JONI: Sure.

SONIA: It's a crying shame. Two girls who love to laugh. We bleed our guts. And you know, Joni, what the biggest crime is—you know what the real shame is? We're not getting any younger.

(*Blackout.*)

END OF PLAY

THREE GUYS
AND A BRENDA

Adam Bock

Three Guys and a Brenda was originally produced by the 24 Hour Company at the Atlantic Theater in New York City on March 15, 2004. It was directed by Garret Savage with the following cast:

BOB	Julie Shavers
JOE	Carla Rzeszewski
RANDALL	Jama Williamson
BRENDA	Tami Dixon

Three Guys and a Brenda won the Heideman Award and received its world premiere at Actors Theatre of Louisville's 30th Anniversary Humana Festival of New American Plays on April 1 and 2 of 2006. Made possible by a generous grant from the Humana Festival, and presented by special arrangement with William Morris Agency, LLC, this play was directed by Steven Rahe with the following cast and staff:

JOE	Suzanna Hay
BOB	Keira Keeley
RANDALL	Cheryl Lynn Bowers
BRENDA	Sarah Augusta
SCENIC DESIGNER	Paul Owen
COSTUME DESIGNERS	John P. White
	Stacy Squires
LIGHTING DESIGNER	Paul Werner
SOUND DESIGNER	Benjamin Marcum
PROPERTIES DESIGNER	Mark Walston
STAGE MANAGER	Debra Anne Gasper

ASSISTANT STAGE MANAGER	Heather Fields
ASSISTANT STAGE MANAGER	Paul Mills Holmes
DRAMATURG	Julie Felise Dubiner

All production groups performing this play are required to include the following credits on the title page of every program:

> *Three Guys and a Brenda* received its world premiere in the 2006 Humana Festival of New American Plays at the Actors Theatre of Louisville.

CAST OF CHARACTERS
BOB: A man, played by a woman.
JOE: A man, played by a woman.
RANDALL: A man, played by a woman.
BRENDA: A woman, played by a woman.

SETTING
At work.

Before this, BOB, JOE, *and* RANDALL *were watching TV waiting for their shift to start.*

> *Now:* BOB *and* JOE *are onstage. They are crying.*
> RANDALL *walks across stage, crying. Exits.*
> BOB *and* JOE *continue to cry.*
> RANDALL *walks onstage. He is still crying. He has a roll of toilet tissue. He hands out tissue. They are all crying.*
> BRENDA *walks across stage. They try not to/don't cry when she is onstage. She exits.*
> *They cry again. Deep breaths.*
> *They sniff. They sniff. They sniff.*
> BRENDA *enters.*

434 *Adam Bock*

BRENDA: You guys are on second shift right?

JOE: Yeah Brenda.

BOB: Yeah that's right.

BRENDA: Joe, then when your shift starts, then you and Bob are going to show Randall what to do with the new machine, ok?

JOE: Ok.

BRENDA: Ok?

BOB: Yeah ok.

JOE: Ok sure.

BRENDA: Ok then.

(*Exits.*)

JOE: (*Deep breath, doesn't cry.*) Fucking animal nature shows.

BOB: I know.

JOE: They get me every time.

RANDALL: She's so beautiful.

JOE: She is.

BOB: She is Randall.

JOE: Yes she is.

RANDALL: Isn't she Bob? She's beautiful!

BOB: She is Randall.

RANDALL: I have to tell her she's beautiful.

BOB: I don't know Randall.

JOE: I don't know.

BOB: What do you think Joe?

JOE: I don't know about that Bob.

BOB: Yeah me neither I don't know either.

JOE: Might not be appropriate. In the work environment.

BOB: Right.

JOE: Right?

BOB: In the work environment.

JOE: This being work.

BOB: Right.

RANDALL: I have to.

BOB: Well if you have to, you have to.

JOE: That's right.

BOB: If you have to, you have to.

JOE: Right.

BOB: Right.

JOE: But I don't think you're going to.

BOB: Nope.

JOE: Right?

BOB: Nope!

RANDALL: I have to.

BOB: Joe here might.

JOE: That's something I might tell her.

BOB: Right. Joe might.

JOE: I might. I might say something to her like

BOB: Like

JOE: "You're beautiful!"

BOB: Right!

JOE: But I don't know whether you'd say something like that.

RANDALL: I am too. I am too going to say something like that
    to her!

JOE: Well.

BOB: Well.

JOE: Well ok then.

RANDALL: Because I think she's beautiful.

BOB: Well.

JOE: Ok then.

RANDALL: And I'm going to say it.

BOB: Ok then.

JOE: Ok.

(RANDALL *exits.*)

JOE: Think he's going to tell her?

BOB: Nope.

JOE: I'm not watching any more of those nature shows. They're too sad.

BOB: Yeah I know. Me neither.

JOE: They're too fucking sad. They make me sad.

RANDALL: (*To audience.*) Thing that's hard about being a guy? You always have to tell the girl "Hey you're great" or "Hey I think you're great" or "You're great" or "You're great" and "Would you maybe want to go out?" and that's hard. Plus it's hard to have to shave all the time. That's hard too.

JOE: (*To audience.*) Plus it's hard to pick a good deodorant.

RANDALL: (*To audience.*) Yeah that's hard too.

JOE: (*To audience.*) Plus guys? Plus we have to carry everything.

RANDALL: (*To audience.*) Right.

JOE: (*To audience.*) Especially heavy things. Like sofas.

RANDALL: (*To audience.*) Yeah that's hard.

BOB: (*To audience.*) Plus

JOE: (*To audience.*) Plus you have to drive all the time.

RANDALL: (*To audience.*) Yeah. And that.

BOB: (*To audience.*) Plus

JOE: (*To audience.*) You have to drive on really long trips, to the beach, to visit your family, and then back from the beach. And if a tire blows you have to take it off, you have to put the spare on. Plus you have to pay.

RANDALL: (*To audience.*) For everything.

BOB: (*To audience.*) Plus

JOE: (*To audience.*) Plus sometimes you don't understand something and that can make you feel stupid and so you have to pretend you understand it. That can be hard. (*Pause.*)

BOB: Yeah.

RANDALL: Yeah. (*Pause.*)

JOE: (*To audience.*) That can be hard. (*Pause.*)

RANDALL: (*To audience.*) Mostly it's hard though saying "I think you're great" and "Would you maybe like to go out" and then you have to wait and find out what the answer is. That's hard.

(BRENDA *enters.*)

Um. Brenda?

BRENDA: Give me a second.

(BRENDA *exits.*)

RANDALL: Guys. Don't bust my chops.

JOE: I didn't say anything.

RANDALL: Don't bust my chops.

(BRENDA *enters.*)

Hey Brenda?

BRENDA: I said just give me a.

(*She exits.* JOE, BOB, *and* RANDALL *stand.*

RANDALL *looks at* JOE *and* BOB.

BRENDA *enters.*)

Yeah ok?

RANDALL: Oh yeah so. Um.

BRENDA: Yeah?

RANDALL: Guys?

JOE: Oh yeah.

BOB: What?

JOE: Ok. Come on.

BOB: What?

JOE: Bob come on.

BOB: Oh yeah yeah ok!

JOE: Ok!

BOB: Ok.

(*They exit.*)

RANDALL: Yeah so Brenda?

BRENDA: Yeah ok?

RANDALL: So.

BRENDA: I have work Randall.

RANDALL: Um.

BRENDA: Yeah ok so, what?

RANDALL: Um.

BRENDA: I have work.

(*Turns to exit.*)

RANDALL: I think you're beautiful.

BRENDA: What?

RANDALL: Um.

BRENDA: That's not funny.

RANDALL: What?

BRENDA: That's not funny.

RANDALL: I'm not being funny.

BRENDA: That's mean. That pisses me off. That really truly pisses me off.

RANDALL: No I do.

BRENDA: I have a lot of work. And you're pissing me off.

RANDALL: No I do. I think you're beautiful. I think you're beautiful like a. Like something beautiful. Like the sun in the sky. Like a lake. Like the sunshine on a lake in the early evening right before the sun goes down and everything is calm. And the water's calm. That's what I think.

BRENDA: Shut up.

RANDALL: No I do.

BRENDA: Like a lake?

RANDALL: Like the sunshine. On the lake.

BRENDA: Really?

RANDALL: Yeah really.

BRENDA: Really?

RANDALL: And I think If only I could kiss her I'd be happy.

BRENDA: Really?

RANDALL: Yeah.

BRENDA: You think if you kissed me, you'd be happy?

RANDALL: Yeah.

BRENDA: You want to kiss me?

RANDALL: Yeah.

BRENDA: And that would make you happy?

RANDALL: Yeah.

BRENDA: Just a kiss?

RANDALL: Yeah.

BRENDA: Ok so.

RANDALL: Really?

BRENDA: So?

(*They kiss. Should be a good smooch.*)

RANDALL: (*Softly.*) Yeah. That made me happy.

BRENDA: I have work.

RANDALL: Ok.

BRENDA: I have work.

RANDALL: Ok. Ok.

(*She exits.*)

JOE: (*To audience.*) I told my wife I loved the sound of her voice on the phone. And I do. I still do.

BOB: (*To audience.*) I gave my girlfriend a smooth stone I found on the side of the road.

JOE: Right?

BOB: Yeah.

(RANDALL *smiles.*)

(*The three men sit.*)

END OF PLAY

TIRADE

Mary Louise Wilson

Tirade was first performed by Denny Dillon at the Odd Fellows Theatre in Olivebridge, New York, on May 30, 2009, with the author directing. Earlier versions entitled *Actress* and *Rave* were performed by Nicole Quinn and Mary Louise Wilson in Actors & Writers' 2002 and 2004 Shorts Festivals.

An actress of indeterminate years stands before us. She has a somewhat grandiose manner and a slight note of injury in her voice.

I don't like to blow my own horn, but I have some standing in the theater community. I am not exactly chopped liver in this town. People know my work, I know people, people know me. In fact, I was at a peak, an all-time high in my career.

I had just opened in my one-woman show *Tra-La!*, an evening of song and anecdote based on my life in the theater You probably saw the reviews? "A benchmark performance," "A comedic watershed," "Pitch-perfect," blah blah blah.

And then this other show opened off-Broadway; *Sick!* A cancer play. And apparently, the lead, Dorothy Dibble, was nude during the entire evening. Well, in the first act she wore a hospital gown with the back open, but in the second act she was nude. And bald.

Nevertheless, *Sick!* was a big hit. You can't beat a cancer play. Audiences love it, they love watching somebody spit into a basin and die for two acts.

Nude and bald. That's acting. Fine! I don't begrudge that. To Each His Own, I say, and Hooray for everybody. I was too busy performing in my own hit to pay too much attention anyway.

It was just that I didn't necessarily want to hear about her show all the time. Every other minute someone was asking me, "Have you seen *Sick!* yet?" I was still recovering from my opening night when my sister called from Alabama: "I just heard about this wonderful play *Sick!* Have you seen it?" Well of course

I hadn't seen it! I was performing *Tra-La!* eight times a week and in between I had to have complete bed rest! I called my oldest friend in Boston about coming into town to see my show and she said, "Okay, but can you get me tickets to *Sick!?*"

And then this other thing started happening: this old theater queen who lives in my building attacked me in the lobby. "Guess who just moved in down the street?" I started to say I heard Meryl Streep had bought a house nearby when he screamed at me, "Not HER, Dorothy Dibble!" I arrived at my neighborhood hair salon and Jeffry the stylist hooted, "You just missed Dorothy Dibble!"

Even the doorman. One night as I was leaving the building I distinctly heard Jahmeal the doorman say, "Dorothy Dibble." I grabbed his lapels. "What did you just say?" The poor man has a very thick accent. I let go when I realized he was saying "Door thing. Jiggle."

But, I mean, why do people think one actress is just dying to hear about another actress, anyway? Is one pipe fitter thrilled to know about another pipe fitter's work?

But it wasn't just the people in my neighborhood. Of course you've heard of Nicky LaPlant, the stage director? Nicky is one of the savviest, most wickedly funny people on the planet. Well one night we were having one of our little dinners together and he was babbling away about all the things he was doing, dropping names left and right and suddenly I hear him say "lunch with Dorothy Dibble." I was shocked. "I didn't know you knew her," I said. "Oh yes, darling," he purred, "Dorothy and I are quite, quite close." Now I have known Nicky since we were both lobsters in a summer stock production of *Alice in Wonderland* and I never heard him mention the woman's name before.

And then another dear friend, the set designer George St. George, who absolutely adores me, always telling me how fantastic I am to the point of embarrassment, he called to invite me to his annual Christmas party. It's always a lovely, elegant affair, never more than twelve of us; he said "Nathan's coming, and Marion and Merle, Philip Seymour and Dorothy—"

"Dorothy?" I gasped. "Tell me it's not Dorothy Dibble!" And he gushed, "Oh but it is! *The* Dorothy Dibble! Isn't she marrrvelous?" This woman had become intimate with all my intimates.

Even my classical theater buddy, Alma Osgood, the famous British snob and vocal coach who is forever going on about Shakespeare and classical training and steak-and-kidney pie. Suddenly Alma starts mentioning "Dottie" in every other breath: the Royal Academy and Dottie, Sir Ian and Dottie, Dottie and spotted dick. I was being Dottied to death. Suddenly "Dotties" are dotting everybody's conversation.

One day when Alma put Dottie in the same sentence with Dame Judy, I exploded. "What is the big deal with this woman, anyway? Has anybody ever seen her act?" And Alma rose to her full four feet and shouted, "Dorothy Dibble is a wonderful woman!"

What exactly was the implication here? That I was *not* a wonderful woman?

Dottie was apparently overflowing with the milk of human kindness. A veritable cow.

The thing that galled me was, I *had* seen her act years ago. It wasn't as if she just popped out of somebody's ear, you know. She had been around for years. Way, way off-Broadway. Performing in broom closets and deserted grocery stores in her one-person show about Mamie Eisenhower. One day when I happened to be on the Lower East Side I went into this grocery to buy an orange and I actually saw her Mamie. All I can tell you is, I was gob-smacked with tedium. There was something going on up there, but I'm damned if I can say what it was. All the nuance and depth of an ironing board. With the voice of Bela Lugosi.

When *Sick!* finally closed I assumed the furor over this woman would wane. But it was like gnats. An infestation. Dorothy Dibble was metastasizing.

She started showing up on letterheads for theater benefits, on fund-raising committees. She was sitting on advisory boards. She was in my mail, inviting me to five-hundred-dollar-a-plate dinners.

There was no escape. She was everywhere, like some ghastly perfume. No matter where I looked she was sounding off about climate change, or saving trees, or starring in two plays at the same time. She was on the front page of the *New York Post*. The pictures showed her frantically hailing a cab to get from one theater to the other, or in her dressing room frantically climbing out of one costume and into another. The AP picked the article up and it ran all over the country. My sister in Alabama cut it out and sent it to me.

I had to get away; get out of the city. Get as far away as possible from the overinflated world of show business where everything is either brilliant or a bomb, a touchstone or a laugh-fest or a love song. When my show closed, I went to Tuscany. I made friends with a lovely Italian couple and one night they invited me to dinner. We were sitting out on the hill overlooking Firenze, lazily chatting, sipping our Bellinis, and suddenly in the cross talk I thought I heard something. That name. Dottie. No. It couldn't be. "Dottie?" I sort of croaked. "Ah, si, si! La bella donna Dibble!" My hosts knew her. They all knew her.

The next morning I left for Egypt. I had a sudden desire to see the pyramids.

By the time I got back home Dorothy Dibble was appearing on two television series at the same time. She was running for president of the Screen Actors Guild. Her platform was clean air.

I opened the *Times* to a full-page ad for world peace and there she was between Kofi Annan and Desmond Tutu. Dorothy came out against clitoral mutilation on *The Charlie Rose Show*.

And all this time I never ran into her. Not once. Not that I wanted to, I really, really did not want to come face-to-face with this person. And I had the oddest feeling she knew this. We were always just missing each other—she would have just left the same party or restaurant where I was. And then, one day, it happened. I was sitting in the reception room of a casting office waiting to audition. The door opened and I heard the casting woman say, "Bless you for coming in, Dorothy," and then I heard a low, lugubrious voice say, "Tell your cute hubby hello for me," and then she turned, and there she was, standing right in front of me.

For a second our eyes locked, then she looked away. She didn't know who I was! Or did she? There was something, I swear there was a glint in her eye. She did know! I had to do something. I could not have this woman not acknowledge me!

She was moving toward the elevator. I heard myself yelling, "Dorothy Dibble! Hi! It's Tootie Perkins! *Tra-la?*"

She looked stony-faced for a second and then she broke out into this blinding smile. "Of course I know who you are!" she intoned. "I didn't think you recognized *me*!"

"How could I not know who you are?" I heard myself gushing, "and your fabulous show *Sick!*? I was *dying* to see it! I mean, I was *sick* that I—I mean, I was *beside* myself that I missed it because of *my* show!"

"Well I saw *your* show," she said—she must have come to a Wednesday matinee—"and it was one of the most brilliant afternoons I have ever spent in the theater."

Then she bowed. Like this. (*Deep bow to the floor.*) She said, "Your performance was thrilling. Exquisite. Beyond perfection." The elevator came. I got in with her.

She continued telling me how wonderful I was all the way down to the lobby and out onto Sixth Avenue. I couldn't seem to manage to get a word in edgewise. And I have to confess, I was so—*pumped up*. I felt like I was on helium. I don't remember what happened next. We just sort of floated to Spitto's; you know, where the theatrical in-crowd hangs out. I don't remember what I ate or drank, I was woozy with praise. According to Dottie, I was spellbinding, heartbreaking. Even my hands could act. My feet could bring tears to the eyes.

These words were tumbling over me and my head was hanging humbly lower and lower over my french fries when I happened to glance up and just for a minute there I thought I saw something. I thought I caught a *glint* in her eye. Something *steely*. I wasn't sure.

Just then she excused herself to go to the ladies' room and the minute she was gone I felt my head clear a little. And that's when it hit me; she was trying to kill me with compliments!

I felt my gorge rising. I had to fight this. I couldn't go under again, I had to stop her. Then I saw her making her way back across the room, waving to tables, stopping occasionally to kiss Sarah Jessica here and Liev there, and then she was looking down at me with that blinding smile, intoning in that sepulchral voice of hers, "Oh, Act-tress..." and I felt myself turning to jelly again. I had to fight back! I grabbed her jowls. "Your face is a benchmark of emotion!" I yelled. "Not since Brando has an acting style so completely altered a generation!" I didn't know what I was saying. I just lifted things from old Ben Brantley reviews—not necessarily her reviews—and spewed them at her. "Your scenes are a series of watersheds! You render an explosive effect! Your searing gestures galvanize the scenery!"

She began to wobble. She was faint. "I need air," she gasped. I let go of her cheeks. We left the restaurant and fell into a cab.

All the way downtown we pummeled each other with praise. She called me a legend in my own time, I called her the Duse of our day. I had no idea there were so many good things to say about anybody.

The cab pulled up to her building. We wrestled over who would go through her door first; she finally shoved me through, yelling, "Pearls before swine!" As I went past her I shot back, "Age before beauty!" And then right there in the foyer we grappled. I grabbed her ankle and roared, "Great bones!" She grabbed my hair and growled, "I'd give my right tit for hair like this!" I twisted around and got her by the neck. We fell to the floor. I got my leg over her, pinned her arms down and hissed, "You were incredible in that scene with the doctor!" She groaned, "I will never forget the way you moved your hand when you were telling the story about your nephew!" and butted her head into mine—hard.

I passed out for maybe two seconds and when I came to she was up and getting something; a gun, maybe. Or a poster for me to sign. I reached out and blindly felt around for something, a heavy object. I managed to get up and just as she turned around I screamed, "That thing you did with your IV drip was hallucinating!" and clobbered her with her Tony Award. She dropped like a felled tree. I went closer. She didn't seem to be breathing. I said, "Dorothy? Your timing is inimitable." She didn't move. I said, "Dorothy, can you hear me? You are luminous." She didn't stir. I moved quickly, wiped my fingerprints off her leg, her Tony, and opened the door. Then, just as I was leaving, I turned back and said one last thing. "Dorothy? You know when you were fiddling with your catheter and wailing at the top of your lungs? You really stank it up!" And then I let myself out.

END OF PLAY

UNCOVERED

Caleen Sinnette Jennings

Uncovered was first presented as a staged reading at the Kennedy Center Page-to-Stage Festival, September 7, 2009. Producing Company: African Continuum Theatre Company, Washington, D.C.

CHARACTERS

TANTE MABEL PRIDEAUX: (Mid- to late fifties.) Former resident of a lovely suburban street in New Orleans.

LUCILLE PRIDEAUX VERNON: (Thirties) Mabel's daughter and resident of Manhattan.

TIFFANY FIELDS: (Thirties) Mabel's niece and resident of Manhattan.

SETTING

The site of what was Tante Mabel's home in New Orleans, two years after Katrina hit. All three women wear rubber gloves and work clothes. There are three large trash bags filled with items. Everyone swats at mosquitoes.

This play is dedicated to those who survived and to those who perished in hurricane Katrina

At rise, LUCILLE *is alone, digging onstage, discarding items here and there. She wipes the sweat from her neck and face, and looks up with hostility at the brutal sun. After a beat,* TIFFANY *enters from offstage left, carrying three bottles of water and looking somewhat cooler.* LUCILLE *glances at her watch.*

LUCILLE: If it ain't Miss Tiff.

TIFFANY: Sorry. Fell asleep in the car and got a crick in my neck. Here.

(TIFFANY *extends the water bottle to* LUCILLE, *who takes it and drinks gratefully.*)

Where is she?

LUCILLE: Behind the garage.

TIFFANY: Isn't that dangerous?

LUCILLE: She had to pee.

TIFFANY: I'm holding mine till we get back to the hotel. I left the air con on and the motor running. (*Calling offstage.*) Tante Mabel? (*She swats at mosquitoes.*) I'm a damn hors d'oeuvres platter. (*Pointing to her bites.*) Look at this. Here, here, and here. One even got down in my bra! I'll be glad to get gone. She finished with all this?

LUCILLE: I sure am. Let's wrap the crap and put a bow on it.

TIFFANY: This is tough on her, Cille. Be gentle.

(*She sees* MABEL *approaching.*)

   Shhhhh.

(MABEL *enters carrying a rock.*)

LUCILLE: What's that for?

MABEL: I need a favor.

TIFFANY: Whatever you want as long as it's back at the hotel. What do you ladies say to a cool shower, a cold beer and a hot filé gumbo?

MABEL: When we're through here.

LUCILLE: And that would be now. There's nothing else left, Mama.

(LUCILLE *picks up a rusty object and tosses it away.*)

MABEL: Put that in the bag.

LUCILLE: (*Picking it up.*) But it's nothing but rust.

MABEL: Well, it's my rust. Put it in the bag.

TIFFANY: What is it?

MABEL: I made Papa Prideaux his first cup of coffee as a married man in that pot.

TIFFANY: Oh, it's a coffeepot.

MABEL: Fresh brewed with a lot of chicory. Just how he liked it. That first morning, that first day of our lives together.

(MABEL *marks out the areas she refers to.*)

The stove was here. The sky turned pink out my window right over here. Got the coffee beans from the bin down here. Cups from the hooks under the shelves that were here. Walked out on the porch over here. Put the coffee down on the little table he had made right here. Sat in the two chairs on either side, sipping and laughing and waving at the Pearsons on their porch over there. Ella Pearson just sliding her greedy eyes up and down Papa's skin too. I saw her. But he was mine. Just sipping and loving that coffee out of my brand-new pot. Smiling and crinkling the corners of his eyes. Tilting back his chair and me scolding him and him laughing and scooping me in his arms. And us leaving our coffee cups and climbing our stairs over here. Never did make it to church that Sunday. If it weren't for that coffeepot you're turning your nose up at, you might not even be standing here, Miss Lucille.

TIFFANY: That's so romantic.

LUCILLE: I truly appreciate it, Mama. And if that's what it is, we'll find a special place for it. (*She puts the rusty pot in the bag.*) Well, Tiff's got the air con running, so...

(LUCILLE *and* TIFFANY *start dragging loaded trash bags toward the car offstage.* TIFFANY *stops, turns around, and looks at the site of the house.*)

TIFFANY: Good-bye, 211 Derbigny and the summer of 1986. And to Tante Mabel's beignets, and June Bug Pearson's kissing me behind the garage.

LUCILLE: Good-bye, 211 Derbigny and Papa Prideaux's switch off that bush over there, and watermelon off Mr. Granville's truck, and nights of stars and crickets and Mama humming over that bowl of snap beans. And when George Bush, Michael Brown and the entire FEMA administration go to hell, and that's exactly where they're going—may it look just like this. Amen. (*Pause. Softly.*) Mama, put the rock down and say good-bye now.

MABEL: I need something from the glove box.

LUCILLE: What glove box.

MABEL: (*Gesturing offstage right.*) In Papa's Buick Skylark.

LUCILLE: Yeah, well the only problem about getting into the Skylark is that there's a garage on top of it. (*Lightly.*) I know we're strong black women and all, but the car's crushed.

MABEL: Only on one side.

(MABEL *makes a move toward the car offstage right.* LUCILLE *blocks her path.*)

LUCILLE: I don't want a scene about this, Mama.

MABEL: (*Brandishing her rock.*) You just have to break the window on the driver's side.

TIFFANY: Now Tante Mabel, Cille and I juggled a lot of things in our lives to do this for you. But now, hard as it is, it's time to say good-bye. That's what this has always been about—

letting go of this part of your life. We know it's painful and we're here for you.

MABEL: And I appreciate everything you girls have done. (*Indicating the trash bags.*) But the most important thing is what's in the glove box.

LUCILLE: Wish you'd told me that two days and three trash bags ago.

TIFFANY: You see that the garage is perched up on the Skylark, Tante Mabel. So we have to let go of whatever is in there. Maybe we should all just go on and have a great big old cry.

MABEL: Papa came to me in my dream last night. Said I have to get it.

LUCILLE: Here we go...

MABEL: Say I need to go in the glove box and take what's in the bag. Say if I hold it to the sky and turn three times, then put it to my heart, it'll heal the ground.

(LUCILLE *starts dragging the trash bag toward the car stage left.*)

LUCILLE: Motor's running, time's a-wasting and you know I ain't down with the hoodoo.

(TANTE MABEL *lies down on the ground.*)

TIFFANY: Oh no.

LUCILLE: Now, Mama, you get up from there. (*Pause.*) You want everyone to see you acting crazy like this? You want the neighbors saying Mabel Prideaux came down from New York and lost her natural mind?

MABEL: All my neighbors gone. Gone for a thousand miles.

LUCILLE: Come on, now, people. We gotta go.

TIFFANY: (*Crossing her legs and bouncing.*) Seriously.

MAMA: I'll go when I get it.

(LUCILLE *takes* TIFFANY *aside.*)

LUCILLE: Any more great ideas? I told you to let her remember it the way it was and mourn. Seeing this has been too much of a shock. She tossed and turned all last night.

TIFFANY: She's been going downhill, Lucille. She needed these objects for closure.

LUCILLE: (*Sarcastically.*) Of course, Dr. Phil. I'm sorry I mistook you for my cousin Tiffany the hospital cafeteria worker. (*Pause.*) I appreciate your help, Tiff, don't get me wrong. You've been more like another daughter than her niece, and Lord knows I think of you as a sister. But the ultimate decision is mine.

MABEL: I don't know what you're whispering but it ain't gonna matter.

LUCILLE: She's going on the antidepressants.

TIFFANY: Medication is not the cure-all.

LUCILLE: She's got her rusty coffeepot. Time to do it my way. Let's wrap the crap and put a bow on it.

TIFFANY: Be gentle, Lucille.

LUCILLE: You know how I get when I'm hot, tired and evil, Mama. Don't make me leave you out here.

MABEL: Leave me here to die and bury me with Papa.

TIFFANY: We're not leaving you, Tante Mabel. Listen, is there money in the glove box? I know, how Papa Prideaux used to squirrel money away everywhere. Is it money? 'Cause if it is, it's gonna be molded and rotting in that glove box by now.

MABEL: What I want with money?

(TIFFANY *talks as she exits offstage right toward the Skylark.*)

TIFFANY: What did Papa Prideaux say in the dream?

LUCILLE: Where the hell are you going?

MABEL: (*Sitting up on her elbow.*) It's in a small black drawstring bag.

LUCILLE: (LUCILLE *yells to* TIFFANY *offstage.*) That's police tape, Tiffany! What part of "DO NOT ENTER" is unclear?

(MABEL *tries to go to* TIFFANY *offstage.* LUCILLE *blocks her path.*)

Would you stay here, please, Mama? Do you know how dangerous this is?

TIFFANY: (*Offstage.*) The whole passenger side is crushed.

LUCILLE: (*To* TIFFANY.) A garage will do that to a car. What do you think it's gonna do to you?

TIFFANY: (*Offstage.*) The driver's door is okay structurally but it won't open.

MABEL: (*To* TIFFANY.) Take my rock and break the window.

LUCILLE: (*To* TIFFANY.) No! If the car shifts it'll bring the garage right down...

(*Sound of glass breaking.*)

MABEL: (*To* TIFFANY.) All right!!! Now go in through the window and slide across the seat!

LUCILLE: Tiffany, don't you even think about!...Don't you!... You did NOT just climb in that window!

MABEL: Praise Jesus, she's in!

(LUCILLE *gets out her cell phone and dials* 911.)

LUCILLE: I'm holding you responsible if anything happens...

MABEL: (*To* TIFFANY.) It's in the back left-hand corner of the glove box.

(LUCILLE *and* MABEL *talk simultaneously.*)

LUCILLE: (*Into her cell phone.*) Yes, good afternoon, Officer. This is Lucille Prideaux Vernon and I'm calling from 211 Derbigny in the Ninth Ward. I'm here from New York to help my mother recover some items and my cousin Tiffany has just gone through the window of my father's Buick Skylark which is under a garage...

MABEL: (*Praying.*) Lord Jesus, Prideaux, don't let anything happen to this child. She and Lucille are all I've got in the world.

She's in your service, Prideaux. Protect her, guide her. (*She begins to sing a spiritual loudly.*)

LUCILLE: Mama, please!

(*Suddenly* MABEL *jumps up and claps her hands.*)

MABEL: That's it!

(LUCILLE *is dumbstruck for a second, then speaks into her phone.*)

LUCILLE: I'm sorry, Officer. The situation seems to have...I think she's all right...

(TIFFANY *enters. Her clothes are dirty and she has minor abrasions. She proudly holds a black drawstring bag and gives it to* MABEL.)

MABEL: Thank you, baby! This is just how it looked in my dream!

LUCILLE: I'm sorry, sir. We won't need you after all.

(*She disconnects and speaks to* TIFFANY.)

TIFFANY: Well that was a taste of hell. I am seriously out of shape.

LUCILLE: Are you out of your mind?

TIFFANY: No sense coming all the way down here for closure and not getting it.

LUCILLE: We need to put some disinfectant on those cuts.

TIFFANY: Can we find a bathroom first?

(*They turn to grab a trash bag but are stopped in their tracks by the sight of* TANTE MABEL *holding something aloft in her palm and walking in a large circle and humming.)*

What's she doing?

LUCILLE: Who knows. You know I hate that hoodoo crap. What was in the damn bag anyway?

TIFFANY: I was scared to look. Felt like a marble or something.

(LUCILLE *and* TIFFANY *approach* MABEL *gingerly.*)

LUCILLE: Time to go, Mama.

MABEL: Give me a minute.

TIFFANY: What are you doing, Tante Mabel?

MABEL: Letting him see.

TIFFANY: God?

MABEL: Papa Prideaux.

(LUCILLE *blocks* MABEL*'s path and takes her gently by the shoulders.*)

LUCILLE: I don't do crazy, Mama, and neither do you. Lord knows there's enough grief to drive us insane. But we've always gotten out of the car one stop before Nutville. I won't let you go there now.

MABEL: I'm not crazy, daughter. This'll make sure.

(MABEL *smiles at* LUCILLE *and puts something in* LUCILLE*'s palm.* LUCILLE *looks at it, screams, drops it, and jumps back several paces.*)

LUCILLE: Oh, my God!

TIFFANY: What is it? What is it?

LUCILLE: (*Pointing.*) Look there! I'm not touching it!

(TIFFANY *walks over to examine the object.*)

TIFFANY: Is that an eye?

MABEL: Yes, sugar.

TIFFANY: (*Picking it up.*) It's glass.

LUCILLE: Keep it away from me.

TIFFANY: What was this doing in the glove box?

MABEL: It was Papa Prideaux's.

TIFFANY: Papa Prideaux had a glass eye?

LUCILLE: What?!

MABEL: (*Laughing.*) He was way too handsome and too proud to let folks know. He learned how to turn his head so the eyes always looked in the same direction.

LUCILLE: No way. My papa did NOT have a glass eye.

MABEL: A piece of shrapnel in Vietnam did it. He was one of the lucky ones. He came home. I was the only one who knew. Each night before he went to sleep he put it in that jelly jar by his bed. Told me if anything ever happened, that would be the piece of him left to look out for me. When he died at the Dome, wasn't no more I could do for him.

But I damn sure wasn't gonna take out his eye in front of all those strangers and embarrass him. I buried him in that eye. But Papa came to me last night in a dream to say he had a spare in the glove box.

(*Pause.* TIFFANY *and* LUCILLE *look at each other, dumbfounded.*)

TIFFANY: Wow!

LUCILLE: Yeah, okay. Whatever. This is the icing on the gravy. Can we go now?

MABEL: Hush a moment, daughter.

(*She holds the eye aloft in her palm, looks upward, and calls.*)

Papa Prideaux! All you saints and angels! Mother Goddess, Father God and all the African diasporic deities—see us here. Bless this ground and the people buried in it. Bless the bodies in the bayou and the limbs under levees. Bless the blood and bones that shadow us. Protect your sorrowful children. Bring us hope in the days of our hereafter. Bring us peace in the rhythms of our heart. Look kindly on these your three daughters—you host of beatific spirits. Consecrate this ground with your love. Weave your promises through the fabric of our pain. Nourish our hollowness with your songs. May the wind carry your kisses to our hungry lips. May the sun beam your knowledge into our shivering souls. May you look kindly on this ground of remembrance and imprint the soil with a token of our having been here at all. Give us your kindly regard. Keep us in your wise and loving vision. Now and forevermore. Amen. And, Prideaux...I'm gonna shine up that coffeepot and put your eye in it. You come back to my dreams, you hear. I won't be so scared of you now. Merci, mon cher mari. Mon amour toujours.

(*Silence.* LUCILLE *and* TIFFANY *are still, almost hypnotized.* MABEL *breaks the spell by putting the eye into her brassiere, grabbing a trash bag, and dragging it stage left toward the car.*)

Let's go, girls. That motor's running and Tiffany's about to wet her pants.

LUCILLE: But, Mama...how did you...where did he...?

TIFFANY: Let's go, Lucille. Nothing more to be said. Tante Mabel done wrapped up the crap and put a bow on it!

(*All three exit, pulling their trash bags.*)

END OF PLAY

A VERY VERY SHORT PLAY

Jacquelyn Reingold

A Very Very Short Play was first produced by Ensemble Studio Theatre, William Carden, artistic director, June 2008, in their *One-act Marathon*. It was directed by Jonathan Bernstein. Producer, James Carter; set design, Maiko Chii; costume design, Molly Rebuschatis; lighting design, Evan Purcell; sound design, Shane Rettig. The actors were:

JOAN	Julie Fitzpatrick
ROGER	Adam Dannheisser

CHARACTERS
ROGER: Thirties.
JOAN: Thirties.

PLACE
On an airplane.

TIME
Now.

AUTHOR'S NOTE
Joan and Roger should be played by actors of average height. In the Ensemble Studio Theatre production the underlined stage directions were prerecorded, then played, as if spoken by the pilot.

A woman sits on an airplane. She is reading a book. A man sits next to her. They are midflight.

ROGER: I'm sorry to ask, you look so content so calm so reasonably relaxed I'm sorry to ask. Your wrist is just so, and your shoes are just right, what are they pumps, mules, puels? I'm sorry to ask, but that shaft of light is hitting your hair and making it glow. And I know, I do, look at me not exactly coiffed, 'cause this crazy way of getting from here to there makes me well want to die, with its clouds and oh God the sky, I can't help it I'll stop, the rhyming I'll drop. But the question's still in here: I'd love to know yet I hate to ask, but you, you are the smallest woman I've ever seen. So in between the pretzels and the plastic cup of cola, while we're madly flying over Massapequa toward Madagascar, with Anawanda on the right and Alabama on the left, I am compelled while I eat my salted nuts, and if you don't mind, it's a nervousness of mine, take out my hibachi and grill shrimp kebabs: just how tall or small are you, and how delicate are your ankles when they're undressed and, what, if I dare ask, is your name?

JOAN: I was trying to read.

ROGER: Yes, of course, reading. I should read, too. I love to read, don't you? I mean. Let me try again. And then I'll leave you be, but you are so, well, so well, petitely proportioned.

I don't mean to be fresh. Fresh is not a word that is used on me. But maybe, with your book, you would like a pear, a peach, a giant seedless watermelon? I know the seeded is tastier, but the seeds on the plane, with the size of the seats, is, well, not so good.

JOAN: I don't think you should cook on the plane. Really. A flame. A hot burning flame would be, just think of the heat and the oxygen. I'm reading!

ROGER: What are you reading?

JOAN: About a lawyer who is also a judge. A heroic man who would do anything for the small people of the world.

ROGER: I'm a lawyer.

JOAN: Coincidence.

ROGER: Perhaps there's some sense in coincidence.

JOAN: Excuse me.

ROGER: How 'bout a cream puff?

JOAN: I shouldn't.

ROGER: I'm a lawyer. I could argue that and win. So trust me. It's a chocolate one. Very chocolate. It's more chocolate than I can describe. What's your name? If you don't tell me, I'll make it up. You are Tiny Teena. You are Teenie Tyna. You are Itty Lily. You are Eenie Meenie. You are Lilly Putia. You are—

JOAN: Joan.

ROGER: Even better. How tall are you, Joan?

JOAN: About a foot.

ROGER: Ah. That means your foot, then, is far less than a foot.

JOAN: It does.

ROGER: That means your toes could fit in my nose.

JOAN: It does.

ROGER: That means your—

JOAN: I thought you weren't fresh.

ROGER: I'm not. I'm freshly flawed, flaught, fraught, fnaught, fmaught—. Try the puff please please please.

JOAN: Okay. If it will quiet you down.

(*He feeds her the cream puff piece by small piece, into her tiny mouth. It is the best puff she's ever had.*)

ROGER: Well?

JOAN: Well.

ROGER: More?

JOAN: Just a bit. (*He feeds her. While eating.*) May I ask: how tall are you?

ROGER: I'm twelve feet, eight inches.

JOAN: Wow. That means.

ROGER: It does.

JOAN: What's your name, big lawyer who carries so much food?

ROGER: Roger.

JOAN: We never could, you know, Roger, it would never work. How could it would it? Work? Impossible.

ROGER: Keep eating.

JOAN: I mean the mechanics. Even if I fell for you. Or you fell for me. I mean. You would fall a lot farther. And I would fall only a little. That would be dangerous. For you.

ROGER: Danger is my middle name.

JOAN: And your last name?

ROGER: Shmeck.

JOAN: Oh, come on. (*He shrugs.*) Enough, Roger Danger Shmeck. I don't have room. For more.

(*She stops him from feeding her.*)

ROGER: Just a little. Bite. From the inside, where it's sweetest and softest and nothing like it seems.

(*He tries to feed her the cream from inside the puff.*)

JOAN: I'm full.

ROGER: Try this.

JOAN: What is it?

ROGER: Arroz con pollo.

JOAN: I can only eat so much.

ROGER: You could fit in more, if you danced on my knees. Or jogged in my hair.

JOAN: I've been through this before.

ROGER: Not with me. See, my thighs are wide, my head is flat, my heart is large.

JOAN: I cannot see your heart.

ROGER: But I bet you can hear it.

(*She listens; she cannot hear it.*)

JOAN: I only hear the plane.

ROGER: Look, I brought seeds that we can plant then watch them grow. I have chicks that we can raise till they give eggs for a soufflé. Try this.

JOAN: What is it?

ROGER: Pickles for a picnic. Brisket for a barbecue. It's the middle of June, it's the beginning of summer. A taste for everyone. And for everyone who doesn't have a someone, or only has the wrong one, there's always the hope for the real one, even when, or especially if, it's impossible, it would never work, it couldn't work, it can never be. But if it were you, I would thank you every day. So, take another bite. Joan. When you think you can't, open your mouth and taste what I have.

JOAN: Well. Roger. Danger. Shmeck. I might. I will. But only if you'll pick me up so I can adjust the little blower near the light button. It's driving me crazy.

ROGER: Gladly.

(*He picks her up over his head, she reaches for the blower button and aims its airstream at his face. He pulls her down to him. They kiss. Her tiny lips on his right eye. Then on his left eye. Then lips to lips, though his cover half her face. He almost tosses her across the plane, he's so happy, but instead, he puts her back in her seat.*)

I never knew such citrus lips.

JOAN: And I thought only small was beautiful.

ROGER: And I thought you never meet anyone you ever want to talk to on a plane. You know, it's always the kind of guy that won't shut up, that goes on and on and all you want to do is watch the bad movie and pray the plane doesn't crash and—

JOAN:—Shut up my sweet-tasting lawyer with too much food and lushest lips.

ROGER: Show me your ankles.

JOAN: If you show me yours.

(*They take off their shoes and socks, show each other their ankles. The roof and the walls and the floor of the plane disappear. And they are flying high, ankle to ankle. Then JOAN picks ROGER up, over her head, as they soar up into the sky.*)

END OF PLAY

THE WHOLE TRUTH
& NOTHING BUT THE
BLUETOOTH

Laura Shaine

The Whole Truth & Nothing but the Bluetooth was first presented in a staged reading at Actors & Writers in Olivebridge, New York, on September 29, 2007, as part of an evening *Midnight City*—extreme comedy written and directed by Laura Shaine. The cast was as follows:

EVA MARIE	Sigrid Heath
MEL	Sarah Chodoff

A not-so-young woman, MEL, *is preparing, not just for a date, but for* THE *date. She is studying herself in a cheval glass, a freestanding mirror, and speaking on a Bluetooth phone to her best friend,* EVA MARIE, *who can be offstage, or in an isolated light, also on a Bluetooth phone connector.*

MEL: I'm so scared; I feel like canceling, I haven't been on a date...in...in nine years! I had almost sincerely given up...except this tiny itsy bitsy pilot light stayed on and now I know it was a flame—This is it! He's the One! But I feel like I could throw up if he kisses me...That's attractive, huh? I can't believe he's even interested—You should see him, Eva Marie—He is...He is everything—he's smart, he's talented...I hate to say this as it sounds shallow—he's RICH! He is creative but he invested! He's retired but still working! He has his own business, his own apartment, his own house in the country...and...his own boat! He's my age! Oh, maybe three years younger and in amazing shape. I don't know if he works out or if it is natural, but you can see his pecs through his shirt...they flex...The shirts look custom-made, because his biceps bulge beyond normal size! Omigod, *everything* bulges. It was natural bulge, I just know it—He had no time to take Viagra—I felt that flag go up on the mailbox when he kissed me good night on the street! I almost dragged him in then, but I thought—No, I have to get ready! I have to prepare, so that's when he asked me out for tonight, and I said—YES! I bought a new dress and had a bikini wax! I dyed my hair and went tanning even though

I know it's terrible. I haven't felt like this since I was...thir-teen! He's cute! He's hot!

EVA MARIE: Guys our age are not hot...at best they are...tepid.

MEL: Okay...no, not tepid...*warm!* His eyes...oh, Eva Marie, they kindle and spark...When he looks at me, his face kind of goes...*soft*...

EVA MARIE: Yeah, well, he is in love...wow I didn't think that still happened. I thought love was diagnosed now—as a disease...That it is the up stage of bipolar!

MEL: I feel it too—when I look at him, or even think about him!

EVA MARIE: You're GONE!

MEL: So should I risk it?

EVA MARIE: Risk what?

MEL: You know. Full disclosure? Nudity! Omigod. I am going to faint. I feel...convulsions coming on, they are real, Eva Marie...I am going to become an epileptic!

EVA MARIE: You can't BECOME an epileptic, you either are one or you're not, and you would know by now.

MEL: I don't know—so much else has...gone wrong with my body, you know the whole truth—you're the only one who knows! How can I stand naked before this perfect buff man? I'm not perfect! I'm...I'm pretty damaged at this point; I am "as is." He'll run, he'll set an Olympic record getting out of my apartment!

EVA MARIE: He won't run, Mel. Male horniness can be...immune to a lot. They see "naked," it doesn't matter about the details.

MEL: In this case, the details are from Columbia Presbyterian! Oh, Eva Marie...I'm scared! You know...the left one, is gone.

EVA MARIE: It's okay—you had reconstruction. He might not even notice in his blind lust.

MEL: He'll notice. There's no nipple. And the reconstruction has...well...failed. It kind of deflated and sank a long time ago...collapsed like a bad underdone cupcake. Eva Marie, it isn't attractive. Even I can't look. And that's only the top half. How do I tell him about my hips?

EVA MARIE: You don't have to! They're replaced! They work perfectly. You said yourself—You can swivel.

MEL: Yes, hips of steel bearings and rollin'! "Watch out for me, guys, I am a serious threat!" Get between these thighs, and you'll remember it.
    There are fine-line scars, but even THAT is NOT the problem! The problem is with replaced hips, you can't assume...the usual positions. The first thing the hospital gives you is a chart—It's like...a choking poster! With Xs over your pelvis...Not this way, or that way...Not my favorite ways! What do I do? Hang the poster—"forbidden positions"—over the bed, and hope for the best? What if we get carried away and my hips fall out? Hip replacement! It sounds so...geriatric!

EVA MARIE: You are many things, but you are NOT geriatric. Connect it to a sports injury. That sounds vital. Oh, it's probably irrelevant what's been replaced or how you look— you know they all like a b...(*She doesn't say blow job.*) Just get out your bib and tucker and suppress your gag reflex, and romance will bloom! Just be honest. You're honest and funny—that will matter MORE! Your charm and wit will carry the day...Do you really think at our stage, a man is primarily looking for tits and ass?

MEL: No, but I bet he'd like them to be there.

EVA MARIE: ... Trust me, it's not essential—you offer more interesting assets—Would YOU care if he was down a testicle, or even two?

MEL: No. It wouldn't matter...at all. You always make me feel better!

EVA MARIE: Yeah.

MEL: So it's going to be fine? We've been telling each other everything will be fine for thirty years...is it really true? We've been saying we're beautiful and lovable to each other for three decades...what if THAT isn't...

(*The door buzzer rings.*)

Here he comes! Well, hello hello! Don't you look nice. Listen, I have a few things I have to tell you before, you know *before*...Have a drink, make it a stiff one!...Well, here goes...this is a little embarrassing but I know you can handle it...(*She laughs.*) What's left of it!

(*Lights blink, seductive music plays.*)

(*A time change can be assumed to have occurred*—MEL *has vanished, the stage is empty. She can be heard offstage.*)

MEL: I'll be out in a second—I'm just changing into something more comfortable, actually it isn't more comfortable...but it's going to hide everything we just discussed...I am so glad, none of it makes a difference! I was so scared! Well...

(*She enters, still finishing her sentence.*)

Here I am...

(*The room is empty; the man is assumed to have fled.*)

(*Finishing in heartbreak.*)...*was.* (*She cries out from her soul.*) Oh, Eva Marie!

(*THERE IS A TERRIBLE SILENCE.* MEL *falls to her knees, gropes for the Bluetooth.*)

Eva Marie! May Jane! He left! He just left without saying good-bye! Where are...YOU? Eva Marie, Eva Marie!

(*There is no answer, and* MEL *lies on the floor, sobbing.*

Lights up on EVA MARIE, *who has also fallen to the floor, her Bluetooth extender lying near her face...She too is in extremis.*)

EVA MARIE: (*Whispering.*) What about me, Mel? What about me?

MEL: Eva Marie—Eva Marie? If you don't answer...I'll...

EVA MARIE: (*Pauses for two seconds, as she considers not answering; then she reattaches the Bluetooth and responds, flat but comforting.*) I'm here.

MEL: (*...Looking up, brightening.*) I'm...glad.

END OF PLAY

THE WOODS ARE FOR SUCKERS AND CHUMPS

Megan Mostyn-Brown

The Woods Are for Suckers and Chumps was first performed at the Stella Adler Summer Conservatory in the summer of 2009. Melissa Ross directed the following cast:

MANDA	Alice Oshima
ZOE	Daniella De Jesus

The woods. MANDA, *sixteen, sits in front of a pile of sticks and leaves. Aside from her hooded sweatshirt she is dressed totally inappropriately for a camping trip. She unsuccessfully tries to start a fire by rubbing two sticks together.*

MANDA: Ugh . . . screw it.

(She tosses the sticks aside and curls up near the small pile of sticks, pulling her sweatshirt closer around her and her hood up over her head.

ZOE, *sixteen, enters carrying a set of directions. She stops and stares at* MANDA.)

ZOE: What're you doing?

MANDA: I'm dying of hypothermia. Leave me alone.

ZOE: Why don't you just make a fire?

MANDA: I tried. That whole rubbing-two-sticks-together thing is total crap.

ZOE: Use a lighter.

MANDA: I lost my lighter in the grass somewhere.

ZOE: Oh.

(*Beat.*)

Where's everybody else?

MANDA: Adnan and Chelsea are doing it somewhere behind a bush or something. And Leila thinks she found some 'shrooms so everyone else went down to check it out.

ZOE: How do they know they're not poisonous?

MANDA: Huh?

ZOE: The mushrooms. How do they know they're the fun, hallucinate-your-face-off kind and not the oh-shit-you're-dead-cuz-they're-poisonous kind.

MANDA: Toby has a book... or something... that tells you.

ZOE: Oh. Yeah. I guess he would.

(*Beat.* MANDA *sits up.*)

MANDA: Wait a minute. I thought you weren't speaking to me anymore.

ZOE: I'm not. I found the directions to the tent but they're in French.

MANDA: Oh. Well I don't take French so—

ZOE: Duh. I wasn't looking for *your* help.

MANDA: Ohhh-kay. Well unless you have a lighter or magically know how to make a fire appear you can like step off till everyone gets back.

ZOE: Fine.

MANDA: Good.

ZOE: Okay.

(MANDA *lies back down on the ground and pulls her hood down farther.* ZOE *sighs disgustedly.*)

You know, this is why I'm glad we're not friends anymore.

MANDA: What?

ZOE: This. Like the way you act 'n' shit. It's like so . . . monumentally depressing. I mean you make shit harder for yourself and everyone else.

MANDA: No I don't.

ZOE: It's supposed to be a fun trip. The least you could do is like pretend you want to be a part of things.

MANDA: Well if you remember, the last time I 'shroomed I thought I turned into a gorilla and Toby convinced me to eat seventeen bananas. I didn't crap for a week so excuse me for not jumping at the chance to do it all over again. Now if you're done being a major bitch I'd like to go back to being cold.

(*Beat.*)

ZOE: I mean who even wears ballet flats and a miniskirt on a camping trip?

MANDA: I'm sorry I guess I missed the memo that you had suddenly turned into Little Miss Nancy Nature.

ZOE: I know about nature.

MANDA: You live on the Upper West Side.

ZOE: So? You live in Brooklyn Heights.

MANDA: So?

ZOE: So at least I know what to wear. And for your information I have been camping.

MANDA: Passing out in Central Park after too many Smirnoff Ices at Leila's sweet sixteen does not like count as camping.

ZOE: Screw you. I went once with my dad before he died.

MANDA: Oh. I didn't know that. My bad I guess.

ZOE: Yeah. I guess.

(*Beat. They stare at each other for a moment. Then* MANDA *turns away as:*)

MANDA: (*Mumbling.*) It still doesn't make you some kind of expert.

ZOE: What?

MANDA: Just because you went once when you were like six doesn't mean you get to act all judgmental and like you know everything about everything. But then again you're always acting like that so I shouldn't expect anything different.

ZOE: I am not always—

MANDA: Yes you are. If someone was like, "Hey I'm gonna go to Bermuda and eat a shit sandwich and then dance naked

with the cast of *Twilight*" you'd be like "I did it. It's been
done and I probably did it better than you."

ZOE: I hated *Twilight*.

MANDA: That's not the point, *Zoe*.

ZOE: Then what is the point, *Manda*.

MANDA: The point is you don't ever let people have their own
experiences.

ZOE: What does that even mean.

MANDA: It means that whatever anyone else's experience is, yours
was always better and theirs is always shit.

ZOE: Well when it comes to you that's pretty much true.

MANDA: Ugh...see this—this is why we're not friends anymore.

ZOE: No we're not friends anymore because of that text you sent
about me to the entire junior class.

MANDA: And why do you think I did that?

ZOE: Because you are a miserable, selfish cow who wants everyone to feel as hateful about themselves as you do.

MANDA: No.

ZOE: Then why?

MANDA: You should know.

ZOE: Well I don't. So like enlighten me.

MANDA: Zachary Bevaccio.

(ZOE *shakes her head as if she can't believe she has to have another conversation on the subject.*)

> You knew it was my first time doing...it...and how much
> I wanted it to be with him...and then it was terrible and
> he was a douchebag and said all that crap about me to his
> friends...and you were just like, "I told you so."

ZOE: Well he is a douchebag. And I did tell you so.

MANDA: The point is it was a like a way big shitty experience
and as my best friend you were s'posed to like comfort
me...not scold me and then like go on and on about how
awesome your first time was.

ZOE: I did not go on and on—

MANDA: Yes you did. It was like the moon got reborn and—and
cymbals crashed and the—the Lucky Charms elf threw
colorful marshmallows at you while Mariah Carey hit a
high note.

ZOE: That is ridiculous. I did not say that.

MANDA: Well of course that's not like specifically what you said
but that's what it sounded like to me.

ZOE: Because you are ridiculous.

MANDA: No I'm not.

ZOE: You are ridiculous and overdramatic and I was right
when I told Leila she shouldn't invite you cuz you'd ruin
everything.

MANDA: You told Leila not to invite me?

ZOE: Yes and you know as usual I was right.

MANDA: Screw you.

(MANDA *pushes* ZOE.)

ZOE: Did you just push me?

MANDA: Yes. And I'll...do it again...if I need to.

ZOE: I can't believe you just pushed me.

MANDA: Whatta ya gonna do about it?

(MANDA *pushes her again.*)

ZOE: Don't touch me.

(ZOE *pushes* MANDA. MANDA *pushes her back.*)

   Stop it.

(ZOE *pushes* MANDA.)

MANDA: You stop it.

(MANDA *pushes* ZOE.)

ZOE: You stop it.

(ZOE *pushes* MANDA.)

MANDA: You started all of this.

(MANDA *pushes* ZOE.)

ZOE: No. You started all of this.

(*They both grab onto each other's hair and begin turning in a circle, tugging at each other and trying unsuccessfully to kick each other. It is the worst attempt at a physical fight and in fact looks more like some bizarre dance.*)

MANDA: Ow you're hurting me.

ZOE: Yer hurting me.

MANDA: Let go.

ZOE: You let go.

MANDA: You let go first.

ZOE: Okay how 'bout we let go on the count of three.

MANDA: Fine.

ZOE/MANDA: One ... two ... three ...

(*They both let go and rub their heads. Pause. They don't look at each other.*)

ZOE: This is stupid.

MANDA: I know.

ZOE: We shouldn't be ...

MANDA: Yeah.

(*Pause.*)

ZOE: I ...

MANDA: What?

(ZOE *stares at her toes as:*)

ZOE: I'm sorry about what happened with Zach. I didn't...
ummm... mean to like... make you think otherwise.

MANDA: Thanks. Sorry... about... you know, the text.

ZOE: Thanks.

(*Beat.*)

If it's any consolation...

MANDA: What?

ZOE: When I... you know... with Dante... there were no cymbals and Mariah Carey was definitely not hitting a high
note.

MANDA: Really?

ZOE: Yeah... I ummm... exaggerated.

MANDA: Oh.

ZOE: A lot.

MANDA: Oh.

(*Beat.*)

My mom was wrong.

ZOE: About what?

MANDA: She said the woods were for suckers and chumps.

ZOE: Your mom used the phrase "suckers and chumps"?

MANDA: Yeah.

ZOE: Your mom is weird.

MANDA: I know, right?

(*They maybe laugh a little. Beat.*)

ZOE: We should ummm probably go look for everyone else.

MANDA: Yeah.

(ZOE *starts to head off.*)

    Zo.

ZOE: Yeah.

MANDA: I'm glad Leila didn't listen to you. I'm glad she invited me.

ZOE: Yeah. Me too.

(*They smile at each other.*

Blackout.)

END OF PLAY

YOU HAVE ARRIVED

Rob Ackerman

You Have Arrived was first presented at POP, a benefit for At Hand Theatre Company, 2008.

CHARACTERS
DAN: In his twenties.
KRISTIN: In her twenties.
CYNDI: Up to you.

SETTING
A car at night (two chairs side by side).

DAN *sits in the driver's seat and peers out, looking for someone. On a low stool in front of him, to his right, sits* CYNDI, *a GPS navigator. Her head is at the height of the imaginary dashboard and her eyes are fixed forward in concentration. She has two chimes in her lap, and right now she rings them: bing-bong.*

CYNDI: "You have arrived."

(DAN *speaks to the back of* CYNDI's *head. Here and throughout the play, she's determined to remain impassive, a machine.*)

DAN: Fuck. Where is she? I don't know why I even try.

(KRISTIN *steps out of the shadows.*)

KRISTIN: Dan?

DAN: Oh. Hey. Kristin.

KRISTIN: Hey.

(DAN *climbs out, kisses* KRISTIN's *cheek, helps her in.*)

DAN: Gosh, I couldn't see you over there.

KRISTIN: I told you I'd be here. Red scarf. Converse sneakers.

DAN: Yeah, you did.

KRISTIN: And you found me, Dan. Way to go.

DAN: Well, I didn't. (*Points to* CYNDI.) She did.

KRISTIN: She?

DAN: My navigator.

KRISTIN: Oh, wow, look at that.

DAN: I always get lost in all these tiny streets—Stanton, Rivington, Ludlow—but she knows where to go.

KRISTIN: "She's" a computer.

DAN: No, she's not. She's a receiver, a transponder, a cartographic data display device with calibrated voice prompts. She's a navigator, a global positioning system is what she is, really.

KRISTIN: A computer, Dan.

DAN: Yeah, I guess.

KRISTIN: A computer is not a person. You can't personify.

DAN: (*Nervousness.*) Oh, I loved that. In high school. No. I guess it was actually seventh grade. Mister Trowbridge. He made us learn all those words. Words of literature. Made us feel all scholarly and philosophical and poetical. I remember all the words. Personification. Alliteration. Irony. (Irony was the best. I loved irony. "The laughter of the gods.") Oh, and euphony . . . and metonymy.

KRISTIN: Metonymy?

DAN: That's when one thing stands for something else. Like if you say, "Damn, that BMW just rear-ended me!" It didn't actually rear-end YOU, it rear-ended your old Subaru Outback, you know?

KRISTIN: Does your navigator stand for you, Dan?

DAN: No. She's a she. I'm a he.

(*Through the following,* DAN *focuses his attention on the back of* CYNDI's *head and uses his index finger to enter commands.*)

CYNDI: "Main menu."

KRISTIN: Oh, I like her voice.

CYNDI: "Enter address."

KRISTIN: Wow. She's got a great voice. Does she have a name?

DAN: Cyndi. Yeah. She's Cyndi.

KRISTIN: I like that. Do you really call her Cyndi?

DAN: I do now.

KRISTIN: Is she easy to use?

CYNDI: "My addresses."

DAN: Like an iPhone, kinda, you play with her touch screen and tell her what to do.

KRISTIN: "Hey, Cyndi. I'm on a blind date. Take me to Williamsburg."

DAN: Basically.

CYNDI: "Previous destinations."

DAN: A lot of times I have to go to work at five in the morning and hunt for some house in Far Rockaway and a MapQuest printout just doesn't cut it, so I'm like, "If these things ever go below two hundred bucks I'm getting one."

CYNDI: "Route."

KRISTIN: And she was...?

DAN: One ninety-nine ninety-nine. They're even cheaper now, of course, and they've got better ones that tell you what street you're turning onto and stuff, but she's all right. I mean, she gets the job done.

CYNDI: "Calculating route."

(DAN *starts driving.*)

DAN: So how long have you known Tim?

KRISTIN: I dated him, in high school.

DAN: Was it serious?

KRISTIN: It kinda was.

DAN: He told me you were cute. (*Beat.*) You are cute.

CYNDI: "Left turn in point two miles."

KRISTIN: Thanks, I guess.

DAN: So you're a "graphic designer"?

KRISTIN: Well, sort of. I know Photoshop and HTML. I do a lot of temp work.

DAN: Join the club. Isn't it weird how there are some things in school that are totally useful, and others that are such total crap you're like, "Why do they even bother?" You know, like word problems.

CYNDI: "Make a left."

(DAN *turns the wheel sharply and* KRISTIN *flinches.*)

DAN: Fuck. Shit. Sorry.

KRISTIN: No, that's okay.

DAN: Where was I?

KRISTIN: Word problems.

DAN: Oh. Yeah. Okay, word problems are like, "If Jack is meeting Sally and it's rush hour, then what time should Jack depart?" But who cares? Jack can call Sally's cell and say he's running late. She's probably got an issue of the *New Yorker* in her purse—she can deal with sitting there and having a Frappuccino. You can't expect Jack to start crunching a bunch of numbers. I mean, Jesus. Math is fucked.

KRISTIN: And metonymy is useful?

CYNDI: "Left turn in point two miles."

DAN: Sure, Cyndi, whatever you say.

(KRISTIN *studies the GPS screen.*)

KRISTIN: I like how she shows us where we are. We're this little arrow, just moving along. There's the river. You can see the bridge.

CYNDI: "Make a left."

(DAN *turns carefully. Bing-bong:* CYNDI *rings her chimes.*)

DAN: The background is black because it's nighttime. In the daytime the screen is all green and blue and if there's a golf course anywhere in the vicinity, she always lets you know. Whoever made this thing is really big on golf courses and country clubs.

CYNDI: "Remain on the current road for one mile."

KRISTIN: Oh-kay.

DAN: Yeah, it always weirds me out when she says that. Makes me want to make a quick turn just to tick her off, see how she reacts. But she won't react, she'll just say "Calculating route." That's how she copes with human frailty.

KRISTIN: "Calculating route."

DAN: Anything goes wrong, she never gets angry, never loses patience, just says...

KRISTIN: "Calculating route."

CYNDI: "Remain on the current road."

(CYNDI *rings her chimes again.*)

DAN: Her chimes mean we've hit some sort of satellite coordinate, I think. But she doesn't always ring her chimes.

You can't count on it. Sometimes she does, sometimes she doesn't. She's a little loopy like that.

CYNDI: "Keep to the right in one mile."

KRISTIN: You know, people used to do just fine before they had these things. Ernest Shackleton saved a whole stranded expedition in Antarctica with nothing but a compass and a sextant.

DAN: Good for him.

KRISTIN: I majored in math with a concentration in geography.

DAN: So I guess you like word problems?

KRISTIN: I love them.

CYNDI: "Keep to the right."

DAN: I am keeping to the right, bitch.

KRISTIN: Don't talk to her like that.

DAN: She's a machine.

KRISTIN: No, she's Cyndi.

DAN: Look, I don't have a sextant like Shackleton. And I can't even find my way around Brooklyn much less Antarctica. I always end up in Greenpoint circling that stinky sewage treatment plant and that's not the best way to start a date.

KRISTIN: Neither is being insulting to women, Dan.

DAN: Cyndi is not a woman.

KRISTIN: She sounds like a woman.

CYNDI: "Right turn in point two miles."

KRISTIN: Take Kent Street.

DAN: (*Raises a hand.*) Wait for Cyndi.

CYNDI: "Make a right."

(CYNDI *rings her chimes and* DAN *turns.*)

KRISTIN: You trust a machine over me—what's your problem?

DAN: You know, it's hard being a guy sometimes. First girls get taller and get boobs and all we get is zits, then they turn out to be smarter and more mature and they're too cool to call us back or call each other bitches.

KRISTIN: We call each other bitches, we just don't like it when cute guys call us bitches.

DAN: Am I a cute guy?

KRISTIN: Lemme get back to you on that.

CYNDI: "Right turn in point three miles."

DAN: Thank you, Cyndi.

KRISTIN: Good. That's better.

(*A quiet moment, and then . . .*)

DAN: I'm sorry about your cat. Tim told me. Mushroom.

KRISTIN: He was great. He was twelve. I had him since sixth grade.

DAN: I'm really sorry.

KRISTIN: Thanks.

(*They both breathe.*)

DAN: There's one thing Cyndi says.

CYNDI: "Make a right turn."

DAN: One thing I really like.

KRISTIN: What?

DAN: You'll see. She'll say it when we get there. (*Beat.*) It's one of those phrases that means more than it means.

KRISTIN: Irony?

DAN: Yeah. It's positively fraught with irony. The good kind.

KRISTIN: She better not call anybody a bitch.

CYNDI: "Approaching destination on the right."

KRISTIN: You know what you've got, Dan? You've got this weird resentment. You rush to judgment on the basis of stuff that's not there, like, I don't know, like ghosts of girlfriends past or something.

DAN: I don't know what you're talking about.

KRISTIN: Look, I'm on this date with you, and I kinda hate you, but Tim said you're a good guy, so let's just try to make the best of it, okay? I'm just me. I just met you. And I'm not the girl who hurt your feelings.

DAN: Hurt my feelings?

KRISTIN: I'm hoping that's what happened. I'm hoping there's a real reason you're being such a jerk. We're both nervous. Are we gonna like each other, hate each other, hook up? That has yet to be determined. But chill out. Having fun is more important. Having fun might possibly be the most important thing in the world, and almost everyone is pretty bad at it. Now, *that's* ironic.

DAN: Uh-huh.

KRISTIN: How do you feel about fun, Dan?

DAN: I, I'm okay with it.

KRISTIN: So am I.

DAN: Kristin…

KRISTIN: Yeah.

DAN: Let's have fun.

(CYNDI *rings her chimes.*)

CYNDI: "You have arrived."

(*Blackout.*)

END OF PLAY

YOU KNOW
WHO ELSE I HATE?

Mark O'Donnell

CHARACTERS
TWO MEN: Drunk, his pal.

A seedy blue-collar bar in Idaho, late night. DAVE *is a truculent drunk, more ridiculous than evil.* HIS PAL *is more passively blotto.*

DRUNK: You know who I hate? I hate those people up in India. All wrapped up in blankets and towels. Why can't they wear normal clothes?

HIS PAL: I think it has to do with their religion. It's, like, always Halloween there...

DRUNK: Speaking of looks, you know who else I hate? Guys who grow goatees! Ugh! What is that? I say, grow a real beard, or else shave like a soldier!

HIS PAL: Wull... Uncle Sam has a goatee.

DRUNK: Hey! You shut up about Uncle Sam! Anyway, what he has, that's something else. That's old-timey, like what the devil has. (*Pause.*) Speaking of goatees, you know who else I hate? The French.

HIS PAL: Yeah, well, the French...

DRUNK: I was in this park, and this French guy was calling his dog, and he was calling it in French! *Venez-ici! Venez-ici!* I hate that. I mean, it's one thing if they want to talk to each other in French, but to force a poor dog to learn it, that's just cruel.

HIS PAL: And where was this?

DRUNK: Over in France. I was there by accident. Plane crash or somethin'. (*Pause.*) I mean, talking in French, that is so phony! (*Pause.*) Speaking of dogs and phonies, you know who else I hate? Those stuck-up guys who wear sunglasses whenever they walk their dogs! Like they were movie stars or something! "I'm glamorous, look at me!" And what I hate even more, these same guys make their dogs wear these real tight harnesses, so the dog can't run or jump or anything!

HIS PAL: Ummm...I think you're talking about blind people there...

DRUNK: Is that what they're called? I hate them. And speaking of show-offs, you know who else I hate? Those guys who are too high-and-mighty for regular bicycles! No, they have to sit on their asses and ride chairs with big wheels, like they were the king passing in parade! "All hail me!"

HIS PAL: Uhhhh...I think you're talking about crippled people there...Or handicapped, specially challenged...

DRUNK: Is that what they're called? I hate them.

HIS PAL: Well, hate, I don't know why you'd...

DRUNK: And speaking of show-offs, you know who else I hate? Those kinda small, skinny, pale guys with the long hair. You know, the ones who insist on opening their shirts in public and nursing those real tiny little guys with no hair? Ugh!

HIS PAL: I, uh, I think you're talking about women there... And, uh, babies...

DRUNK: Is that what they're called? I hate them. I hate foreigners.

HIS PAL: (*About to pass out.*) Oooooh...

DRUNK: The thing about foreigners, you never know what they're thinking. At least with you and me, you know all the thoughts I'll ever think already!

(HIS PAL *passes out; his head clunks to the table.*)

The guy can't hold his liquor.
I hate him.

(*Lights fade.*)

END OF PLAY

CONTRIBUTORS

ROB ACKERMAN (*You Have Arrived*) is a widely produced play-wright whose works include *Origin of the Species*, made into an award-winning independent film starring Amanda Peet; *Tabletop*, Drama Desk Award for Best Ensemble; and *Icarus of Ohio*, chosen for the hotINK International Festival of New Plays at NYU's Tisch School of the Arts.

BILLY ARONSON'S (*Reunions*) short plays have been produced in seven Ensemble Studio Theatre Marathons and published in five volumes of *Best American Short Plays*. His full-length *First Day of School* received a Bay Area Critics Circle award for Best Original Script, 2009. Also: original concept/additional lyrics for *Rent*, book for *Click Clack Moo*, scripts for *Beavis & Butt-head* and *Courage the Cowardly Dog*. www.billyaronson .com.

JOHN AUGUSTINE'S (*PeopleSpeak*) plays include *Kent, CT* at the Zipper; *Back to Canton* at E.S.T.; and *Scab Writes a Song* at HOME for Contemporary Theatre. Also at HOME was *Augustine's Confessions*, an evening of one-acts including *Siobhan* (published in *Take Ten*) and *Window of Opportunity* (included in *Best American Short Plays of 1993–94*.) Recently *Father's Day* and *PeopleSpeak* premiered at the popular Summer Shorts Festival in NYC. www.JohnAugustine.net.

PETE BARRY (*Nine Point Eight Meters per Second per Second*) has authored and coauthored numerous plays, including *Drop*,

Hangman, The Banderscott, Early Morning in the Tenement, Sex with a Mathematician, and *Signs from God.* He is a cofounder of the Porch Room, a film and theater production company. Pete lives in the Lehigh Valley, Pennsylvania, with his wife, Jean, and his daughter, Lia.

DAN BERKOWITZ (*Sourpuss*) is co-chair of the Alliance of Los Angeles Playwrights and former L.A. regional rep of the Dramatists Guild. He's written a lot of stuff that's been produced, and hopes to write a lot more before he croaks. http://danberkowitz.com.

ADAM BOCK's (*Three Guys and a Brenda*) plays include *The Receptionist* (MTC, Trinity Rep, Studio Theater, Outer Critics nomination); *The Drunken City* (Playwrights Horizons, Outer Critics nomination); *The Thugs* (Soho Rep, OBIE Award); *Swimming in the Shallows* (Second Stage, Shotgun Players, three BATCC Awards, Clauder Award); *Five Flights* (Encore Theater, Rattlestick, Glickman Award); *The Typographer's Dream* (Encore Theater); *The Shaker Chair; Three Guys and a Brenda* (Heideman Award); and *We Have Always Lived in a Castle,* a musical with Todd Almond.

ERIC COBLE (*H.R.*) wrote some other plays too. *Bright Ideas, The Dead Guy, Natural Selection, For Better,* and *Southern Rapture* have been produced off-Broadway and other places, including productions at Manhattan Class Company, the Kennedy Center, Playwrights Horizons, and Actors Theatre of Louisville's Humana Festival. He also stares fondly at his Emmy nomination, the AT&T Onstage Award, and National Theatre Conference Playwriting Award.

PHILIP DAWKINS's (*Nothing*) plays include *Edgar and Ellen: Bad Seeds; The Skokie Detective Charter School* (Northlight Theatre Academy, www.playscripts.com); *Yes to Everything!* (Around the Coyote; ARS Nova); *Ugly Baby* (Chicago Vanguard/

Strawdog); *A Still Life in Color* (TUTA); *Saguaro* (Estrogen Fest, Estrogenius); *Perfect* (Side Project). Philip teaches playwriting through Chicago Dramatists, and kung fu to little, tiny children through Rising Phoenix, HI-YAH!

ANTON DUDLEY'S (*Getting Home*) productions include *Substitution* (Soho Playhouse); *Slag Heap* (Cherry Lane Theatre); *Honor and the River* (Walnut Street Theatre); *Letters to the End of the World* (Theatre Row, NYC); *Cold Hard Cash* (Williamstown Theatre Festival); *The Lake's End* (Adirondack Theatre Festival); *Antarctica* (Cleveland Public Theatre); and *Davy & Stu* and *Pleaching the Coffin Sisters* (both at Ensemble Studio Theatre). His work is published by Playscripts and Heinemann Press.

CHRISTOPHER DURANG'S (*Funeral Parlor*) plays include *A History of the American Film* (Tony nomination), *Sister Mary Ignatius Explains It All for You* (OBIE Award), *Beyond Therapy*, *Baby with the Bathwater*, *The Marriage of Bette and Boo* (OBIE Award, Hull Warriner Award), *Laughing Wild*, *Durang/Durang*, *Betty's Summer Vacation* (OBIE Award), *Mrs. Bob Cratchit's Wild Christmas Binge*, *Miss Witherspoon* (Pulitzer finalist), *Adrift in Macao* with Peter Melnick, and *Why Torture Is Wrong and the People Who Love Them*. www.christopherdurang.com.

LIZ ELLISON (*Gabrielle*) is a Pittsburgh-based playwright and screenwriter. She has been awarded a Steven Bochco Fellowship, the Eleanor Frost prize, and the Alexander Laing screenwriting award. Her play *The Minute Hand* was named a semifinalist for the O'Neill's National Playwrights Conference. She is a graduate of Dartmouth College and holds an MFA in dramatic writing from Carnegie Mellon University.

HALLEY FEIFFER (*Thank You So Much for Stopping*) wrote *Easter Candy*, produced at the Cherry Lane Theatre (Young Playwrights' Festival XXII); her play *Passion Fruit* was performed at the Edinburgh Fringe Festival. Her film and TV credits as an actress include *The Squid and the Whale*, *Margot at the Wedding*, *The Messenger*, *Gentlemen Broncos*, *Flight of the Conchords*, and the HBO miniseries *Mildred Pierce*.

PETER HANDY (*Friendship*), a native New Yorker, is a graduate of both Sarah Lawrence College and the dramatic writing program at Mason Gross School of the Arts. He has worked as writer, actor, director, and producer in a variety of productions on both coasts. His play *East of the Sun and West of the Moon* is published by Samuel French, Inc.

JEFFREY HATCHER's (*Murderers*—"*Match Wits with Minka Lupino*") plays have been produced on Broadway, off-Broadway, throughout the United States, and abroad. They include *Three Viewings*, *A Picasso*, *Scotland Road*, and *Compleat Female Stage Beauty*, as well as adaptations of *The Turn of the Screw*, *The Government Inspector*, *Dr. Jekyll and Mr. Hyde*, and *Tuesdays with Morrie* (with Mitch Albom). Film/TV: *Stage Beauty*, *Casanova*, *The Duchess*, and episodes of *Columbo*. He is a member of the Playwrights Center, Dramatists Guild, Writers Guild, and New Dramatists.

AMY HERZOG (*Christmas Present*) is the author of *After the Revolution*, produced at the Williamstown Theatre Festival and at Playwrights Horizons in 2010. Other productions: Ensemble Studio Theatre, ACT in San Francisco, and the Yale School of Drama; readings/workshops: MTC, NY Stage and Film, Arena Stage in D.C., Soho Rep, and others. Amy is the 2010 playwright-in-residence at Ars Nova. MFA, Yale School of Drama.

MIKHAIL HOROWITZ (*Mere Vessels*) is the author of *Big League Poets* (City Lights, 1978) and two collections of poetry. He has been performing poetry, music, comedy, political satire, and pataphysical acrobatics professionally since 1973, and his work is included on more than a dozen CDs, including *The

Blues of the Birth (Sundazed Records). His day gig? Redacting academic wapdoodle at Bard College.

DAVID IVES (*The Blizzard*) is probably best-known for his evenings of one-acts, collected as *All in the Timing* (Vintage Books) and *Time Flies* (Grove Press). His full-length work to date has been collected in *Polish Joke and Other Plays* (Grove). He is also the author of two young-adult novels, *Monsieur Eek* and *Scrib*. He lives in New York City with his wife, Martha.

CALEEN SINNETTE JENNINGS (*Uncovered*) is a professor of theater at American University, Washington, D.C. She received a Heideman Award from Actors Theatre of Louisville for her play *Classyass*, and a $10,000 grant from the Kennedy Center's Fund for New American Plays for her play *Inns & Outs*. Her other plays include *Playing Juliet/Casting Othello*, *Elsewhere in Elsinore*, *Free Like Br'er Rabbit*, and *Chem Mystery*.

EAN MILES KESSLER (*Brotherly Love*) is a BFA graduate of Rutgers University, Mason Gross School of the Arts. Acting credits include: *Hamlet* (Hamlet, Player King, Priest) on London's Globe Stage; *Roll Your Own* (Willy) off-off-Broadway at Where Eagles Dare; and *Dei-GAH* (Charlie and Harlan) at Rutgers University. He is also a lead writer for the New York–based theater company Inertia.

DAN KOIS (*The Rumor*) is the author of *Facing Future*, a book about the Hawaiian singer Israel Kamakawiwo'ole. He is a film critic for the *Washington Post*, a contributing writer at *New York* magazine, and a contributor to the *New York Times*, *The Village Voice*, *Slate*, and *The Awl*. A retired improv comedian, he lives in Arlington, Virginia, and is writing a book about church.

ERIC LANE'S (*Curtain Raiser*) plays have been published and performed in the United States, Canada, Europe, and China.

Eric has won a Writers Guild Award, the Berrilla Kerr Award, and the La MaMa Playwright Award. Publications include *Ride, Heart of the City* (Dramatists Play Service), and *Dancing on Checkers' Grave* (Playscripts), and *Early Morning* in *Best American Short Plays 2008–2009* (Applause Books). www .ericlanewrites.com

DREW LARIMORE (*The Anniversary*) is a playwright who currently lives in New York. His minimusical *Whahoo!* is published through Heuer Publishing Company, and his ten-minute play *The Quintessential Rapport* was a finalist in the 2002 National Ten-Minute Play Competition. Drew has worked with the Telluride Playwrights Festival, Ensemble Studio Theatre MCC Playwrights Coalition, and was a 2010 Finalist for the O'Neill's National Playwrights Conference.

MARK HARVEY LEVINE (*The Rental*) has had hundreds of productions of his plays from New York to Seoul to Sydney to Prague, and his work has been translated into French, Hebrew, Japanese, and Portuguese. Evenings of his work have played in Amsterdam, Los Angeles, Boston, and Indianapolis. *Aperitivos*, an evening of his plays in Portuguese, played in Brazil from 2005 to 2007. www.markharveylevine.com.

WARREN LEIGHT (*Norm-Anon*) wrote *Side Man*, which won the Tony Award for Best Play 1999. His other theater work includes *Glimmer, Glimmer & Shine, Fame Takes a Holiday, No Foreigners Beyond This Point*, and *James and Annie. Dark, No Sugar*, a collection of his one-act plays, is published by Dramatists Play Service. He was coexecutive producer on *Law & Order: Criminal Intent*, and is executive producer on *Lights Out*.

ELIZABETH MERIWETHER (*Particleboard*) wrote *The Mistakes Madeline Made*, which premiered at Naked Angels Theater and was subsequently produced at Yale Rep and published by

Dramatists Play Service. Other plays include *Heddatron*, an adaptation of *Hedda Gabler* featuring live robots, which was produced by Les Freres Corbusier and is published by Playscripts; *Nicky Goes Goth*, which premiered in the 2004 New York Fringe Festival; and *Oliver*, which will be workshopped by the Vineyard Theatre.

MICHAEL MITNICK'S (*Life Without Subtext*) recent works include *Babs the Dodo*, a voyage through home shopping and loneliness; *Elijah*, an adventure story; *Learning Russian*, a tale of identity theft; *Spacebar: A Broadway Play by Kyle Sugarman*, a play about a bar in outer space; and *The Current War*, a musical about the race to light up the globe. He has an MFA from the Yale School of Drama.

MEGAN MOSTYN-BROWN'S (*The Woods Are for Suckers and Chumps*) plays include *Girl*, *The Secret Lives of Losers*, *Lizards*, *The Rest of Your Life*, and *Objects Are Closer Than They Appear*. She is published by Samuel French, and *Girl* can be found as a podcast on iTunes. She lives in New York City and is a member of LAByrinth Theater Company.

MARK O'DONNELL (*You Know Who Else I Hate?*) won a Tony as the coauthor of the musical *Hairspray*, and was nominated again for *Cry-Baby*. His other plays include *That's It, Folks!*, *Strangers on Earth*, and *Fables for Friends*. His novels include *Getting over Homer* and *Let Nothing You Dismay*. His humor and cartoons have appeared in the *New Yorker*, *Spy*, and many other publications.

NICOLE QUINN (*Sandchair Cantata*) has written for HBO, Showtime, and network television. Her short-play collection *odds&ends* is published by Playscripts. Nicole wrote and directed *Racing Daylight*, which stars Academy Award nominees Melissa Leo and David Strathairn and is distributed by Vanguard Cinema International. At present she is lost two million years in the dystopic future with the novel *The Gold Stone Girl*.

WAYNE RAWLEY (*The Scary Question*) was the 2010 Faith Broome Playwright-in-Residence at the University of Oklahoma. Productions include *Live! From the Last Night of My Life*; *Money & Run: An Action Adventure Serial for the Stage*; *God Damn Tom,* a present-day adaptation of *The Seagull*; and an adaptation of *1984*. His play *Controlling Interest* was produced by the Actors Theatre and is published in the collection *Laugh Lines: Short Comic Plays*.

THERESA REBECK (*The Contract*) is a widely produced playwright and novelist. Her work has been produced on Broadway and off-Broadway, and she has had several world premieres at the Williamstown Theatre Festival and the Humana Festival for New American Plays. She has won numerous awards for her work in theater, television, film, and fiction. For more information, please visit www.theresarebeck.com.

JACQUELYN REINGOLD's (*A Very Very Short Play*) plays *String Fever*, *A Story About a Girl*, *Acapulco*, *Girl Gone*, *Tunnel of Love*, and *Freeze Tag* have been seen in New York, Los Angeles, across the country, and in London, Hong Kong, and Bosnia. Awards: NYFA, EST/Sloan Foundation, Kennedy Center. Published: *Things Between Us*; *Women Playwrights: The Best Plays 2003*; *Best American Short Plays*. Wrote for HBO's *In Treatment* and *Law and Order Criminal Intent*. MFA, Ohio University. www.jacquelynreingold.com.

EDWIN SÁNCHEZ's (*Ernesto the Magnificent*) productions include *DIOSA* at Hartford Stage; *Unmerciful Good Fortune* at Intar Theater (Princess Grace Playwriting Award in 1994); *Barefoot Boy with Shoes On* at Primary Stages; *Icarus,* produced by Fourth Unity, Actors Theater of Louisville (as part of their Humana Festival), San Jose Rep, and regionally throughout the United States; and *Trafficking in Broken Hearts* and *Clean*, both at the Atlantic Theater in New York.

LAURA SHAINE (formerly Cunningham) (*The Whole Truth & Nothing but the Bluetooth*) is a playwright, journalist, and author of eight books. Ms. Shaine's fiction and nonfiction have appeared in the *New Yorker* and the *New York Times*. She has seven full-length plays including *Sleeping Arrangements, Beautiful Bodies*, and *Bang*. She is widely produced and has several other short plays in the Vintage anthologies *Take Ten, Take Ten II, Leading Women*, and *Laugh Lines*.

NINA SHENGOLD (*Double Date*) has had short plays produced on five continents. Her seven-play evening *Finger Food* and the ensemble play *War at Home: Students Respond to 9/11* are published by Playscripts. She multitasks as a novelist, screenwriter, journalist, and editor. www.ninashengold.com.

JANE SHEPARD (*Long Distance*) is the recipient of multiple awards for her plays and film writing, including a Writers Guild Award nomination for her Showtime original movie, *Freak City*. Two collections of her plays appear in print, including the popular *Kickass Plays for Women*. Full information can be found at www.Kickass-plays.com.

SAMARA SISKIND (*Bar Mitzvah Boy*) is a Florida-based playwright who simply adores the art of the short play, having penned several other shorter, faster, funnier plays, including *Blind Date, I Was a Teenage Prom Queen*, and *Little Play of Horrors*. Samara's work has also been featured in *Plays: The Drama Magazine for Young People* and in volume two of *Young Women's Monologues from Contemporary Plays*.

DARYL WATSON'S (*Snap*) works include *Prime Time, The Blueberry Hill Accord*, and the collaborative play *Game On* ("*The Best*" and "*Signature*"). He was also a cocreator and writer for the

Disney TV series *Johnny and the Sprites*. Daryl holds a BFA in drama with a second major in English and American literature from New York University.

BARBARA WIECHMANN's (*36 Rumson Road*) plays have been produced at theaters in New York City and at colleges and universities around the country. She is the creator of the television show for kids *Naturally, Sadie*, which aired on the Disney Channel for three seasons; a New Georges affiliated artist; and an alumna of New Dramatists and HARP. Barbara is a graduate of Hamilton College.

MARY LOUISE WILSON (*Tirade*) cowrote the award-winning play *Full Gallop*, which had a successful run off-Broadway and subsequently in London, Paris, Sweden, Australia, and Brazil. She has written articles for the *New York Times*, *American Theatre*, and the *New Yorker*. Her short plays have been published in *Take Ten: New 10-Minute Plays* and *Take Ten II*, and in her short play collection. *Theatrical Haiku* will be published by Dramatists Play Service.

GARTH WINGFIELD's (*Mary Just Broke Up with This Guy*) plays include *Flight* (Lucille Lortel Theatre); *26 Dates . . . and Counting* (Barrow Group); *Dating Games* (New York City and Los Angeles); *Are We There Yet?* (New York City and London); *Daniel on a Thursday* (New York City and Los Angeles). Lots of one-acts. Garth's plays have been published by Samuel French, Vintage Books, Smith & Kraus, and Playscripts, Inc. Television: Showtime's *Queer as Folk* and ABC's *Clueless*.

GARY WINTER (*I Love Neil LaBute*) is a member of Obie Award winner 13P. His plays have been produced or heard at the Chocolate Factory, the Flea, the Cherry Lane Alternative, HERE, PS 122, defunktheatre, Playwrights Horizons, the Long Wharf, and Little Theater. From 1998 to 2008, Gary served as literary manager of the Flea Theater, where he currently helps organize pataphysics workshops for playwrights. MFA, NYU.

ELIZABETH WONG (*Ripper Girl*), playwright/director, was a sitcom writer for *All American Girl*, starring Margaret Cho; a Disney Studios writing fellow; and a recipient of the Tanne Foundation Award for artistic achievement. Her plays include *Letters to a Student Revolutionary*, *Kimchee & Chitlins*, and *China Doll*. She has written musicals for the Kennedy Center and Honolulu Theatre for Youth. Her short comedy, *Finding Your Inner Zulu*, premiered in Chicago in 2010.

DANA YEATON (*Men in Heat*) is the recipient of the Heideman Award from the Actors Theatre of Louisville and the New Voice in the American Theatre Award from the William Inge Theatre Festival. His plays include *Midwives*, *Redshirts*, *Mad River Rising*, and a new two-person musical comedy, *My Ohio*. He teaches at Middlebury College and was founding director of the Vermont Young Playwrights Project.

ABOUT THE EDITORS

ERIC LANE and NINA SHENGOLD have been editing contemporary theater anthologies for more than twenty years. Their other titles for Vintage Books include *Laugh Lines: Short Comic Plays*, *Under 30: Plays for a New Generation*, *Talk to Me: Monologue Plays*, *Plays for Actresses*, *Leading Women: Plays for Actresses II*, *Take Ten: New 10-Minute Plays*, and *Take Ten II: More 10-Minute Plays*. For Viking Penguin, they edited *The Actor's Book of Contemporary Stage Monologues*, *The Actor's Book of Scenes from New Plays*, *Moving Parts: Monologues from Contemporary Plays*, *The Actor's Book of Gay and Lesbian Plays* (nominated for a Lambda Literary Award), and *Telling Tales: New One-Act Plays*.

ERIC LANE'S award-winning plays include *Ride*, *Heart of the City*, *Floating*, *Times of War*, *Cater-Waiter*, and *Dancing on Checkers' Grave*. His plays have been published by Dramatists Play Service, Playscripts Inc., Applause Books, and the Foreign Language Press (Beijing). Eric wrote and produced the short films *First Breath* and *Cater-Waiter*, which he also directed. Both films screened in over forty cities worldwide. For TV's *Ryan's Hope*, he received a Writers Guild Award. Honors include the Berrilla Kerr Playwriting Award, the La MaMa Playwright Award, and fellowships at Yaddo, VCCA, and St. James Cavalier in Malta. Eric is an honors graduate of Brown University and artistic director of Orange Thoughts, a not-for-profit theater and film company in New York City.

www.ericlanewrites.com

NINA SHENGOLD writes in many genres. Her books include the novel *Clearcut* (Anchor Books, 2005) and *River of Words: Portraits of Hudson Valley Writers* (SUNY Press, 2010) with photographer Jennifer May. Shengold won the Writers Guild Award for her teleplay *Labor of Love*, starring Marcia Gay Harden; she also wrote *Blind Spot*, starring Joanne Woodward and Laura Linney, and three other TV movies. Her plays have been published by Playscripts Inc., Broadway Play Publishing, and Samuel French. She is books editor at *Chronogram* magazine, and her good twin has a thriving career as a pseudonymous young adult author.

INDEX BY CAST SIZE

PERMISSIONS ACKNOWLEDGMENTS

Anton Dudley: *Getting Home* by Anton Dudley, copyright © 2011 by Anton Dudley. Reprinted by permission of the author.
Inquiries contact: Anton Dudley, dudley2@adelphi.edu.

Christopher Durang: *Funeral Parlor* by Christopher Durang, copyright © 1995 by Christopher Durang. Reprinted by permission of The Carsey-Werner Company/Kalola Productions, Inc.
Inquiries contact: Dramatists Play Service.

Liz Ellison: *Gabrielle* by Liz Ellison, copyright © 2011 by Elizabeth Ellison. Reprinted by permission of the author.
Inquiries contact: Liz Ellison, lizell@alum.dartmouth.org.

Halley Feiffer: *Thank You So Much for Stopping* by Halley Feiffer, copyright © 2011 by Halley Feiffer. Reprinted by permission of the author.
Inquiries contact: Jessica Amato, The Gersh Agency, 41 Madison Avenue, New York, New York 10010, 212-997-1818, fax: 212-391-8459, jamato@gershny.com.

Peter Handy: *Friendship* by Peter Handy, copyright © 2011 by Peter Handy. Reprinted by permission of the author.
Inquiries contact: pfranciscoblue@gmail.com.

Jeffrey Hatcher: *Murderers ("Match Wits with Minka Lupino")* by Jeffrey Hatcher. Copyright © 2008 by Jeffrey Hatcher. All rights reserved. Reprinted by permission Paradigm Agency.
Inquiries contact: Dramatists Play Service.

Amy Herzog: *Christmas Present* by Amy Herzog, copyright © 2008 by Amy Herzog (*Christmas Present* was first produced at the Ensemble Studio Theatre, New York, in 2008). All rights reserved. Reprinted by permission of William Morris Endeavor Entertainment, LLC.
Caution: Professionals and amateurs are hereby warned that *Christmas Present* is subject to a royalty. It is fully protected under the copyright laws of the United States of America and of all countries covered by the International Copyright Union (including the Dominion of Canada, and the rest of the British Commonwealth), the Berne Convention, the Pan-American Copyright Convention and the Universal Copyright Convention as well as all countries with which the United States has reciprocal copyright relations. All rights, including professional/amateur stage rights, motion picture, recitation, lecturing, public reading, radio broadcasting, television, video or sound recording, all other forms of mechanical or electronic reproduction, such as CD-ROM, CD-I, information storage and retrieval systems and photocopying, and the rights of translation into foreign languages, are strictly reserved. Particular emphasis

Theresa Rebeck: *The Contract* by Theresa Rebeck, copyright © 1999 by Madwoman in the Attic, Inc. Reprinted by permission of the author.
Inquiries contact: Creative Artists Agency, Attn: George Lane, 162 Fifth Avenue, 6th Floor, New York, New York 10010.

Jacquelyn Reingold: *A Very Very Short Play* by Jacquelyn Reingold, copyright © 2009 by Jacquelyn Reingold. Reprinted by permission of the author.
Inquiries contact: Mark Subias, 1 Union Square West, #913, New York, New York 10003.

Edwin Sánchez: *Ernesto the Magnificent* by Edwin Sánchez, copyright © 2011 by Edwin Sánchez. Reprinted by permission of the author.
Inquiries contact: edwinplaywright@aol.com.

Laura Shaine: *The Whole Truth and Nothing but the Bluetooth* by Laura Shaine, copyright © 2011 by Laura Shaine Cunningham. Reprinted by permission of Bret Adams, Ltd.
Inquiries contact: Bret Adams, Ltd., 448 West 44th Street, New York, New York 10036, Attn: Bruce Ostler, 212-765-5630, www.bret adamsltd.net.

Nina Shengold: *Double Date* by Nina Shengold, copyright © 2011 by Nina Shengold. Reprinted by permission of the author.
Inquiries contact: Phyllis Wender, The Gersh Agency, 41 Madison Avenue, 33rd Floor, New York, New York 10010, 212-997-1818, pwender@gershny.com.

Jane Shepard: *Long Distance* by Jane Shepard, copyright © 2008 by Jane Shepard. Reprinted by permission of the author.
Inquiries contact: Jane Shepard, janershep@aol.com.

Samara Siskind: *Bar Mitzvah Boy* by Samara Siskind, copyright © 2007 by Samara Siskind. All rights reserved. Reprinted by permission of Playscripts, Inc.
To purchase acting editions of the play, or to obtain stock and amateur performance rights, you must contact: Playscripts, Inc., http://www.playscripts.com, email: info@playscripts.com, phone: 1-866-NEW-PLAY (639-7529).

Daryl Watson: *Snap* by Daryl Watson, copyright © 2007 by Daryl Watson. All rights reserved. Reprinted by permission of Playscripts, Inc.
To purchase acting editions of the play, or to obtain stock and amateur performance rights, you must contact: Playscripts, Inc.,